Natural Ethical Facts

Natural Ethical Facts

Evolution, Connectionism, and Moral Cognition

William D. Casebeer

A Bradford Book
The MIT Press
Cambridge, Massachusetts
London, England

Set in Sabon by UG / GGS Information Services, Inc. Printed and bound in the United States of America.

Library of Congress Cataloging-in-Publication Data

Casebeer, William D.
Natural ethical facts : evolution, connectionism, and moral cognition / William D. Casebeer.
p. cm.
Includes bibliographical references and index.
ISBN 0-262-03310-0 (alk. paper)
1. Ethics, Evolutionary. I. Title.

BJ1311.C37 2003
171'.7—dc21

2003042226

The sharphoofed moose of the north, the cat on the housesill, the chickadee, the prarie-dog,
The litter of the grunting sow as they tug at her teats,
The brood of the turkeyhen, and she with her halfspread wings,
I see in them and myself the same old law.

Walt Whitman, *Leaves of Grass* (1855)

Philosophy ought to imitate the successful sciences in its methods, so far as to proceed only from tangible premises which can be subjected to careful scrutiny, and to trust rather to the multitude and variety of its arguments than to the conclusiveness of any one. Its reasoning should not form a chain which is no stronger than its weakest link, but a cable whose fibres may be ever so slender, provided they are sufficiently numerous and intimately connected.

Charles S. Peirce, *Some Consequences of Four Incapacities* (1868)

Contents

Preface and Acknowledgements

I have been told it is inappropriate to begin a paper or (heaven forbid) a book with an apology. So: I apologize . . . not just for ignoring this piece of advice, but also for attempting a project whose scope and nature precludes thorough examination in a single volume, let alone a whole series of books. I beg your indulgence, and hope that by the end of the book you will understand why I think writing it was necessary, despite its myriad shortcomings and truncated discussions of theses that deserve a far more elaborate defense.

a short introduction to a complex subject

very difficult to make Bringing this book to completion has been a distributed cognitive enterprise of the first order. Many scholars have been involved in the intellectual labor required to integrate the core ideas of the project into an organic whole. In particular, Paul Churchland, Patricia Smith Churchland, Jeff Elman, Georgios Anagnostopoulos, and Joan Stiles were kind enough to read original drafts in their entirety when the project was merely embryonic; they all provided useful feedback and encouragement, and the structure of the book owes much to their groundbreaking work in this area in the past decade. Paul and Pat Churchland in particular have been sources of constant inspiration; their willingness to see (with Paul's mentor Wilfrid Sellars) how things (in the *largest sense*) fit together (in the *largest sense*) is but one reason why their philosophy *about* philosophy is and will continue to be instrumental in helping us cope with the challenges presented by the brain and mind sciences. In addition, the scholars Larry Arnhart, William Rottschaefer, Louis Pojman, P. D. Magnus, Wayne Martin, Carl Sachs, Carl Ficarrotta, David Schiller, Joseph Cohen, David Barash, and Bill Rhodes all provided useful critical feedback on pieces of the manuscript at various stages. Of course, the factual errors and mistakes in reasoning

fledgling subject

a large scale science

that remain are all my own, while most of what is true and good in the book is theirs. My thanks are also due to the excellent editorial staff at The MIT Press, particularly Tom Stone and Paul Bethge, whose patience and advice I very much appreciate.

Raising a family while writing a book can be problematic; I lovingly thank my wife Adrianne for her intellectual and emotional support and for the tremendous efforts she has placed into raising our three children (Jonah, Mara, and Linnae) when I was otherwise preoccupied. My greatest hope is that this project can contribute in some small way to making the world that they and other children grow up to inhabit a better, more sane place.

My heartfelt thanks to all those whose ideas and attitudes have otherwise made their way into this book, particularly friends, philosophers, and cognitive scientists from the University of California at San Diego, the University of Arizona, and the United States Air Force Academy. You know who you are—it's an honor to be among your company. Finally, I thank the United States Air Force (and, in turn, the American taxpayer) for funding my graduate education, and for the daily reminder that supporting and defending the U.S. Constitution is a worthy use of heartbeats.

1
Natural Ethical Facts

Why Care about Natural Ethical Facts?

Evolutionary biologists have been at work for more than 100 years telling us about our nature as evolved, embodied creatures. Cognitive scientists have been plumbing the depths of the mind for 50 years, discovering the neural and computational roots of complex behavior and cognition. For more than 2,000 years, moral philosophers have been plugging away at big-picture normative theories regarding how we ought to conduct ourselves and, ultimately, what the point of this blooming and buzzing confusion of life and mind is. Until relatively recently, however, work at the intersection of these three areas of inquiry was difficult to find. Scientific theories of life and mind have had relatively little contact with normative moral theory, and moral philosophers, when they have made contact, have often expressed disappointment with the results. Why is this? What can we do to ensure that fruitful consilience between our best theories in the cognitive sciences, evolutionary biology, and ethics is the norm rather than the exception? Addressing these issues by showing how there can be useful interactions between science and ethics is the critical issue facing the sciences. As we cast about for a post-Enlightenment normative anchor, if we are to prevent backsliding into dogmatic supernatural and non-naturalistic conceptions of the moral life, it is imperative that we demonstrate the possibility of intelligent, useful interactions between the human sciences and human ethics.

This book is an attempt to show that, theoretically speaking, there is no reason to rule out a scientific naturalized ethics *tout court*, and that, practically speaking, by taking into account recent developments in evolutionary biology and the cognitive sciences, the outlines of one promising form of such an ethics can be sketched. It will be a pragmatic neo-Aristotelian virtue theory, given substantive form by both conceptions of function from evolutionary biology and connectionist conceptions of thought from cognitive science. The rough structure of the book follows from the unfolding of this admittedly synoptic thesis.

Moral Judgments, Connectionism, and the Cognitive and Biological Sciences

The naturalization of ethics has been a problematic enterprise for moral philosophers. Historically, there are several reasons why this is so. For one, theoretical arguments regarding the impossibility of a systematic reductive relationship between the natural realm and the normative realm have stymied attempts to unify the two spheres by those sympathetic to such a union. In addition, the cognitive capacities we use to grasp moral knowledge have been thought by some to be far too subtle for "mere" empirical explanation by a scientifically informed theory of cognition. Finally, some previous attempts to construct a scientifically informed moral theory, and thus remake ethics into a science, have been too simplistic (or have been painted as such by critics) to do justice to the full range of our considered moral intuitions and our reasonably informed moral judgments. As a result, much of the work in the naturalization of morality has taken place in metaethics rather than in normative moral theory, leaving the latter bereft of empirical content. And very little research has attempted to relate the latest findings of the cognitive sciences to moral psychology and moral judgment, let alone normative moral theory, in any systematic fashion.

This isolation has had a debilitating effect on both the empirical plausibility of normative moral theories and the societal impact of the biologically informed cognitive sciences. Our normative moral theories would be greatly enriched if the questions they posed were empirically tractable, and the breadth of our cognitive and biological sciences would be enhanced if they were to offer plausible reconstructions of our cognitive capacity to reason about, grasp, and accede to moral norms. Such an enrichment and enhancement also would pay dividends external to the academic professions, giving us alternate strategies for framing and resolving moral conflicts and allowing us to improve our methods for cultivating moral knowledge by enhancing the effectiveness of our collective character-development institutions.

My project embodies a synoptic reconciliation of the sciences of cognition with a fully naturalized conception of morality. I argue that we can improve our understanding of the nature of moral theory and its place in moral judgment if we better understand just what morality consists in. Such an understanding will best be informed by treating morality as a natural phenomenon subject to constraints from, influenced by, and ultimately reduced to the sciences, particularly the cognitive sciences and biology. Treating morality as a matter of proper function, biologically construed (e.g., at least partially fixed by our evolutionary history), with a concomitant emphasis on skillful action in the world, will also shed light on just what kind of creatures we must be (cognitively speaking) if we are to possess knowledge about morality so taken. Connectionist accounts of cognition can best accommodate this style of knowledge and can also account for other gross moral psychological phenomena, giving them ample explanatory power and making them the centerpiece of moral cognition. The nature of morality and the picture of moral cognition I defend are rooted in a pragmatic construal of knowledge and in a modern, biologically informed neo-Aristotelianism. Exploring these roots, particularly as they manifest themselves in John Dewey's theory of moral deliberation, will shed light on the role of moral theory in such a scheme and will help distinguish this approach from less fruitful and more purely sociobiological undertakings. Finally, I discuss objections and draw out some practical implications, regarding the nature and form of our collective character-development institutions and our methods for moral reasoning that arise from taking this approach seriously.

The Way Forward

In chapter 2, I discuss and rebut two popular arguments against a reductive and naturalizable account of morality: the naturalistic fallacy and the open-question argument. I contend that both arguments fail, primarily because they rely on an outmoded analytic/synthetic distinction. Arguing for a continuum of analytic and synthetic judgments, thus demonstrating that moral knowledge and scientific knowledge are commensurable, will open the way for a reductive naturalistic account of morality. I accomplish this by recapitulating W. V. O. Quine's arguments against the analytic/synthetic distinction. I also present the basics of Dewey's theory of moral deliberation, arguing that his conception of "ends-in-view" effectively demonstrates the continuity of scientific and practical knowledge with moral knowledge. The conception of morality I thus offer will be cognitivist and realist but will nonetheless constraint our ability to systematize moral theory. Moral conclusions, I will argue, follow abductively from properly construed non-normative premises. Our moral judgments are part and parcel of our web of beliefs. If the proper reductive relationship between moral terms and natural terms is captured by a theory that relates the two in a fecund way, then inferences from non-normative premises to normative conclusions will not be excessively licentious.

In chapter 3, I articulate the basics of such an approach, rebutting the "error-theory" arguments against a moral science articulated by John Mackie. Moral claims should be reduced to functional claims technically construed, hence the shared roots with an Aristotelian view of the world. Such functional claims should be treated as they are in biology and the life sciences, with a suitably modified Wright-style teleonomic analysis: a Godfrey-Smith-flavored "modern-history" theory of functions. Such a theory will thus take advantage of the explanatory power of the neo-Darwinian synthesis. Some functional facts about human beings fully fix normative claims; others will only constrain the possible state space of moral options. A small percentage of the decisions we face may have no effect at all on functional concerns, in which case we are (morally speaking) simply free to choose. The basics of this account will thus allow some flexibility in the normative structure of our lives. My account also has the resources necessary to distinguish itself from hedonistic, egoistic, desire-satisfaction, and utilitarian theories of morality, particularly after I make some crucial distinctions (including the difference between proximate and distal functions and the difference between ahistorical and historical functions). On this picture, moral facts are not "queer" and unscientific, nor is morality globally relativistic and dramatically contingent. We can in good conscience be moral realists and yet embrace an acceptable form of humility regarding our ability to know the good; such humility reflects not only constraints on our cognitive economy but also constraints on the form of norm-fixing evolutionary processes in nature. Ultimately, this approach makes empirical and scientific investigation of moral normativity possible. I also examine contemporary work done in the same vein, including more purely sociobiological and Darwinian approaches to morality. I focus primarily on modern accounts, ranging from Larry Arnhart's theory to E. O. Wilson's, although I briefly discuss wrong-headed evolutionary ethical theories, such as those offered by Herbert Spencer and the Social Darwinists. I discuss similarities and differences between these approaches and my own, concluding that the account on offer has strengths that the other approaches lack.

In chapter 4, I draw on resources from connectionist accounts of cognition and from the embodied cognition movement to articulate a purely biological notion of moral judgment that bridges the "normativity gap." Using resources from these two approaches, it becomes possible to specify a conception of judgment that harmonizes with the account of moral knowledge discussed in chapter 3. A purely biological notion of judgment is possible, and such a notion comports well with the idea of judgment as the cognitive capacity to skillfully cope with the demands of the environment. Thus, moral judgment is possible only in systems that learn in a natural computational manner, whose nature is at least momentarily fixed,[1] and that exist in an environment where demands are placed upon the organism. Having good moral judgment amounts to being able to accomplish cognitive tasks that enable one to meet the demands of one's functional nature. Morality is therefore a matter of "knowing how" more than a matter of "knowing that." Some of these cognitive capacities can be captured in "representation-free" neural nets that are best described in the language of dynamical systems theory; others require traditional connectionist distributed representations. Some advanced forms of moral reasoning may require a model-theoretic account of reasoning. I discuss what mental models look like in connectionism, postulate how they can accommodate more advanced aspects of moral cognition, and point out their essential connection to action in the world and embodiment in an organism. Certain high-level aspects of connectionist mental models may lend themselves to a truth-functional analysis rooted in a symbolic redescription of network activity, but such a redescription will be possible only in certain instances and should not be reified into a categorical demand placed upon normative action and its associated psychology. I draw connections between this discussion and Dewey's account of moral deliberation, which I sketched in chapter 2. I also offer a useful typology of moral characteristics that follows from this account, distinguishing between those objects of science that are the proper subjects of moral *cum* functional concerns, and between creatures that are able to effectively model their environment and their relationship to it (and that can hence formulate their own moral science). This generates a continuum among living things that have functions, ranging from simple moral agents (for example, most insects) to maximally robust moral reasoners (most social creatures with a significant range of behavioral repertoires, especially—but not only—human beings).

In chapter 5, I use the explanatory power of a connectionist approach to account for other gross features of moral reasoning. The interaction of advances in connectionist accounts of thought and traditional issues in moral cognition and psychology is an interesting one, as heretofore disparate phenomena in the latter can be unified by an account from the former. Connectionism can serve as a platform on which to reconstruct several high-order moral cognitive phenomena, including moral knowledge, moral learning and conceptual development, moral perception and the role of metaphor and analogy in moral argument, the appearance of staged moral development, the possibility of *akrasia* (acting against one's best considered judgment), the presence of moral systematicity, moral dramatic rehearsal and moral motivation, and moral sociability. A connectionist account of moral cognition best unifies the neurobiology and cognitive psychology of morality and sheds new light on traditional issues in moral psychology, including questions about the motivational efficacy of moral claims, the affective aspect of moral reasoning, and the importance of moral exemplars. I support these contentions with reference to the exponentially increasing body of modeling work in artificial neural networks. Finally, I briefly examine the literature relating brain structure and function to these models, identifying key components of the several cognitive systems that jointly constitute our capacity to be maximally robust moral reasoners.

In chapter 6, I draw together themes from the preceding five chapters, examining how naturalizing morality by way of evolution and connectionism may affect our moral theories, our moral practices, and our moral institutions. Where does this attempt at reduction leave traditional moral theory? On the one hand, some aspects of moral theory—particularly an appropriately naturalized Aristotle and large parts of Dewey's attempt to develop a pragmatic ethic—remain components of the moral life; on the other hand, certain traditional moral theories do not fare as well, at least if they are taken to be universally applicable. A Kantian approach, for example, has at best heuristic value but at root makes demands that are psychologically unrealistic. I conclude that it functions well as a device for drawing attention to the strong conditions necessary to enable social reasoning to occur, but that it fails to appropriately accommodate primary functional concerns. This pragmatic approach recognizes a healthy limit to the usefulness of grand moral theory: its existence can be explained, but its limits are outlined. Ethical reasoning becomes a species of pure practical knowledge and as such is responsive to the demands of the present. Just as pragmatic epistemology is a process-oriented philosophy, so too is a pragmatic ethics that draws on the useful portions of previous moral theorizing, insofar as they are informed by and illuminate the issues raised by functional *cum* biological concerns. This emphasis on proper function is rooted in an Aristotelian account of the nature of humanity and requires the defense of at least a "soft essentialism," which I offer here by adverting to the findings of the neo-Darwinian synthesis. Though we might think that one of the primary lessons of Darwinism is that there is no such thing as a species essence, I argue that population thinking serves as a healthy corrective to the idea that our functions are immutable and that all of us must possess exactly the same functional natures. I discuss the similarities between this explicitly pragmatic approach and an Aristotelian virtue ethic, arguing that the two are successfully unified with very little remainder and that the neo-Darwinian synthesis can give biological bite to Aristotle's contentions about the limits of moral theorizing. I conclude chapter 6 by using the aforementioned approach as a tool to critique character-development institutions and to illuminate cases of moral conflict. I address real-world case studies in ethics that demonstrate how this conception has the ability to contend with these objections directly and not just abstractly. I focus first on whether an individual should develop deep or wide friendships (modern-history

WHAT REALLY WORKS???

functions call for deep friendships) and second on how we should structure our societies (modern-history considerations lead to liberal democratic forms of organization). In more abstract and general terms, my account restores an emphasis on habituation and mindfulness that our social institutions would do well to attend to. I examine the implications of this view for character development and moral education, arguing that it propels to the forefront a narrative-driven case-study approach to moral education, a solid grounding in the biological and sociological dimensions of the human situation, a careful tending of the institutional environment in which moral action is situated, a demand for consistency between articulated principles and practical actions, and a healthy flexibility in the practical application of rules and regulations. Nothing teaches like experience, and so the proper environment for moral experience must be carefully cultivated and maintained by institutions of moral education and character development. Such a process is demanding and requires those engaging in it to stay informed of the results from a large number of fields of empirical inquiry.

In chapter 7, I address the remaining objections to the aforementioned approach and outline its additional strengths. It must answer some hard questions usually put to more traditional sociobiological undertakings that any naturalistic account of morality must deal with. Among the grounds for concern are the perceived lack of robust and genuine normativity in the approach, some purportedly morally repugnant "entailments" of the position, an argument that the position demands its own rebuttal for heuristic "Platonic noble lie"-style reasons, and an argument that the position is empty of useful moral content. In the conclusion of this chapter, I outline several areas where there is a notable absence of empirical work or where more empirical work is needed; these areas include the connectionist modeling of moral cognition, applied moral cognitive psychology, moral anthropology, the neurobiology of moral cognition, and biologically informed game-theoretic approaches to skillful coping. I also discuss the need for further exploration of more traditionally philosophic topics, such as alternatives to a simple-correspondence account of cognition. A biological and neurobiologically informed pragmatic ethic holds the most hope for being the unifying procedural glue that can successfully hold together otherwise disparate and possibly mutually antagonistic approaches to the moral *might not change the way people think*

life. Although moral progress using this approach is not a given, I highlight its essentially optimistic character and hold out hope for reconciliation between the humanities and the sciences. *hopes this will succeed*

'Naturalism' and 'Ethics': Problematic Terms?

Before I begin my discussion of the naturalistic fallacy, there are several terms whose use demands clarification so that the nature of this *individual definition* approach is clear. These include 'naturalism' and 'ethics'. (Entire books have been written about the definition of these terms, so my discussion will be concise.) *quick definition*

'Naturalism'

The principal approach that I will use in the book is best typified as a *naturalism* form of methodological naturalism, by which I mean that the method- *use* *meant* ological and epistemological assumptions of the natural sciences should *standards* *based* serve as standards for this inquiry. If at the end of the inquiry we feel *of other* *from* compelled to postulate the existence of a non-naturalistic entity or *sciences* *experiment* process, so as to best explain the results of our study, then our method- *claim the* *standard)* *existence* *from* ological naturalism will have led us to a denial of ontological natural- *of* *natural* ism. However, I don't think this will be the case, and for the moment we *beyond* *sciences* should hold our methodological naturalism close so as to see if norma- *the world* *would* tivity can be derived without postulating "spooky" non-natural entities *i.e. influen* *be beyond/* (gods, a noumenal realm, and so on). Of course I will avail myself of the *by some* *disproof.* ontologies postulated by the natural sciences during the course of this *higher* *of non-* inquiry, but this will be done with requisite sensitivity to moral experi- *power* *naturalism* ence, and with the fallibilistic view that the ontologies of our current *doesn't want* *will use* sciences might be wrong, so, although the project will presuppose onto- *to bring in* *the authors* logical naturalism to a certain extent, naturalist methodologies are still *only speculat* *assumed* the primary constraint. *some aspects unable to be proved w/* *things)* *forces* *evidence + some methodical can be used* *take* *advant.* *certain* *of* *principles* *required* *can be* *sensitivity)* *proved* *assumed*

will probably not happen

Dewey (1902, p. 142) provides a nicely succinct definition of naturalism: "The theory that the whole of the universe or of experience may be accounted for by a method like that of the physical sciences, and with recourse only to the current conceptions of physical and natural science; more specifically, that mental and moral processes may be reduced to the terms and categories of the natural sciences. It is best defined

naturalism: moral + mental ideas can be explored with experimental procedures negatively as that which excludes everything distinctly spiritual or transcendental. . . . ”

Some of the traditional methodological and ontological theses of naturalism will be actively defended in this paper; others will be assumed. For example, I will actively defend a realist conception of morality, whereas I will simply assume that there are no miracles and there is no extrasensory perception (at least until evidence demands that we change these assumptions). In other words, my defense of certain traditional tenets of naturalism will take place against the background of (a) uncontroversial findings from the sciences (e.g., no ESP), (b) controversial but eminently defensible findings from the sciences (e.g., the explanatory power of connectionist approaches to cognition), and (c) the interesting points of conflict between fields of inquiry not generally considered to be part of the sciences (e.g., certain assumptions about the nature of ethical claims) and the sciences of cognition and life.

Gerhard Vollmer's list of the traditional ontological and methodological theses of naturalism (taken from his "Naturalism, Function, Teleonomy," as published in Wolters 1995) is worth quoting in full:

A) Only as much metaphysics as necessary!

B) As much realism as possible!

C) For the investigation of nature, the method of empirical science is superior to any other.

D) Nature (the world, the universe, the real) is, at bottom, constituted of matter and energy, both temporally and causally.

E) All real systems—the universe as a whole included—are subject to development, to evolution, to assembly, and disassembly. That's why any modern naturalism is an evolutionary naturalism.

F) Complex systems consist of and originate from less complex parts.

G) The real world is interconnected and quasi-continuous.

H) Instances transcending all human experience are conceivable, but dispensable for the consideration, description, explanation and interpretation of the world.

I) There are no miracles.

J) There is no extrasensory perception.

K) Understanding nature doesn't transcend nature itself.

L) There is a unity of nature which might be mirrored in a unity of science.

The naturalization of ethics would thus entail making ethics consistent with this list of statements and thereby showing how knowledge of the normative can be derived and justified using this methodology and ontology. As Vollmer notes, every thesis on this list deserves explication and refinement, but I hope they are intelligible without this and that they serve as useful guideposts for present purposes.

Jay Garfield (2000, p. 423) distinguishes between strong naturalism and moderate naturalism. Strong naturalism requires more than mere consistency (which is demanded by even the weakest forms of naturalism); it also requires entailment or some form of reduction to more fundamental and already unproblematically naturalized theories. Moderate naturalism would require (1) consistency, (2) that the research be guided by the methodological canons of the sciences, and (3) that there be (in Garfield's words) "plausible explanatory strategies for linking the theories, explanations and theoretical perspectives" of the body of knowledge being naturalized to the remainder of science. In my case, I will be happy if I achieve a moderate naturalization, but I keep in mind the goal of strong naturalization as a regulative ideal. This reflects my suspicion that mere supervenience relations, though acceptable in a developing science, often are used as an excuse not to explore the phenomena in question in more depth, or, in the worst of cases, merely restate a problematic relation rather than "solving" it.[2] In sum, we should expect that a plausible naturalization of ethics would explain the essential nature of moral judgments, their subject matter, and how we come to make them. Such a naturalization would make full use of background knowledge from the sciences, especially (at least in the case of this book) from the cognitive sciences and evolutionary biology.

The Natural Method

Keeping the background knowledge of the pertinent sciences in mind while constructing a theory has been given a name by Owen Flanagan: the Natural Method.[3] Though Flanagan uses it to triangulate on a theory of the nature of the mind (paying attention to results from the associated departments of the cognitive sciences, as well as to first-person phenomenology), there is no principled reason why the process couldn't be applied to any phenomenon of interest. Flanagan (2000, p. 14) characterizes the Natural Method as follows: "The idea is to keep one's eye, as much as is humanly possible, on all the relevant hypotheses and data sources at once in the attempt to construct a credible theory. The natural method involves seeking consistency and equilibrium among different modes of analysis applied to the study of some . . . phenomenon." Flanagan's prescription derives in part from Quinean considerations about confirmatory holism. Insofar as these considerations also drive my inquiry (as will become evident at the end of chapter 2), it is no surprise that the method I advocate for framing theories of morality is, in essence, the Natural Method.

Two Desiderata for Naturalization

To summarize the desiderata for naturalism (for comparison to the conclusions of chapter 7), naturalizing ethics would therefore consist in producing (1) an account of moral normativity that roots normativity in nature, where the content of nature's ontology is (provisionally[4]) provided by the methodological canons of the natural sciences, and (2) an account of our capacity to grasp and accede to these norms that is rooted in the best theoretical frameworks that the mind sciences have to offer.

'Ethics'

What does the subject matter of the study of morality consist in? Broadly speaking, it is the study of what we ought to do, what we ought to intend, or what kind of people we ought to be, all in the largest sense—how ought we live our lives? The three traditional theoretical approaches to ethics have been thought to answer these questions in turn: utilitarianism[5] focuses primarily on the consequences of actions (as they relate to the production of pleasure and the reduction of pain), deontology concentrates on what duties we owe to one another (and, in its most famous Kantian version, on what duty-filtered maxims or intentions we ought to form in our minds), and virtue theory considers what states of character we ought to cultivate in ourselves. In the course of this book, I discuss all three of these theories as they relate to naturalization, particularly virtue theory.

There are many more fine-grained distinctions to be made here, beginning with the difference between instrumental reasoning and reasoning

oh so what do we have to get done now

about final ends. On the one hand, we can ask what we ought to do given some desire or project; such a question is one of means and involves instrumental reasoning. What is the best means or instrument I can use to accomplish my goal? On the other hand, we can ask what we ought to desire or what projects we ought to have; such a question is one of ends and involves practical reasoning about *final* ends. Naturalized systems of ethics, particularly modern approaches, are often accused of dealing only with the former, and hence of not dealing with ethics proper at all. In this project, I intend to deal with both instrumental and final norms, although the distinction often obscures the true nature of moral reasoning and can cloud inquiry. Rather than construing "grand theory" ethics as the search for final ends, we should seek explanatory unification of reasoning about both instrumental and final ends.

how does biology affect how we deal with the long + short term?

Some authors draw a distinction between morality and ethics. For example, Bernard Williams argues that morality is a subset of ethics, and that the former concentrates on obligation whereas the later deals with larger questions.[8] Others argue that ethics is a specialized body of knowledge applicable only to certain roles, and that morality is actually the larger term; there can be "military ethics" or "medical ethics," both of which derive their content from more general *moral* considerations.[9] I am dubious about the work done by drawing these distinctions, at least for this project (although in other contexts, such a distinction might be eminently useful). For present purposes, then, the terms 'ethics' and 'morality' will be used interchangeably, and no particular substantive inferences about the project should be drawn from my use of one term instead of the other.

the two are the same for this project

Final Context

Philip Kitcher offered an enlightening list of potential alternative goals for those who would "biologicize" ethics. Kitcher formulated the list while attempting to discern the exact nature of the project encompassed by E. O. Wilson's sociobiology, which Kitcher criticized in his 1985 book *Vaulting Ambition*. Kitcher's piercing critique of Wilson is a healthy corrective to both excessive ambition and vagueness, though

naturalized ethics sometimes only address things in context of short term decision making

code that a flynt(?) free was to decide yes vs. no

ethics are used in certain situations as a set of rules

morality being larger

who should we be?

sometimes the separation of the two distorts stuff

morality = what should we do vs. ethics = more close(?) people who are nicer

should be logical, attainable and specific

Wilson's program has much about it that is worth admiring.[10] Kitcher (1985, pp. 417–418) postulates four possibilities for "biologicizing" (E. O. Wilson's neologism) morality:

A. Evolutionary biology has the task of explaining how people come to acquire ethical concepts, to make ethical judgments about themselves and others, and to formulate systems of ethical principles.

B. Evolutionary biology can teach us facts about human beings that, in conjunction with moral principles that we already accept, can be used to derive normative principles that we had not yet appreciated.

C. Evolutionary biology can explain what ethics is all about and can settle traditional questions about the objectivity of ethics. In short, evolutionary theory is the key to metaethics.

D. Evolutionary theory can lead us to revise our system of ethical principles, not simply by leading us to accept new derivative statements—as in (B)—but by teaching us new fundamental normative principles. In short, evolutionary biology is not just a source of facts but a source of norms.

Though it is a stretch to say that any single science (let alone evolutionary biology) can do all these things, I will claim that collectively the sciences can accomplish A–D.[11] The methodologies and the ontologies of the science are up to the task, particularly if our approach is subtle. In particular: I think the cognitive sciences have the leading role in A; both cognitive science and biology can contribute to B; the evolutionary sciences—evolutionary biology, ecology, systematics, etc.—can answer C (I will defend a version of realism using those resources); and both cognitive science and evolutionary biology can answer D (they reaffirm an appropriately naturalized virtue ethic, such as that developed by Aristotle and Dewey, and they can inform normative principles in interesting and enlightening ways). Minimally, and relatively uncontroversially, this book will make a contribution to A and B. Maximally, and controversially, it will also make a contribution to C and D.

So, on to certain pieces of philosophical undergrowth that must be cleared out before the project can begin in earnest, beginning with the naturalistic fallacy. Is ethics explanatorily autonomous from the sciences? Can a valid argument be given that has only factual premises and a normative conclusion? Doesn't the nature of the concepts of "normative" and "empirical" preclude any meaningful interplay between the two, and if it does, what kinds of interaction are prohibited? Depending on our answers to these questions, we may be able to rule out naturalization from the start.

2

Clearing the Way for Reduction: Addressing the Naturalistic Fallacy and the Open-Question Argument

Metaethics: Cognitivism and Non-Cognitivism

The status and the nature of moral claims have been topics of controversy in metaethics for as long as the field has existed as an independent arena of inquiry; settling arguments about these issues is in fact the metaethical *raison d'être.* One way of resolving disputes regarding just what it *is* that moral judgments make claims *about* is to ask whether such judgments are truth evaluable.[1]

The non-cognitivist argues that moral judgments are not truth evaluable because (for example) they are merely expressions of attitudes or emotions—in much the same way that "jealousy" is not a truth evaluable claim (as jealousy does not refer to anything independent of the emotional state of the person experiencing jealousy), neither are moral claims. This "boo-hurrah"[2] metaethical view stands in opposition to cognitivism, the school of thought according to which moral claims are indeed truth evaluable. The cognitivist claims that, just as the statement "This dog's mass is 20 kilograms" can be true or false, so too can the statement "This act is immoral." Though most ethicists today adopt cognitivism as a default position,[3] there is still heated debate within the cognitivist camp regarding just what should happen next.[4] Though many cognitivists want to be good reductive naturalists too, the seeming irreducibility of moral claims to perfectly ordinary and empirically tractable ones has presented an "anti-reductionist roadblock" past which many have been afraid to travel.

The arguments for irreducibility have driven some philosophers, such as George E. Moore, to abandon naturalism about ethical claims; others, such as John McDowell, have become non-reductive naturalists.

Some non-cognitivists even offer these irreducibility arguments as a strong motivation for abandoning cognitivism. By my lights, however, the two main historical arguments against reduction, Hume's "naturalistic fallacy" and Moore's "open question argument," fail to establish such a roadblock. Supporting this claim will pave the way for an explanation of my particular brand of reductive cognitivism—there is such a thing as a moral fact, and such facts are complexes of functional claims, where functionality is given a thoroughly naturalistic interpretation.

The Naturalistic Fallacy and the Open-Question Argument: Barriers to Naturalization?

In this chapter I will argue that both the naturalistic fallacy and the open-question argument fail. Each, either implicitly or explicitly, relies on the distinction between analytic and synthetic statements for its force. Insofar as we have good reasons (thanks to Quine and Dewey[5]) to doubt that such a distinction exists, anti-reductionism has lost much of its force. I will end the chapter with a survey of the nature of the relationship between empirical statements and moral theories. Although the use of normative language does capture a unique and important aspect of the world (namely, planning by organisms to achieve ends), it does not point to an ontological barrier that somehow separates the natural world from non-natural normativity. The leap from 'is' to 'ought' becomes an ever-so-tiny web-of-belief-driven inference when the objective correlates of normative terms are appropriately scientifically explicated, and when we view "ought" statements as recommendations about the habits humans and other organisms need have if they are to relate in fruitful ways to those objective correlates.

Terminology

Before I offer a brief exposition of the naturalistic fallacy and the open-question argument, I should clear up some terminology. Although Hume was the first to note the seeming invalidity of inferring an 'ought' statement from a list of 'is' statements, he did not actually use the phrase "the naturalistic fallacy." Rather, G. E. Moore (1902) popularized these words in his discussion of his own "open question argument." Moore's argument was directed specifically against attempts to naturalize the term 'good', whereas Hume's argument applied more generally to all norma- tive terms. Following most other philosophers, I will thus treat the open-question argument as a species of a naturalistic fallacy, giving Hume credit for the general argument and Moore credit for the specific one.[6]

What Is Not at Stake

Before examining Hume and Moore's arguments, let me briefly detail what exactly is *not* at stake in the debate. This is crucial, as wrong-headed refutations of the naturalistic fallacy can do more harm than good for naturalism in ethics. First, no reasonable naturalist in ethics would deny that certain states of affairs in the world are good and others are bad. The point of a naturalistic ethics is just to give a natural yardstick against which to measure such affairs. Thus, it won't do to say in response to the naturalist "You can't infer from the fact that x exists that x is good," as any plausible naturalistic ethical theory will be in agreement. For example, we can't infer from the fact that there is inequality that inequality is good. The question is: Will the norm that we use to criticize inequality originate in nature, or will it originate and be justified supernaturally? Second, no reasonable naturalist in ethics would argue that naturalism in ethics entails the elimination of normative language from our vocabulary. It might very well be that normative terms (such as 'ought' and 'should'), when given the appropriate theoretical explication, are proxies for sets of empirical statements (or, more richly, as statements about what would happen if we behaved in certain ways—that is, as scientific statements), but that is not to say that we should then use these statements rather than the normative terms in everyday discourse. When embedded in the appropriate theory, such normative terms will have explanatory power and pragmatic use. We might have to reform or modify some of our moral concepts, true, but there is no need to dispense with moral language as a result.

What Is at Stake

What is at stake is the nature of the relationship between normative moral theories and traditional empirical scientific theories. Both of the arguments I discuss in this chapter contend that we have *a priori* reason to think that there can be no legitimate form of strong intercourse between normative theories and empirical theories. Can normative theories be justified with the appropriate sets of empirical statements? Hume says no, as any inference from a list of 'is' statements to an 'ought' statement will be invalid—we cannot expect a normative theory to be supported only by scientific findings. Moore also says no, as we will never be able to reduce the primitive unanalyzable term 'good' to any natural predicate or term. Thus, the arguments turn on the question of legitimate possible relationships between empirical findings and normative theories.

Hume and the Naturalistic Fallacy

Hume first offered a general argument for the existence of the naturalistic fallacy in *A Treatise of Human Nature* (1739),[7] where he discusses the transition from 'ought' to 'is', reminding us that it "is of the last consequence. For as this ought, or ought not, expresses some new relation or affirmation, 'tis necessary that it shou'd be observ'd and explain'd; and at the same time, that a reason should be given, for what seems altogether inconceivable, how this new relation can be a deduction from others, which are entirely different from it." Hume is "surprised" when authors writing about morality who were previously reasoning in the 'usual way' suddenly begin to substitute 'oughts' in places where before only 'is' had been present. Since Hume is often cited as a pre-eminent advocate of a naturalized ethics, one might be surprised to hear him offering this argument. However, in the context of the work, Hume is arguing that moral judgments (as it were) arise not from reason but from our passions. We should not look to reason for the wellspring of morality, for reason is the faculty we use to judge things true or false—it does not motivate us; rather, our *passions*, which are not ratiocinative, move us to act, and therefore only they can adequately ground morality. Thus, Hume is a non-cognitivist about moral claims, and hence the apparent tension between his naturalization of ethics and his formulation of the naturalistic fallacy is only apparent.[8] For the naturalist who would also be a cognitivist, however, Hume's remarks do pose a problem, so much so that the Humean version of the naturalistic fallacy has its own name: "Hume's Law." It would appear that Hume has pointed out a serious flaw in any attempt to reason from the empirical to the normative: that in your conclusion you will make reference to an unexplained term (the 'ought' term) that was nowhere present in the (empirical) premises of the argument. Such an argumentative structure is invalid, as the truth of the premises does not guarantee the truth of the conclusion.[9]

[handwritten: you have an invalid premise and so your conclusion can't possibly be correct]

Moore and the Open-Question Argument

The open-question argument takes a similar approach. In his *Principia Ethica*, Moore argues that all naturalists about ethics are guilty of a common fallacy. They confuse the property of goodness with the things that possess it or with another property that the good things have. To commit the naturalistic fallacy is just to confuse the good with one or both of these other things. Moore offers two arguments to support his claim. One is the open-question argument; the other is an argument from the addition of meaning (the import of this phrase will become clear later). First, I will examine the open-question argument.

[handwritten left margin: goodness ≠ good things]

[handwritten right margin: the naturalistic fallacy comes out of the idea that good things are good]

If goodness were identical with another property, then every competent speaker of a language would consider it an ill-formed question to ask if the property in question is itself good; this would be akin to asking a fluent English speaker "Are birds birds?" But in fact we do not consider questions of the type "Is x good?" (where x represents your favorite contender for the reduction of the moral property "good") to be nonsensical. Thus, if your brand of reductive naturalism is utilitarian, then others can, Moore argues, legitimately and sensically confront you with the question "But is it good to maximize aggregate pleasure?" This indicates that the property in question and the property of being good are not actually identical. It is an open question for *any* natural property as to whether it is good. Moore's conclusion is thus that goodness is and must be a simple, non-natural property.

[handwritten right margin: goodness is not a concrete thing. IF it were then it would be redundant — the "instant gratification" factor]

[handwritten left margin: certain things can be good but it isn't redundant to me so]

[handwritten: goodness is something beyond natural]

The second argument Moore offers is an argument from the addition of meaning. If, for example, 'good' meant *pleasant*, then to say "What is pleasant is good" would provide us with neither additional information nor any extra reason to promote pleasurable states of affairs. But since saying "What is pleasant is good" *does* provide us with additional information and *does* give us extra reason to promote pleasure, then we cannot reduce the good to the pleasurable. Such an argument, Moore

[handwritten right margin: if there is no implicit meaning behind good then what motivates people to do good things?]

[handwritten bottom: good is much deeper than mere pleasure]

says, generalizes to prevent any reduction of the term 'good'.[10] Again, goodness, on Moore's view, is a simple, non-natural property.

Several moral philosophers (including Mark Johnson and Geoffrey Warnock) think that Moore did great damage to ethics by advancing these claims. He set the stage for the emotivism that predominated in early-to-mid-twentieth-century ethics. Johnson (1993, p. 140) summarizes:

> By claiming that empirical evidence about who we are and how we function is simply irrelevant to the fundamental questions of moral philosophy, Moore initiated a serious decline in ethics (and in value theory generally) in this century, from which we are only beginning to recover. Quite simply, he so impoverished and marginalized reason that its only role in ethics was the determination of efficient means to ends and of probable causal connections. As Warnock has summed up, Moore leaves us with a realm of *sui generis* indefinable moral qualities about which reason can say nothing. We are confronted with a "vast corpus of moral facts about the world—known, but we cannot say how; related to other features of the world, but we cannot explain in what way; overwhelmingly important for our conduct, but we cannot say why." [Warnock 1967, p. 16]

Moore and Hume Rely on an Implicit Analytic/Synthetic Distinction

One very important feature of Moore's argument that may be transparent at this point is worth discussing in more detail. Moore is essentially arguing that the good itself is a simple, unanalyzable concept. In *Principia Ethica* (1902, p. 9) he writes: "'Good', . . . , if we mean by it that quality which we assert to belong to a thing, when we say that the thing is good, is incapable of any definition, in the most important sense of that word. . . . It is simple and has no parts." Arguments from open questions and the addition of meaning all imply that the good *qua* good is non-synthetic, a simple property not amenable to reductive theoretical analysis. That is, if I say "The good is the pleasant," the *reason* it makes sense to ask of the pleasant "But *is* it good?"—and the *reason* I acquire additional information and may obtain motivation to promote pleasant states of affairs when someone informs me that the pleasant *is* good— is just that we purportedly learn something new when we append the concept "good" to the concept "pleasant" (or whatever our contender for naturalization is). The good is *not analytically given* by any natural definition. If we think that there is no clear distinction between analytic and synthetic statements, and if we think that even simple statements about the good are revisable in light of experience, then we will have gone a long way toward defusing Moore's in-principle objections to a naturalized ethic.

Interestingly, among Moore's belongings when he passed away was a new preface for a never-written second edition of *Principia Ethica*. This preface was published posthumously. In it, Moore spends a considerable time backing away from some of the claims he seems to be making in the text, concluding with this startling statement: "Some such proposition as this, namely, that G [the Good] is not identical with any natural or metaphysical property (as now defined), was more or less vaguely in my mind, I think, there is no doubt. . . . I was, I think, certainly confusing this proposition to the effect that G is not analyzable in one particular way, with the proposition that it is not analyzable at all." This is an incredible admission—we learn that Moore did *not* intend for the open-question argument to establish *a priori* that G could not be a natural property. Thus, Moore's argument boils down to this: We haven't been given a perfect naturalistic ethic *yet*, to which all but the most partisan naturalists about ethics would agree, myself included (although, with others, I think an appropriately scientifically updated Aristotle comes very close). Strangely, I have not been able to find a single work about the open question as it relates to evolutionary accounts of morality that discusses these interesting admissions. Since Moore examines only two naturalistic accounts of the meaning of 'Good' in his book (namely, hedonism and Herbert Spencer's evolutionary ethics), his conclusions suddenly seem much less grand. More realistically, his point becomes that Hedonism and Spencerian ethics are not good candidates for a reduction of moral properties to naturalistic properties. I agree, as do many other naturalists. Nonetheless, despite these clarifications, Moore *still* insists that "ethical propositions do involve some unanalysable notion, which is not identical with any natural or metaphysical property." I assume that the reason there hasn't been more discussion of these remarks is that they are taken from a posthumous manuscript.

In any case, Hume similarly relies on an implicit analytic/synthetic distinction. We find the new copula 'ought' strange and confusing, apparently, because it references concepts that are not analytically identical to those referenced by the copula 'is'. If it were, on popular accounts of what analyticity consists in, we could, by the law of substitution,

merely replace 'ought' with 'is' in the conclusion of the fallacious naturalistic argument and go on our merry way. But such a story about why
we *don't* substitute 'is' for 'ought' relies on our ability to clearly distinguish analytic from synthetic statements—that is, on our capacity to
delineate meaning independent of factual content. If there is no clear
distinction to be drawn between these two types of statements, then
there must be another reason why we find the inference a strange one. It
could be that only empirical statements of the *proper* kind, namely those
informed and organized by an appropriate naturalized ethical theory,
can productively inform a normative statement. But an admission that
our logic can be informed by experience—that the laws of logic are open
to revision in light of recalcitrant experience—amounts to an admission
that the laws of logic are not analytic. Thus, our intuitions that Hume
is on to something with the naturalistic fallacy are driven by either
(a) implicit analytic/synthetic distinctions or (b) an inappropriate theory
of naturalized ethics. Quine effectively undercuts (a), and the purpose of
this book is to provide more support for a theoretically fecund notion of
naturalized ethics, so (b) is not a threat to the project.

There is another sense in which Hume's argument reduces to Moore's
argument. One could grant that it is illegitimate to make an inference
from an 'is' to an 'ought', but only if, as Hume implicitly assumes, you
do not *define* 'oughts' in terms of 'is' statements (e.g., "One *ought* to do
what *is* pleasurable"). Hume's argument then relies on Moore's argument for its force: you can't give a naturalistic definition of the good,
and so the naturalistic fallacy will forever remain a fallacy.

The secondary literature on the naturalistic fallacy is large. However,
it would be a fair summary to say that contemporary philosophers of a
non-naturalistic stripe accept one version or another of either the
Humean or the Moorean naturalistic fallacy. I will spend a good part of
the remainder of this chapter outlining two possible responses to Hume
and Moore. One draws on the explanatory resources of Quine, the
other on a little-discussed account of moral reasoning proffered by
Dewey. By my lights, Quine and like-minded philosophers such as Nelson
Goodman and Morton White[11] make short work of the analytic/synthetic
distinction. In doing so, they remove a crucial premise necessary for
Hume and Moore to cleanly separate the empirical and the normative.
Similarly, Dewey's philosophical method tends to dissolve dualisms of

all kinds, including the analytic/synthetic distinction; nowhere is this clearer than in his discussion of means-ends reasoning. Though which means is most effective to a given end may be "merely" a matter for empirical demonstration, it may also be, if Dewey's picture of moral judgment is at all correct, an empirical matter as to which ends we ought to have *impliciter*.[14] Dewey and Quine are thus cozy bedfellows, which should come as no surprise since both fall under the pragmatist umbrella.

The upshot of Quine's and Dewey's responses to Hume and Moore will be that all of our beliefs, including seemingly analytic ones, are open to revision based on recalcitrant experience. If our beliefs are appropriately (that is, pragmatically) formed, so-called analytic statements are nothing more than extremely well confirmed scientific facts. Any attempt to argue that "come what may, we can never infer norms from empirical judgments," as both Hume and Moore do, would entrench an indefensible assumption. We should therefore be open to the possibility of a reduction of normative properties to natural, functional properties.

Quine: Rejecting the Analytic/Synthetic Distinction

In "Two Dogmas of Empiricism," Quine attacks two ill-founded beliefs that have conditioned the modern empiricist epistemological project. The first dogma is, of course, the analytic/synthetic distinction. The second is reductionism. The reductionism Quine attacks is not the kind of intertheoretic reduction that I am pressing. Rather, he attacks the reductionism of the logical empiricists, who thought that all meaningful statements were equivalent to logical constructs built out of terms referring to immediate experience. Quine would guardedly approve of the unity-of-science considerations that often drive both the articulation of traditional theories of reduction and more broadly ecumenical theories such as domain integration.[13] I focus primarily on the first dogma, although, as Quine notes, the two are, at root, identical.

Quine first distinguishes between logically true analytic statements and other statements that appear to be analytic but do not obviously share the "logically true" status. An example of a logically true statement is "No unmarried man is married." If we presuppose a class of *will always be true unless the relationship between the words is changed*

"logical particles" (e.g., truth-functional connectives such as 'not' and 'and'), this statement remains true under any reinterpretation of its components (unless, of course, we reinterpret the logical particles themselves).

Quine later demonstrates that even the first class of logically true statements begs the question against the problem of analyticity. But we can set this concern aside for the moment to at least consider whether we can reduce the second class to the first so as to further constrain the bounds of the problem. Quine thus begins his argument with the second class of "analytic statements." His example is "No bachelor is married." At first glance, this statement seems analytic. But how can we demonstrate that it is? One strategy is to reduce this second class of statements to the first class by leveraging definitions. "Bachelor" is *defined* as "unmarried man," so the second statement is actually equivalent, via substitution, to the first. To this, Quine responds "But who defined it thus, and when?" Appealing to dictionaries written by lexicographers begs the question, as those empirical scientists already had a standard for synonymy in mind—that is exactly why they listed 'bachelor' and 'unmarried man' next to each other in their dictionary. Thus, adverting to "definitions" does not adequately analyze the notion of synonymy to which friends of analyticity were appealing in the attempt to reduce definitional truths to logical truths.

can all analytic statements be reduced to analytic statements that are true

any seemingly true statement can be reduced to its false

definitions are synonyms

definitions can be used with logical truths

An alternative explication of synonymy is to equate it with interchangeability. On this view, terms are synonymous if they can be interchanged without loss of truth value. Quine rightly notes that in this case we are concerned only with "cognitive synonymy," not with psychological synonymity (e.g., terms can be cognitively synonymous with regard to the logical structure of the arguments they will support without necessarily calling to mind similar associations in you and me). According to Quine (1953, p. 158), "to say that 'bachelor' and 'unmarried man' are cognitively synonymous is to say no more nor less than that the statement: '. . . all and only bachelors are unmarried men' is analytic." Thus, this move is just question begging yet again. We still have no criteria for distinguishing this purportedly analytic statement from a statement that is true but only contingently so.

The final option that Quine examines for reducing statements of the second class of seemingly analytic truths to statements of the first logically true class relies on semantic rules. By examining and rejecting this final option, Quine undermines any clean distinction between analytic and synthetic statements of *either* class, as logically true statements also lean heavily on the concept of a semantic rule.

One might think that it is only the sloppiness of ordinary language that prevents us from drawing a bright analytic/synthetic line. In an appropriately constructed artificial language, such as a good logic, can't we just define sets of semantical rules that stipulate what statements are analytic? However, as Quine quickly points out, such a move does not offer an analysis of analytical statements but instead solves the problem by fiat; stipulations and truths by fiat can, of course, be wrong. Perhaps then, we can merely add that such stipulations must be *true* stipulations. But this doesn't help, as that amounts to saying that *any* truth can be an analytic truth. Semantical rules would then be distinguished from the statements of (say) a true science merely because they happen to appear on a page under the heading "Semantical Rules" rather than in the "Well-Confirmed Experimental Results" section.

Quine concludes by noting the obvious fact that "truth in general depends on both language and extralinguistic fact." But, crucially, the belief that we can therefore somehow analyze a statement into a linguistic component and a factual component is, as Quine famously puts it, "an unempirical dogma of empiricists, a metaphysical article of faith" (ibid., p. 163).

What of the second reductionist dogma? Quine argues that Rudolf Carnap's attempt to translate sentences about the physical world into sentences about immediate experience (in the technical sense intended by the logical empiricists—for example, that complexes of simple sentences of the form "Quality q is at point-instant x;y;z;t" will latch on to immediate experience and serve to ground all other sentences) implicitly relies on a language/fact distinction. The confirmation of a sentence leans heavily on the fact that one can distinguish the linguistic content of the sentence from the factual content supplied by the basic experience. But it was exactly the inability to demonstrate that such a thing is possible that led to Quine's abandonment of the analytic/synthetic distinction. Quine remarks: ". . . as long as it is taken to be significant in general to speak of the confirmation and infirmation of a statement, it seems significant to speak also of a limiting kind of statement which is vacuously confirmed, *ipso facto*, come what may; and such a statement is analytic. The two dogmas are, indeed, at root identical" (ibid., p. 166).

Of course, Quine remains a good empiricist. He thinks, however, that our empiricism cannot make the simplistic assumptions required to get the project of *logical* empiricism off the ground. Rather, we should view belief formation more pragmatically. Each of us approaches the world armed with our theories (our "scientific heritage") and an ongoing barrage of sensory stimuli. The considerations that guide us in warping our scientific heritage to fit our "continuing sensory promptings" are "where rational, pragmatic" (ibid., p. 168). All our beliefs exist in a web (including our theories about ethics, logic, and the various sciences),[14] and we should not be so arrogant as to think that any of them, even the purportedly analytic ones (or normative ones), are immune to revision in light of experience.

Quine realized that his approach to philosophy would have tremendous implications for ethical theorizing. Indeed, he discussed his thoughts about the relationship between pragmatism and ethics in "On the Nature of Moral Values." With Owen Flanagan, however, I think that Quine did not go far enough in allowing normative theories full play in our web of beliefs.

Quine, Hume, and Moore

Quine's arguments interact with those of Hume and Moore in three significant ways.

First, as was discussed in chapter 1, both Hume and Moore rely in some respects upon a hard and fast analytic/synthetic distinction. If such a distinction cannot be supported, then there is reason to believe that the normative and the natural might be more closely related than they (especially Moore) argued. Recall particularly that Hume's argument relies on Moore's argument for its force. With Quine in hand, we can insist that any *a priori* attempt to isolate the good from natural definition dodges tough questions about theory change: rather than insist that the meaning of good precludes natural definition, why not admit that you have a theory of the good (rather than merely a definition of it), and let such a theory be adjudged as theories are: by their relationship to other theories, and by their encounters with experience?

Second, Quine's arguments also had an impact on *a priori* truth, at least insofar as analytic statements captured a large subset of those truths that could purportedly be justified without appeal to experience. If moral truths weren't those that could be known *a priori,* then we must come to have knowledge of them via experience, which opens the door for a robust empirical/normative interaction.

Third, Quine leveled the playing field with regard to an implicit hierarchy of things known—those things that were certain and were often known with certainty (the rules of logic, the truth values of definitional sentences, moral rules) were not categorically different from those things that were contingent and usually known contingently (the deliverances of the natural sciences). On the Quinean picture, theories about all these entities were conjoined and made responsive to experience. As a result, areas of inquiry that were not previously thought to be amenable to empirical interpretation, such as epistemology, were ripe for naturalization as the old hierarchies collapsed.[15] Likewise for ethics.[16]

Dewey on the Naturalistic Fallacy and Moral Reasoning

John Dewey, one of the founders of modern pragmatism, anticipated much of Quine's work. Dewey was highly sensitive to dualisms of all sorts and the damage that they could do to our interests, particularly when they prevented us from expending our energies appropriately when dealing with our problems. Like Quine's, Dewey's logic was at root a compendium of empirically successful ways to deal with problematic situations; he did not have patience for those who would reify logic, making it a part of the formal structure of the universe that existed independently of reasoning creatures interacting with the world. His ethical theory, and the framework for moral judgment that constitutes its epistemological machinery, also eschews supernaturalism about the ethical and roots moral concerns in the activity of people coping with an environment. In this section, I will briefly discuss the basics of Dewey's moral theory, highlighting especially his appeal to the means-ends continuum, so as to sketch Dewey's conception of a science of morality. I will also gloss his theory of moral reasoning, which establishes the necessity of several crucial cognitive capacities that are especially amenable to connectionist reconstruction.

Dewey's general position on the naturalistic fallacy was that the "is/ought" gap did capture something about moral reasoning: that to articulate norms consisted in discussing intelligent methods of regulating consummatory experience. But Dewey did not think that this implied that there could be neither a science of ethics nor a naturalistic explanation of the ontology of the good and how we comprehend it and regulate it. Crucially, Dewey distinguishes between the desired and the desirable. The presence of a desire for dessert does not mean I ought to eat the dessert; to do so would be to improperly balance my *desire* for sweet food with something *desirable*, namely maintaining a healthy body. In the short term, regulating my experience by giving in merely to what is desired rather than to what is desirable would be disastrous and would lead to non-consummatory experience in the long run. I should regulate my desires and resolve conflicting wants and needs, or I should triangulate a reasonable course of action when faced with apparently conflicting values. The reasoning process that I use to regulate action in this way is the moral reasoning process.[17] But such a process does not rely on a *supernatural* capacity to identify *pre-existing* "eternal norms." And neither does the fact that I have desires on which I ought not act preclude my using positive moral experience as a fallible basis for generating norms and "oughts." Dewey's general approach to ethics is thus consistent with his naturalistic humanism, and with his appreciation for evolutionary theory.[18] As Dewey notes in his introduction to *Human Nature and Conduct* (1922, p. 12), "a morals based on study of human nature instead of upon disregard for it would find the facts of man continuous with those of the rest of nature and would thereby ally ethics with physics and biology."

There is some disagreement in the small secondary literature on this matter. Marga Vicedo (1999, p. 234) insists, using strong language, that Dewey would approve of an evolutionary ethic,[19] whereas Paul Lawrence Farber (1994, p. 113) argues that Dewey rejects evolutionary approaches to ethics as "fundamentally misguided." Scholars such as Farber often support their contentions with quotations from the first edition of the *Ethics* (1908). But a close reading of the second edition (1932) reveals that much of the controversial language that can be construed as eliminating in principle an evolutionary ethic has been removed. Moreover, examination of the context of the remarks in the first edition reveals that they are intended as criticisms of *existing* systems of evolutionary ethics, mainly those proposed by Darwin and by Spencer. Finally, Farber draws mostly upon Dewey's early work, which is tainted with a Hegelian residue from Dewey's early philosophic training. Though Dewey learned the theory of evolution in college and believed it to be accurate, it took almost 10 years for the import of it to leach into his philosophy. Dewey makes several precautionary remarks regarding an evolutionary ethic, but in view of his general approach of having Darwinian considerations inform philosophy *en toto* we have *prima facie* reason to believe that Dewey would be amenable to an appropriately formulated evolutionary ethic.

For Dewey, organisms like ourselves engage in inquiry when we are faced with problematic situations. Such organic, "lived" problems are what spark reflection and issue in choice. Thus, in moral inquiry there are three predominant stages: (1) an agent finding herself in a morally problematic situation, which leads to (2) moral deliberation involving experimental, emotional, and imaginative processes, which then issues in (3) a judgment, choice, or an action. Though all three of these phases are crucial, of particular interest for this chapter is moral deliberation as it relates to imagination.

Dewey on Moral Imagination

Dewey thought that, if we applied ourselves, we would come to regulate our activities intelligently so as to provide an optimum amount of consummatory experience. Although the world (e.g., organisms and environments) contains both value and disvalue, and although we cannot hope to alleviate the latter entirely, we can certainly ameliorate our situation, improving it as much as possible.

Language such as "consummatory experience" should not lead one to think that Dewey or other pragmatists were concerned with maximizing *subjective* happiness or pleasure. For Dewey, values are part of the world-organism relationship, and, owing to the facts of our biology and our evolutionary history, we can come to discover them (although this is not to say that they were there before the organism was). David Brink (1989) argues that accounts of value that make values subjective (such as hedonistic or desire-satisfaction theories) fall prey to a fatal *gedanken* from Robert Nozick. If we had an "experience machine" that we could connect to our brains so as to provide continual satisfaction of our desires, none of us would choose to connect ourselves to this machine. This belies the fact that value is not merely a reflection of our subjective desires but involves interaction with a world that contains value.

One important cognitive method we use to hold an end in view so as to ascertain the consequences of its pursuit (and fix effective means to achieve it) is imagination. The capacity to imagine is crucial for moral reasoning on Dewey's account. In *Human Nature and Conduct* (1922, pp. 132–133), Dewey explains:

> Deliberation is an experiment in finding out what the various lines of possible action are really like. It is an experiment in making various combinations of selected elements of habits and impulses, to see what our resultant action would be like if it were entered upon. But the trial is in imagination, not in overt fact. The experiment is carried on by tentative rehearsals in thought which do not affect physical facts outside the body. Thought runs ahead and foresees outcomes, and thereby avoids having to wait the instruction of actual failure and disaster. An act overly tried out is irrevocable, its consequences cannot be blotted out. An act tried out in imagination is not final or fatal. It is retrievable.

Though at first glance it might appear that Dewey is merely referring to our ability to model events in the world, he is doing more than this, as he has very subtle accounts of what it means to possess a habit. Habits for Dewey are rich cognitive and conative capacities that are influenced by experience and, in turn, influence what we make of experience. Later I will argue that Dewey has in mind a complex of cognitive capacities when he speaks of imagination, only some of which include our ability to engage in mental modeling, and all of which are amenable to connectionist interpretation. In some cases, Dewey's language anticipates radical connectionist, sub-symbolic, and dynamical systems theory approaches to situated action; in addition, some of the otherwise strange language that he uses when describing moral reasoning and character development can be viewed as an anticipation of developments in the cognitive neuroscience of judgment and decision making. Dewey's account and these influences and connections will be explored in more depth in chapter 5.[20]

For the time being, the important thing to note is the existence of a fluid continuum in this picture of moral reasoning between means and ends. A trivial example: I have a quite natural and possibly appropriate desire for ice cream; ice cream is of value to me. I hold fixed this end in view so as to imagine the consequences associated with the consumption of the ice cream. I discover that there are many possible futures wherein I gain an unhealthy amount of weight, and I discover also that in those circumstances many other things I value as consummatory experience would not be available to me—I could no longer fit into the cockpit of my stunt airplane, say, and there is a good chance that I would suffer a heart attack owing to arterial sclerosis. I choose instead to eat an apple, and as I eat apples rather than ice cream I come to enjoy the experience of apple eating and focus approvingly upon it, making it a habit. I react to apples differently now ("Oh, an apple! How delightful!") and have different experiences around them as a result of my initial encounter with and cognition about ice cream.

In this case, my moral imagination has caused me to transform an end in view (consumption of ice cream) into a different end in view (consumption of apples), which at first I conceive of as merely a *means* to the end (remembering that ends are something desirable and not merely desired) of health, but which I eventually transform into an end *in and of itself* also. I finally get in the habit of eating apples, and such a habit is not *merely* the repetition of a bodily movement but rather a rich set of cognitive experiences that transforms my daily activity into something quite different than it was before. A better example: think of exercise. It is no accident that this process of habituation (*richly* construed) is essentially a character-development activity. On this view, the sets of capacities we gain by reasoning morally are more accurately characterized as sets of cognitive skills and habits rather than as linguistic knowledge as such.

Ends become means and means become ends. This process of transformation demonstrates that, according to Dewey, we do an injustice to the world if we construe ends as being fixed, permanent, final and out of the reach of a scientific analysis. Most people look upon engineering as an applied science, and would view it as an expertise that focuses on means, yet we have no bitter ontological struggles about engineering (at least, none that make their way into common parlance, quite unlike ethical ontologies). The transformation of one thing formerly valued as an end into something that is merely a means for another end, and the reverse transformation of ends into means (e.g., at first I enjoy going to the library because I like to read, but later reading becomes a means to enable me to acquire the skill of being able to philosophize) demonstrates that the fact/value distinction is not hard and fast, but rather is one of degree.

In the perfect world, all experience would be continually consummatory. Note that in the analysis of moral function in the next chapter this amounts essentially to being perfectly adapted to the range of environments with which you regularly interact. Note also that if your environment is perfectly stable, being perfectly adapted would abnegate the need for creative abstract thought. On some pictures, if this world were simple enough, cognition would altogether cease to have a function. Peter Godfrey-Smith's 1996 book *Complexity and the Function of Mind in Nature* contains an excellent discussion of these issues as well as illustrative treatments of both Dewey and Herbert Spencer. But, since we do not exist in a perfect world, not all experience is consummatory. However that is not to say that norms can't be grounded in empirical facts about human flourishing, nor is it to say that ends can never be means and vice versa.

In line with these thoughts, Dewey's account is both normative and empirical. It is normative insofar as it represents the way we ought to think about moral matters (that is, in a scientific spirit), and it is empirical insofar as Dewey thought that this was the way we do in fact proceed when engaging in fruitful moral inquiry. It is naturalistic through and through, and the open-question argument and naturalistic fallacy find no purchase on it.

Dewey, Hume, and Moore

The open-question argument merely amounts to a description of one crucial phase of moral experimentation, namely that of testing ends in view to see if they should be adopted as ends proper. However, nothing about this process implies that ends are metaphysically strange or that they are not facts about creatures and environments and their relationships. There is a singular, crucial difference between Dewey's method and Moore's: despite Moore's lament that philosophers too often engage in purely speculative metaphysics, the open-question process at its best is still basically a form of non-empirically informed conceptual analysis. At its worst, it can legitimize armchair metaphysics (as in: not only must we proliferate moral ontological simples, but perhaps there are open questions about every concept at every turn). Dewey, however, intends for moral reasoning to be empirically informed. On his picture, it has a scientific aspect that is missing from Moore's "open questioning." And, as discussed earlier, open-question arguments implicitly rely on the analytic/synthetic distinction, which Dewey, anticipating Quine, rejects as yet another ill-advised dualism.

As for Hume's naturalistic fallacy, Dewey's process of moral reasoning will, he thinks, help us identify those extant values that are worthy of pursuit. These values, though, are discovered by examination of the biological world of organism-environment interaction: they are facts, empirical matters in any reasonable sense of the phrase. Dewey's ethical theory has many points in common with Hume's,[21] although once the teleological aspects of Aristotle are canalized and given limits by a biological analysis of function, we will see that Dewey's project is actually much more like a modern-day virtue theory.

A Pessimistic Coda: Why This Project Is Still Important Even If This Chapter Is All Wrong

Even if Quine, Dewey, and I haven't convinced you that the naturalistic fallacy and open-question arguments do not stand in the way of attempts to sketch a naturalistic account of the content of morality and the form of moral judgment, you still have reason to keep reading. Only the most stalwart anti-naturalist would think that facts about human beings and how they reason have absolutely no bearing on normative concerns, and only a small number of contemporary moral philosophers have taken this position. Even if this chapter seems misguided, we can at least maintain that the biological and cognitive sciences can constrain moral theorizing by identifying the realistic limits of our biological and moral capacities.

Usefully, we can sketch out three possible personality types that embody sets of positions regarding the relationships between science and the norms of morality (since the question is ultimately one of governance, I have used political terms): Separatists, Confederates, Unionists.

Separatists advocate abstinence: there shall be no intercourse between the findings of science and the articulation of norms. What is would be irrelevant to what ought to be; the methods of the sciences would be orthogonal (at best) to the formulation of norms, and there would be no common ground between science and morality. Virginia Held, Kelly Nicholson, and Alvin Plantinga are modern-day separatists.

Confederates are moderately promiscuous: they allow the findings of the sciences to place limits on the demands that norms can legitimately place upon us, or to rule out some moral theories as inconsistent with our best natural knowledge. James Sterba and David Brink are contemporary Confederates.

The fecund Unionists are of two stripes. There are those who think that robust moral norms are part of the fabric of the world and can be constrained by and derived from the sciences. These are the "Conservative Unionists," who wish to subsume ethics by making it into a science. Mark Johnson and Larry Arnhart are Conservative Unionists, as is Owen Flanagan. Sharing similar views about the relationship between science and morality, but disagreeing about what the sciences will tell us about moral nature, are the "Eliminative Unionists," who wish to "unify" science and ethics by eliminating the purportedly illusory subject matter of ethics. Michael Ruse is presiding president of this party; J. L. Mackie is past president, and E. O. Wilson is vice-president.

The point of this section was to make a plausible case for Conservative Unionism. (I will deal with the complications presented by Eliminative Unionism in the next chapter.) Though the inertia of the history of moral philosophy is against Conservative Unionism, the party platform has much to offer. But even if you remain a Confederate, the remainder of this book will be very useful, as it will identify constraints placed upon our normative moral theories by the results of the cognitive and biological sciences. If you are still a Separatist, then it will at least be a provocative read. But I would hasten to point out that your party is growing smaller and more disorganized day by day. The future lies with Conservative Unionism and consilience. Nothing about the term 'Conservative' is mean to imply that the viewpoint won't be progressive. It will be; rather, it merely indicates that the party wishes to maintain the general moral stance, identifying parts of the ethical tradition that are especially useful in view of the findings of science. The view will not be radically eliminative, but neither will all moral concepts be maintained.

Conclusion

I have argued in this chapter that cognitive naturalists about morality have often been stymied in their attempts to fruitfully unify ethics and the sciences by the two non-reductive roadblocks of the naturalistic fallacy and the open-question argument. However, both of these positions rely upon the analytic/synthetic distinction for their force, and the arguments of Quine give us good reason to doubt that such a hard and fast distinction exists. In addition, the theory of moral judgment on offer from Dewey belies the fact that facts and values intermingle and correlate in ways subversive to both roadblocks. "Conservative Unionism" about the relationship between science and norms remains a live option. In the next chapter, I give content to the party platform by outlining a neo-Aristotelian conception of function that is biological and is naturalistic through and through.

3

The Functional Account of Ethics: Functional Explanation in Biology and a Corresponding Account in Morality

Metaethics Again: Mackie's Error Theory

In the preceding chapter, I made a brief case for the possibility of a cognitivist account of ethics that would be consonant with the natural sciences and overcome anti-reductionist arguments. What are we to make of the response that even if everything said thus far is true, it could *still* be the case that our moral theories are wrong across the board because they do not actually refer to objects, states, or properties that *genuinely* exist? In *Ethics: Inventing Right and Wrong*, John L. Mackie, Eliminative Unionist, argues forcefully for an error theory regarding the meaning of moral terms. Mackie contends that our ordinary use of moral language implies that moral values are objective, but that philosophers have not spent enough time investigating the non-conceptual component of this claim to objectivity. This is a case, he contends, where conceptual analysis is, thankfully, not enough, as the argument in favor of such things as objective moral values is far from proven. Despite what common sense and the meaning of moral terms might imply, Mackie thinks there is good reason to believe that there aren't objective values—hence the need for an "error theory" for our moral language. Mackie offers several arguments against the objectivity of values, two of which are found in the historical tradition of moral anti-realism.[1] These two arguments, the "argument from relativity" and the "argument from queerness," have *prima facie* force. Nonetheless, when the appropriate resources are marshaled and brought to bear, they can be just as forcefully rebutted. The resources I have in mind are an appropriately naturalized Aristotelian virtue theory and a contemporary biologically oriented notion of function. Drawing on this strand of the Greek tradition and upon modern philosophy of biology will not only enable us to argue against Mackie's contentions about relativity and queerness; it will also shed light on why a critic of moral realism might be convinced by these two arguments to begin with. In a nutshell: Reducing moral terms to functional terms, and treating the objects to which those terms refer as a contemporarily informed Aristotle would, we can establish a case for the objectivity of moral value *and* simultaneously understand why Mackie might find the case against objectivity initially persuasive. A renaissance in contemporary moral philosophy awaits the scientifically sensitive ethicist—a synoptic view encompassing the essentially functional nature of human morality and emphasizing the importance of developments in the human sciences (particularly the cognitive sciences and evolutionary biology) will shed new light not only on the case for realism about values but also on other long-standing issues in moral philosophy, as I have been concerned to argue.

From Moral Functions to Biological Functions

First, I will quickly sketch outlines of the arguments from relativity and queerness, placing them in their historical context and noting their upshot for moral realism.[2] Then I will briefly summarize a virtue-theoretic answer to these two arguments. Next, drawing on contemporary philosophy of biology and on work recent work in moral realism, I will situate Aristotelian virtue theory in a modern function-laden context, briefly outlining a scheme for naturalization that will make the case for the objectivity of values even more persuasive by leveraging a modern-history theory of functionality. Drawing on an expanded notion of property articulated by Richard Boyd, I will demonstrate how the case for the objectivity of values can be made in a scientifically tractable manner. I will briefly note what implications this set of responses to Mackie has for other issues in ethics and metaethics. Contra Mackie, I will conclude that ethics is discovered, not invented, and that being sensitive to this claim (and what it implies about our methods for discovering moral knowledge) will allow us to improve our ethical theories. The anti-naturalistic roadblocks discussed in chapter 2 can thus be overcome not just in principle but also in fact with the appropriate moral theory. I will conclude by reviewing recent work in evolutionary ethics, using other authors as foils against which to refine and develop the account on offer.

Mackie and the Argument from Relativity

The argument from relativity begins with the premise that moral codes vary from one period of time to another and from one society to another. This variation is often cited by proponents of the subjectivity of values as evidence for the claim that there are not objective values. As an example, in his *Outlines of Scepticism* (300 A.D./1994, p. 38), Sextus Empiricus discusses the variation among morals and customs in the ancient world, offering it as evidence in favor of skepticism about values:

> For example, we opposed custom to custom like this: some of the Ethiopians tattoo their babies, while we do not; the Persians deem it becoming to wear brightly-coloured full-length dresses, while we deem it unbecoming; Indians have sex with women in public, while most other people hold that it is shameful. We oppose persuasion to persuasion when we oppose the persuasion of Diogenes to that of Aristippus, or that of the Spartans to that of the Italians.

Unlike Sextus Empiricus, Mackie (1977, p. 36) notes that "such variation is in itself merely a truth of descriptive morality, a fact of anthropology which entails neither first order nor second order ethical views." This acknowledgment saves him from immediate charges of crude and simple moral relativism of the kind that Rachels responds to effectively in chapter 2 of *The Elements of Moral Philosophy* (1993). A cruder relativism could immediately be rebutted by noting that variation among views about what is constitutive of morality implies nothing about what is actually constitutive of it, in much the same way that variations among the beliefs of poorly informed cosmologists don't necessarily imply anything about whether the Big Bang theory of the origins of the universe is true. However, Mackie (ibid., p. 37) notes that his version of the argument is subtler. He argues that the variations in moral codes do not stem from differences in moral perception; rather, these differences spring from the fact that they are *merely* reflections of various ways of life: "The argument from relativity has some force simply because the actual variations in the moral codes are more readily explained by the hypothesis that they reflect ways of life than by the hypothesis that they express perceptions, most of them seriously inadequate and badly distorted, of objective values." But there is a much-discussed reply to this argument, and it consists in noting that, if variations of the scope discussed by Sextus Empiricus and Mackie exist, all of them can be accounted for by the interaction of basic general principles which are implicit in the moral codes of all cultures with the individual circumstances of a particular culture. These principles, as Sidgwick noted, will beget different particular rules when applied to a given situation owing to the vagaries of individual societal circumstance. And, as Dewey notes, this is what we should expect given the non-fixed nature of experience and the variability of life as lived. Merely because moral codes vary from society to society we should not infer that moral codes are "merely" reflections of ways of life and not more-or-less correct perceptions of objective values.³ Different environments demand different things of the organisms that exist within them. The presence of moral universals is a live debate; nonetheless, recent work in moral anthropology accomplished by Cook (1999) argues that the variation among moral codes oft-cited by friends of relativism and skepticism does not really exist. A careful examination of the anthropological and historical evidence suggests that in fact there are a large number of value universals. And in any case, if this variation is a reflection of coevolutionary adaptation between organism and environment, then it will be justified by principles that spring from an objective functional account of morality.

Mackie is sensitive to this reply, arguing that it does not go far enough in countering the argument from relativity. The objectivist about values has to say that it is *only* these general principles to which the objective moral value of the societal practices attaches. Insofar as our "moral sense" and "moral intuitions" provide the starting point for much of our moral dialogue, it would be wishful thinking on the part of the moral objectivist, notes Mackie (1977, pp. 37–38), to argue that these general principles are what actually guided the production and application of particular societal mores.

However, this burden is not one that the value realist has to live with. The argument is not persuasive as it seems to beg the question against the moral objectivist. Any reasonable theory of moral judgment will have an "error clause"—that is, it will explain why there is moral misperception as well as moral perception. When I discuss my account, it will have an error clause. Additionally, Mackie seems to shoulder the realist about values with a version of the genetic fallacy: since the moral codes of a particular society weren't devised with a general moral principle *explicitly* in mind, they can't *reflect* such general moral principles. Value realists need not accept this burden in order to demonstrate their case, particularly if their moral epistemology can accommodate moral error in a reasonable manner.

Let me continue my explication of Mackie's position by moving from the argument from relativity to what Mackie considers to be an even more persuasive and difficult argument: the argument from queerness.

The Argument from Queerness

The argument from queerness has two components, one metaphysical/ontological and the other epistemological. Mackie (1977, p. 38) summarizes the two components as follows: "If there were objective values, then they would be entities or qualities or relations of a very strange sort, utterly different from anything else in the universe. Correspondingly, if we were aware of them, it would have to be by some special faculty of moral perception or intuition, utterly different from our ordinary ways of knowing everything else." Thus, the metaphysical *cum* ontological component argues that objective values would be very strange creatures indeed, and since strange creatures require strange senses so as to be perceived, their known existence would require the imputation of a very odd faculty on our part. Hence, the epistemological component of the argument is tightly connected to the metaphysical part of the argument. Let us take a closer look at what, by Mackie's lights, objective values would have to be and why this would make them so very odd.

The paradigmatic example of an odd objective value is the Platonic notion of the forms.[4] Knowledge of the "Form of the Good" is such that to know the good will inevitably cause you to do the good. In other words, correct courses of action would have "to be done-ness" built into them, whereas incorrect courses of action have "not to be done-ness" as part of their constituent structure. Mackie's point is that values must have their motivational structure built into them, which seems rather odd insofar as "motivations" as such do not float around in the world waiting to be perceived by moral agents. Mackie is also dubious about the possibility of linking natural features to moral features in a "non-queer" manner. In brief, then, the argument from queerness has both a metaphysical and epistemological component—values are strange things and we would come to know them (*if* we do actually come to know them) in strange ways—and the metaphysical component is supported by two genuinely difficult questions ("How can values be intrinsically motivational without being strange?" and "How can values be linked to natural features in a non-queer manner?"). An appropriately naturalized Aristotelian position, I will argue, can successfully dissipate both the ontological and epistemological queerness of objective values.

A Brief Summary of Aristotelian Ethics

In order to better answer Mackie's arguments, I will first sketch the Aristotelian moral position. This will be admittedly much too brief, and it may border on being oversimplified to the point of being non-representative (although hopefully not in the aspects that are directly related to the case for naturalization that I am making). I avoid many of the difficult finer points of debate in the voluminous secondary literature on Aristotle. For reasons of space, I ask the reader's indulgence.

Aristotle's best-known work in the area of ethics is the *Nicomachean Ethics* (hereafter referred to as the *NE*).[5] In it, Aristotle attempts to give a reflective understanding of human well-being and the "good life." He suggests that flourishing consists in excellent activity (such as intellectual contemplation and virtuous action) arising from an appropriately structured character. David Charles (1995, p. 54) summarizes concisely: "Virtuous action is what the person with practical wisdom would choose; and the practically wise are those who can deliberate successfully towards well-being." Aristotle's ethics thus has a distinctively teleological flavor—in his biological studies, he thought that a thing's nature was determined by what counted as its successful operation; so it is too for his ethics. Ethical statements are ultimately functional statements. In much the same way that a hammer has the *telos* (or end) of hitting nails on the head, and is functioning well when it hits nails on the head excellently, human beings also have a *telos*, and function well when they realize their *telos* in activity. To live the life informed and motivated by practical reason and wisdom is to live a functional life.

Giving Content to Aristotelian Function: What Is Success?

Aristotle believes that success in life is the only intrinsic good—all else is instrumental to the achievement of it. We are successful insofar as we realize our true nature, our one function. We can determine the content of our nature by asking "What is it that distinguishes us from other animals?" Aristotle's essentialist answer: our capacity for robust reason.

The proper function of reason is to enable us to live a functional, flourishing life. If we reason well, have a moderate amount of primary goods (food, water, companionship, etc.), and act on the outcomes of our reasonings over the course of our lives, then we will experience *eudaimonia* (variously translated as happiness, success, well-being, and—my favorite—proper functioning). The person reasoning well will act so as to cultivate those states of being—the virtues—that enable him to function properly. Sarah Broadie (*Ethics with Aristotle*, 1991, p. 37) explains: " . . . an excellence or virtue, as Plato and Aristotle understand that concept, is nothing but a characteristic which makes the difference between functioning and functioning well."

When Aristotle considers what types of lives will lead to eudaimonia, he quickly dismisses the life of pleasure, focusing instead on the two obvious contenders: a life of public service and a life of intellectual contemplation. (Let it not be said that our station in life does not influence our philosophy!) For Aristotle, pleasure refers to something more than mere gustatory or tactile pleasure; rather, pleasure is an awareness of an activity. Whether a pleasure is good, then, depends on what its object is, on what activity it is awareness of—so Aristotle is able to contend that the life spent in pursuit of proper functioning and awareness of it will also be an ideally pleasurable life. Such a life will not be spent pursuing transitory sensory pleasures but will instead have as its focus the two other contenders Aristotle seriously considers: political public service and contemplation. The life of public service is a rewarding life because, as Aristotle famously notes in his *Politics*, humans are political animals, social by nature and living best in groups.[6] However, even that life will be a good one only if the politician is virtuous and just. Thus, the life of contemplation, including contemplation of the virtues, will ultimately be the most admirable and self-sufficiently complete form of human endeavor, as it enables us to realize our essence as *rational* political animals.

Virtues of Character and Virtues of Thought

In the *NE*, Aristotle distinguishes between virtue of thought and virtue of character. Virtue of thought arises from teaching and has its genesis in experience over time. Virtue of character arises from habit (*ethos* in Greek), and such habits can be inculcated by repetition, practice, and punishment (famously, the youth are "steered" with the rudders of pleasure and pain). It is possible for someone to possess virtue of character without possessing virtue of thought, and to do the right thing for the wrong reason or for no reason at all. Virtue of thought, on the other hand, consists in knowing *why* the habit you possess is the proper one to have so as to be able to reason about its possession; when we speak of someone's being of good judgment, what we usually mean is that he possesses virtue of thought. My four-year-old son Jonah, as a result of his fine upbringing, has the relevant virtue of character with regard to brushing his teeth. He brushes them after every meal, habitually; however, he has no theoretical understanding regarding why he brushes his teeth. He has not yet learned of cavities, and he probably could not make the proper theoretical judgments regarding the virtue of brushing your teeth as it relates to other important virtues. He does not have virtue of thought (although I hope he soon will).[7] Usually, we associate virtue of thought with experience and age; it is likely that our moral exemplars, those to whom we go for moral advice, are older rather than younger.

How is it that experience helps us to fix the content of our virtues? Aristotle has a general schema regarding how we should conceive of the moral virtues: adjusting for our individual circumstance, we ought to regard them as lying on the mean between two extremes. Never brushing your teeth, or brushing them only once a day, represents *deficiency*; brushing them six times a day represents *excess*. Thus, for the average person, brushing three times a day would be *proper*.[8] Through experience over time, you come to know how often you ought to brush your teeth (perhaps you lose a tooth or two by brushing too little at first, or perhaps you brush your gums away by brushing far too much at first). This general schema extends to all the virtues, which is why we go to those with experience for moral advice rather than to those without it.

The Golden Mean

Aristotle (*NE*, 1107a, p. 44) defines virtue as "(a) a state that decides, (b) [consisting] in a mean, (c) . . . relative to us, (d) which is defined by reference to reason, (e) i.e., to the reason by reference to which the intelligent person would define it. It is a mean between two vices, one of excess and one of deficiency."[9] Using this definition, Aristotle discusses several virtues and their associated vices of excess and deficiency. These include virtues concerned with feelings, such as bravery (a relationship to fear: the mean between foolhardiness and cowardice) and temperance (a relationship to pleasure and pain: one extreme is insensitivity and the other is intemperance). Virtues concerned with external goods include generosity (a relationship to money, the extremes of which are wastefulness and stinginess) and magnanimity (a relationship to honor, the extremes of which are vanity and pusillanimity). Virtues concerned with the social life include wit (a relationship to humor, the extremes of which are buffoonery and boorishness) and friendliness (a relationship to pleasantness, the extremes of which are flattery and quarrelsomeness) (*NE*, 1107b–1108a). The social virtues are important for Aristotle in view of his picture of human nature. He devotes several pages of the *NE* to a discussion about the nature and value of friendship.

Aristotle also discusses intellectual virtues. These virtues are those that concern our attitudes toward cognition as such rather than our attitudes toward our emotions. He identifies three intellectual virtues that relate to things we cannot hope to change (this qualification will become clear later): scientific knowledge, comprehension, and scientific wisdom. These terms come from Aristotle's discussion of science in his *Prior Analytics* and *Posterior Analytics*. The intellectual virtue of knowledge consists in the ability to make the proper deductions from more basic principles of nature. Comprehension consists in the ability to identify the correct basic principles from which to reason. Wisdom consists in the ability to combine the first two virtues in intellectually fruitful ways, appreciating the truths you successfully deduce. This contemplative activity, Aristotle thinks, is the unique human function and the best activity we can engage in.

Two other intellectual virtues that Aristotle discusses are practical wisdom and skill. These virtues relate to aspects of the world that we can affect and change with our actions. Skill consists in knowing what steps to take so as to bring something into existence (e.g., being skilled at basket weaving). Practical wisdom is the capacity to know what is good for human beings; thus, it includes excellent deliberation. In *The Cambridge Companion to Aristotle* (1995, p. 207), D. S. Hutchinson writes: " . . . practical wisdom is an appreciation of what is good and bad for us at the highest level, together with a correct apprehension of the facts of experience, together with the skill to make the correct inferences about how to apply our general moral knowledge to our particular situation, and to do so quickly and reliably. It is used in our own cases when we are obliged to commit ourselves to some course of action."

Friendship and Sociability

The practically wise will choose to involve themselves in associative activities. People are *zoon politikon* and must live and work in groups if their basic functional needs, including associative needs, are to be met. Not surprisingly, then, Aristotle ends the *NE* with two books on the value of friendship. Aristotle offers at least two reasons why friendship is necessary for our flourishing. First, friends serve as reflections of ourselves and can be used as epistemic yardsticks by which to judge our own flourishing. Self-knowledge is a difficult thing, and having others around can be invaluable to help you decide what the good life consists in and your status with regard to eudaimonia. Anyone with children can appreciate this general fact about close associations. When you spend enough time with them, children become small mirrors that reflect the sum total of many of your habits and dispositions. I've learned much about myself by watching my children. The same can be said for spouses and close friends (although it is sometimes not quite as entertaining to watch them in action). Another reason that friendship and associative activity is a part of flourishing relates to our natures—we are simply psychologically incapable of maintaining sustained interest in activities that promote our flourishing outside of groups. John Cooper (1980, p. 330) summarizes:

Aristotle argues, first, that to know the goodness of one's life, which he reasonably assumes to be a necessary condition to flourishing, one needs to have intimate friends whose lives are similarly good, since one is better able to reach a sound and secure estimate of the quality of a life when it is not one's own. Second, he argues that the fundamental moral and intellectual activities that go to make up a flourishing life cannot be continuously engaged in with pleasure and interest, as they must be if the life is to be a flourishing one, unless they are engaged in as parts of shared activities rather than pursued merely in private, and given the nature of the activities that are in question, this sharing is possible only with intimate friends who are themselves morally good persons.

A Blast from the Past: Aristotle on Mackie

From this skeletal sketch of Aristotle's virtue ethics given above, one can see how a first gloss on an Aristotelian response to Mackie would go. With regard to the relativity of values, one could argue, since virtues are functional in nature, that, at least at the margins, an objective account of what virtues are in fact functional in a given environment will leave room for variation. "It should be said, then," Aristotle notes in the *Nicomachean Ethics* (Irwin translation, 1985, p. 42, 1106a16), "that every virtue causes its possessors to be in a good state and to perform their functions well. . . . The virtue of a human being will likewise be the state that makes a human being good and makes him perform his function well." Although our essential natures will make many virtues necessary for our proper functioning irrespective of our environment, and will constrain the space of possible virtues in interesting ways, there is also a respect in which to be virtuous just consists in knowing how to react in changing situations. As Aristotle stresses, the virtuous person is affected in the appropriate way to the appropriate degree at the appropriate time.[10] Note the *practical* nature of this activity—virtues are sets of cognitive and conative skills. And it may very well be that the intellectual virtue of wisdom consists in having an intuitive grasp of how to optimize functioning when balancing competing, disparate, vaguely identifiable concerns that affect proper functioning. At times, this begins to resemble a process of multiple constraint satisfaction or vector completion—see chapter 5.

Aristotelian ethics *is* concerned with universality, but as ethics is ultimately a practical discipline (much like medicine, for example), it must reach down to and "gather life" from particulars.[11] Thus, we can give a principled account of the objectivity of values that nonetheless allows room for variation in application. The parallels between Aristotle's virtue-theoretic account and Dewey's theory of moral deliberation discussed briefly in the preceding section should be obvious.

With regard to the epistemological queerness of value, Aristotle has a robust moral epistemology. Just as we can come to have medical knowledge, we can come to have moral knowledge; this knowledge will be gained in much the same way that scientific knowledge is—through the application of reason to experience. We would not have to postulate any radically strange "moral sense organ" in order to justify and explain moral epistemology.[12] As for the metaphysical/ontological queerness of values: if values are functional relations, and if we can give a "non-queer" account of what functions are (this certainly seems possible—again, think of medical knowledge), then values will not be these "strange entities" that can't be related to natural facts. They will be perfectly natural entities, tractable within and given explanatory force by a materialist ontology. Of course, we may have to make some assumptions about the nature of values in order for this argument to be convincing. For example, Aristotle's moral psychology allows for the fact that to know the good is not necessarily to do the good. Thus, unlike with Platonic forms, Aristotelian virtue-theoretic functional statements don't have this strange non-natural property of being "intrinsically motivating." Even if this were not the case, though, Aristotle would have a response to Mackie: the motivational aspect of values may seem queer on Mackie's account, but only because Mackie is ignoring their essential relational nature. Functions obtain between organisms and an environment, and so the motivational aspect of a value is not to be found in the environment *per se*, but rather within the organism. This certainly does not mean values are strange, as we can give a perfectly non-spooky naturalized account of what motivation consists in, psychologically speaking. Thus, either way, Aristotle has a response to Mackie.[13] And, as we will see later this chapter and in chapter 4, what is queer is not the "recognition/feeling" complex; that is to be found throughout the animal kingdom. Rather, what may appear to be strange are the relatively abstract properties and objects that we deal in (such as "ribosome") that have no relation to the "feeling/do-this" complex that is bound up with animal perception and so common in nature.[14]

The Aristotelian response to Mackie can be made even stronger by incorporating some of the advances in philosophy of biology that have been made in the past two centuries. Aristotle was the pre-eminent ancient biologist, and no doubt if he were alive today he would take full advantage of the explanatory resources offered by the conceptions of function that are at play in modern evolutionary biology. In the next section, I will flesh out and expand how a robustly naturalized Aristotelian ethic that uses functional concepts from biology can even more effectively address allegations about the relativity and queerness of objective values. I will do this by examining how functions are dealt with in evolutionary biology, and then by detailing Boyd's conception of properties. This conception makes functional properties thoroughly natural and non-strange. Bringing Aristotle up to date, biologically speaking, will have an impact on his moral theory; however, the modifications that are necessary are ones we can live with, and they will make it even more obvious how we could hope to see Dewey's theory of moral judgment as continuous with Aristotle's.

Functions in Evolutionary Biology

Although the philosophic literature that deals with the conceptual analysis of function is huge, two general approaches to functional analysis are seminal, and both are useful starting points when dealing with function in Aristotle. These approaches are typified by Larry Wright's etiological approach to function and Rob Cummins's capacity approach to function. Ultimately, though, I argue that the two approaches are endpoints on a spectrum. "Distal etiological functions" are extremely historically laden, whereas "proximate Cummins functions" fully divorce present function from history altogether, making it "analysis relative." In the end, morally relevant functions will be fixed by the intelligent consideration of the distance we must travel backwards along our functional etiology so as to flourish. For that reason, I favor the modern-history theory of function (a version of a Wright-style analysis advocated by Peter Godfrey-Smith) that limits functional ascriptions to recent adaptive history.

Wright-Style Etiological Functional Analysis

Larry Wright's approach is etiological (or causal) in nature. If, Wright argues, we are trying to explain that the function of X is Z (let's say, the function of scissors is to cut), then what this really means is: X is there because it does Z (scissors exist because they cut), and Z is a consequence or result of X's being there (cutting comes about because you have a pair of scissors).[15] This analysis of function makes sense of many of the functional claims that are made in biology (such as that "the function of the red blood cells is to transport oxygen to and remove carbon dioxide from bodily tissues"). It was elaborated in a selectionist, evolutionary framework by Ruth Millikan (1984).[16] Unlike Wright, however, Millikan sees herself as offering a biological *theory* of function, not merely an *analysis* of functional concepts and language in biology. In view of my emphasis on the lack of a distinction between scientific findings and definitions in chapter 2, Millikan's point is well taken: our story about function ought to be a scientific story, one that relies on substantive biological theories so as to fix function. It should have explanatory power and do genuine explanatory work in our biological *cum* moral theories.

Millikan's addition to Wright's analysis is crucial: in order for an item to have a "*proper* function," two conditions should be met. First (to paraphrase Millikan 1989), the item should have originated as a reproduction of some prior thing or things that (owing in part to possession of the properties duplicated) have actually performed the function in the past, and the item exists because of this or these performances. An object or character that has this property has a proper function.[17] Alternatively, an item could have a *derived* proper function if it exists as a result of being produced by a device or object that produces those items as means to accomplish its proper function. Examples of biological items with proper functions include hearts (which pump blood) and brains (which think thoughts and coordinate action). Biological items with derived proper functions are things like whispered sweet nothings (to attract potential mates) and waggle dances (to get bees to nectar).

Cummins Functions and Causal Analyses of Function

A different analysis, the second seminal notion of function, has been offered by Robert Cummins, who claims that to ascribe a function to something is to "ascribe a capacity to it which is singled out by its role in an analysis of some capacity of a containing system. When a capacity of a containing system is appropriately explained by analyzing it into a number of other capacities whose programmed exercise yields a manifestation of the analyzed capacity, the analyzing capacities emerge as functions" (Cummins 1975, revised version in Allen et al. 1998).

To use our scissors example, when analyzing the system of "dress making," the function of scissors is to cut fabric, for it is only by virtue of scissors being able to do this that a dressmaker is able to fashion a dress. Though this is a useful and pertinent analysis as well for some domains, for pragmatic reasons a suitably modified Wright-style account will prove to be most useful for this project—a "modern-history" theory of function has the advantage of grounding current capacities in an evolutionary past, making it more likely that we will correctly identify and respect the complex of intricate functional norms that constitute our basic biological natures. A Cummins function is relativized to a capacity, not to a history. Capacities will, in turn, be determined by the relationship between very basic physical laws and the appropriateness of the item in question for the capacity. For example, it could very well turn out that, in a system that has the capacity to function as a doorstop, a hammer could serve perfectly well as the component of the system that holds the door open. Relative to the "doorstop system," the hammer has the function of holding the door open. However, we would not find this a satisfying explanation for why the hammer came to have the structure it did (unless, of course, it were modified by the builder of the system so as to function even more effectively in the doorstop system, in which case it would have a derived proper function). Stripping items of historicity may be useful in some analyses of function, but it is explanatorily underpowered relative to an evolutionary etiological account. This is important if you think that our capacities are evolved ones.

An evolutionary etiological account, on the other hand, can both explain why an item has the function that it does, and can, moreover, define what it means for an item to be functioning well in a manner that does not rely purely on capacity. It thus has broader explanatory ambition, and because of this, it will be more useful when giving a naturalistic spin to Aristotelian moral functions.

Endpoints on a Spectrum?

There is one sense in which the capacity account and the etiological account of function are the extreme endpoints on a spectrum of function. We can view a Cummins function as an etiological function devoid of historical content (that is to say, devoid of any content at all, in which case we are free to put any content that we wish into the system—e.g., hammers are doorstops). On the other hand, we can also view the historically deepest etiological account of function as reaching so far back into our evolutionary history that it succeeds in identifying the "primal end," that function that the first genetic replicators on Earth had—that of *merely* reproducing, one of the crucial conditions for there to be adaptedness at all.[18]

Presumably, given the nature of our explanatory project, we don't want to gravitate to either extreme. If we gravitate to the distal, super-historically laden conception of function, then the only content we can squeeze out of function is that the ultimate function is to reproduce.[19] This is not very fruitful or useful, and would be a bad analysis of any *particular* character-driven function; after all, though my eyes may yet contribute to my reproductive ability, their *proper* function on a Millikan analysis is to enable me to see by serving as transducers of light energy to electro-chemical energy. That is how they came to be present in us. On the other hand, if we move instead to the proximate, "instantaneous" analysis of a Cummins function, all historical context is lost. Flippantly, we could say: "What's the function of my eye? I don't know. What do you want it to be?"

Détente: A Modern-History Theory of Functions

Peter Godfrey-Smith has an enlightening analysis of function that steers a path between the Scylla of functional vacuousness (represented by the capacity approach) and the Charybdis of functional single-mindedness (represented by the deep-history proper-function approach).[20] It is an analysis of proper function as well; however, it relates the functions of traits and characters to their recent evolutionary history. As Godfrey-Smith states (1994, version in Allen et al. 1998), "functions are dispositions and powers which explain the recent maintenance of a trait in a selective context." For example, most vestigial traits or characters (such as an appendix) will not have a strong function on the modern-history account. How far back need one go in order for the history to be ancient rather than modern? This is an empirical question, as Godfrey-Smith notes: "The answer is not in terms of a fixed time—a week, or a thousand years. Relevance fades. Episodes of selection become increasingly irrelevant to an assignment of functions at some time, the further away we get. The modern history view does, we must recognize, involve substantial biological commitments. Perhaps traits are, as a matter of biological fact, retained largely through various kinds of inertia. . . . There is no avoiding risks of this sort."

For present purposes, then, a modern-history theory of functions gives us everything we need from the biological use of the term 'function' to naturalize Aristotle. The other conceptions of function are useful—there is *some* sense in which the distal function of all living things is to reproduce, but that is not to say that all of the capacities we exercise have as their immediate *telos* the end of reproduction or that their modern history is to be explained in terms of that capacity. Conversely, we can avoid wholesale and rampant "teleological moral relativism" by denying that the Cummins approach is of use when analyzing the functions of people, morally speaking—not every experience is consummatory, and not everything we do leads to eudaimonia, no matter what angle it is viewed from and no matter what the history of the agent. The Cummins capacity approach is very useful, though, when we are engineering or designing systems (e.g., when we are dealing with a system that has no history but is merely "raw capacity" waiting to be harnessed). But humans, being biologically evolved systems with fascinating developmental trajectories, are most assuredly not ahistorical creatures.

Much of this discussion can be boiled down to the following: Morally speaking, it is not true that anything goes, but neither is it true that our *only* proper function in life is to breed like rabbits.

Crucially, what all these accounts of function do, irrespective of which seems most plausible, is offer a thoroughgoing naturalized conception of function. Functional properties are not "strange" or "odd" properties that could not supervene on matter in any comprehensible way. Rather, functional properties are interesting and conceptually tractable, and they can serve a useful purpose in scientific theories, particularly in the biological sciences. They can serve the same role in the moral sciences—Aristotle can address charges of queerness by availing himself of either of these concepts of function, although Godfrey-Smith's account will be most useful owing to its reliance on a modern evolutionary story. The upshot is that moral facts are functional facts, and functional facts are not queer; we can understand them perfectly well within a materialist ontological framework.

Boyd's Homeostatic Property Clusters

Additional support for this view can be gained by considering a wider view of what it means for a system of characters to have a property. Functional properties might be "spread across" a material system, but this does not imply that functional properties are perforce spooky and unnatural. Richard Boyd's conception of homeostatic property clusters is useful in this regard, and Boyd (1988, p. 117) thinks such a conception of property in fact underlies most functional analysis in the special sciences. Boyd's full explication of "homeostatic property clusters" postulates eleven salient characteristics of these kinds of properties; their gist can be captured in a few sentences and with a few examples. There are natural kinds, Boyd argues, whose natural definitions involve a cluster of properties together with indeterminacy in their extension. For example, the natural kind of "healthy" or "being healthy" involves an organism's implementing several properties (being well fed, being free of pathogenic infections, etc.), and there are many organisms that can be healthy (protozoa, humans, plants, etc.). These property clusters reliably tend to be grouped together by virtue of the functional nature of the natural kind that is being analyzed (hence the term 'homeostatic').

'Healthy' is a property cluster; so, presumably, are 'wealthy' and (crucially for Aristotle) 'wise'. This conception of properties is, again, thoroughly naturalistic, as Boyd is at pains to mention, and involves no radical ontological maneuvers. It coheres well with the functional nature of virtues. Admittedly, Boyd's conception results in a "type non-reductive materialism," but it does at least preserve token reductionism: any particular example of a healthy entity will obviously have a particular material extension, namely the creature in question.

Looked at in another light, Boyd's conception of homeostatic property clusters allows us to group together *families* of functions. Thus, we can argue that the homeostatic property cluster "healthy" consists in organisms that implement manifold functions successfully. However, while different organisms might have different requirements for functioning healthily, this is not to say that the basic physical properties of matter and the general biological principles of organization to which they give rise suddenly become irrelevant; quite the contrary, as form and function constitute an integral package. The multiple realizabilities that face us will thus be of a non-threatening kind and will not be so numerous that a science of function isn't possible, especially since there will usually be tight links between the history of a function-laden character and the form and structure of the character. A parallel situation exists in the mind and brain sciences, where the "bogeyman" of functionality (which maintained that mental states are nothing but functional states of a cognitive system) purportedly threatened to make the study of the brain of no consequence for cognition. But this has not proven to be the case for much the same reason.[21]

Revisiting Mackie

Combining this brief recapitulation of functional analysis and homeostatic property clusters, we can see how an Aristotelian position that is informed by these conceptual developments will be in an even stronger position to rebut Mackie's claims. There may appear to be a rampant relativism of values—in many cases, this is only apparent, but when it is the case, it can be accounted for by the functional nature of virtues, as functions are a result of interactions between organisms and environments. The "fuzzy" multiple realizability of functional claims follows from the fact that the properties picked out by them are homeostatic property clusters—the standards for "health" may vary across organisms, but (contra Mackie) that does not mean that the standards are subjective or that talk about them is laden with error. Value properties are not queer in either the epistemological sense or the metaphysical sense. They are scientifically tractable in the same way that biological notions of function are, and to gain moral knowledge we need posit no "special sense" above and beyond the traditional tools and methods of scientific naturalism. For this reason, it would behoove moral theorists to pay attention to developments in the human natural sciences, particularly, by my lights, the cognitive sciences (moral cognition is an important part of moral comportment and proper functioning for human beings) and biology.[22] In view of recent advances in the human sciences and in the study of cognition, this is an exciting period for moral theorists and one that promises to provide new and interesting answers to old questions, whether they be posed by Sextus Empiricus or John Mackie.[23]

To summarize thus far: Mackie's *Ethics: Inventing Right and Wrong* argues for an error theory regarding the meaning of moral terms. Mackie offers several arguments against the objectivity of values, two of which are found in the historical tradition of moral anti-realism. These two arguments, the "argument from relativity" and the "argument from queerness," have some force; in this chapter, though, I have demonstrated that when the appropriate ancient and contemporary resources are brought to bear these arguments can be effectively rebutted. The resources I have in mind are an appropriately naturalized Aristotelian virtue theory and a contemporary biologically oriented notion of function. Drawing on the Greek tradition as exemplified by Aristotle and on modern philosophy of biology enabled me to not only argue against Mackie but also to shed light on why a critic of moral realism might be convinced by these two arguments to begin with. By reducing moral terms to functional terms, and by treating the objects to which those terms refer as a contemporarily informed Aristotle would, I established a case for the objectivity of moral value and demonstrated why opponents like Mackie might find the case against objectivity initially persuasive. A renaissance in contemporary moral philosophy awaits the scientifically sensitive moral theorist. A reinvigoration of the relationship between the sciences and philosophers of morality will be to the benefit of both groups, and has the potential to shed new light not only on the case for realism about values but also on other long-standing issues in moral philosophy.

James Wallace (1978, p. 25) anticipates the epistemological upshot that the norms of the life sciences might have for morality:

The relevance of the normative aspect of the life-sciences to the study of virtues and human goodness lies in the epistemological relevance of the former. It is not at all tempting to suppose that the norms central to biology have their basis in the emotional responses or the personal preferences either of biologists or of the organisms they study. It does not seem plausible either to hold that biologists derive their knowledge of taxa, modes of life, adaptation, and so forth *a priori* from pure reason. They learn these things, rather, by studying the organisms in question and their lives, bringing to such studies what ingenuity and knowledge of the world they command.

Fleshing Out the Functional Account by Distinguishing It from Other Moral Theories

Now that the basics of the functional account are on the table, we can compare it with other approaches to a naturalized morality, using them as fencing partners against which to develop the nascent account more thoroughly. The theories I consider are close enough to the fledgling account of evolutionary function I have articulated that it will be useful to elaborate the grounds for distinguishing it from them. As they are venerable old moral theories, understanding their content will be useful for the discussion in chapter 6 regarding the opportunistic nature of a functional moral theory.

Hedonistic Accounts and the Function of Emotions

A hedonistic account of morality commends one to do what produces pleasure and prevents pain. This is because pleasure is the sole intrinsic good on this account. Hedonists need not be *hedonistic*—they can have very sophisticated theories regarding just how it is that we maximize pleasure. Thus, a hedonist would not necessarily counsel that one drink wildly every evening, as hangovers are very painful affairs. Historically, hedonists have recommended quite reasonable approaches of moderation to those things that by linguistic accident we associate with the word 'hedonism' (rampant drinking, wantonness, gluttony, etc.). Usually, a hedonistic theory of morality leads one down one of two paths: the egoist path, wherein the pleasures that matter are your own, or the utilitarian path, wherein the pleasures of all sentient creatures are held in equal regard. First, then, I will distinguish the general hedonistic account of morality from the functional account on offer. This will in turn mark an initial difference between the functional account, egoism, and utilitarianism. It will also provide an opportunity to modify the Aristotelian account delineated earlier so as to make it cohere with the biological account of function discussed in the preceding sections.

Accomplishing this requires briefly articulating a Darwinian view of the function of the emotions. I argue that when emotions work well they serve a dual purpose as (1) motivational (2) markers of value. In a world in which our environment was stable and we were perfectly adapted to it, our emotions would not lead us astray; when we encountered a dys-functional situation, we would be viscerally motivated to correct it. We would naturally take pleasure in all functional activities and displeasure in all dysfunctional ones, and character development would not be nec-essary. In this world, emotions would have content driven crucially by the external world, and would be another form of perception, albeit a unique form insofar as they would have strong connections to the human motivational system.[24] In such a hypothetical world, the func-tional account might collapse into hedonism. However, we do not live in such a world, nor, most likely, will we ever. Until we do, it will not be enough to rely *merely* on pleasurable and unpleasurable states of being as representational markers of value and hence functionality. Though they are a critical *starting point* for moral reflection, they can also serve as the problematic that spurs such reflection (think again of the "ice cream" example from chapter 2—it is because ice cream *is* so tasty and because I so strongly desire it that I begin to question its role in my diet). Functionality bears no necessary relationship to pleasure and pain, although in a well-adapted organism pleasure and pain will often serve to highlight functional and dysfunctional states. But not always— biological functions are more complicated than that, alas.

This account of the role of emotions is similar to that offered by Jonathan Turner (2000) and Antonio Damasio (1994). For example, Turner hypothesizes that emotions served as an initial *lingua franca* for ancestral hominids, acting as a base upon which were built the types of regulative social structures that we must have if we are to flourish in environments other than the savannah; primal emotion serves to "mark value" and to motivate, and it is by building upon these less subtle emo-tions with subtler ones, such as "pride" and "shame," that we are able to engineer effective social structures. In a related vein but at a different level of analysis, Damasio's somatic-marker hypothesis (1994, pp. 173–174) postulates that feelings serve to regulate cognition by screening out dys-functional and harmful options from higher cognitive processes: "Somatic markers probably increase the accuracy and efficiency of the decision process. Their absence reduces them. . . . Somatic markers are a special instance of feelings generated from secondary emotions. Those emotions and feelings have been connected, by learning, to predicted future outcomes of certain scenarios. When a negative somatic marker is juxtaposed to a particular future outcome the combination functions as an alarm bell. When a positive somatic marker is juxtaposed instead, it becomes a beacon of incentive."[25]

It is not my purpose at this point to articulate and defend a theory of the role of emotions in reasoning; nonetheless, Turner and Damasio's work—and Joseph LeDoux's (1995, 1996) work on the function of the amygdala—should at least make the initial response to the charge of hedonism a plausible one. Base emotions such as pleasure and pain, and higher-order emotions such as satisfaction, serve to highlight value, where value is cashed out in terms of functionality; they also serve to motivate organisms to act on such identifications, either by filtering out certain options at the beginning or by otherwise weighting cognitive decision-making processes.[26] But this is not to say that emotions will always mark functional states, or that they will filter out only the inappropriate responses.

Desire Satisfaction: Egoistic and Utilitarian Accounts and Agent Relativity

The explanatory pattern used to rebut charges of hedonism will apply across the board to other theories of ethics that the functional account might otherwise resemble at first glance. For example, with regard to desire satisfaction, it is only insofar as our desires are well informed by functional considerations that we ought to satisfy them. In an ideal world, where we were perfectly informed about functional relationships, and where we were all appropriately motivated, proper functioning and satisfaction of desires would be coextensive. Likewise for egoistic and utilitarian accounts of morality, since both are variations on hedonism that leverage some form of sentience to gain moral purchase.

However, egoistic and utilitarian accounts of morality raise a very important question that the functional account has yet to broach: Is it merely *my* functioning that "counts," or ought I seek to maximize the functioning of *all* biological organisms? Egoistic accounts of morality are agent relative (only the agent's pleasure and pain count), whereas utilitarian accounts are agent neutral (if two pleasures are equal, it does not matter, *ceteris paribus*, whether the pleasure is yours or mine; they are equally valuable). Is the account on offer agent relative, or is it agent neutral?

I have two answers to this question. The first is that our answer is irrelevant; it simply doesn't matter. Owing to an admittedly contingent fact about human beings, we will maximize our own well-functioning by entering into relationships with others wherein we help them function well. It could have been the case that our biological functions were best met by our being solitary (e.g., there are possible worlds wherein we are the human equivalent of Tasmanian devils, associating with others only long enough to reproduce, shunning packs and going our own way otherwise). However, this hypothetical solitary creature would not be anything like a human being—it would have no need for language, for example, and it would not partake of cultural and social evolution, as it would not have access to artifacts, tools, and other products of group cognition. Its cognitive capacities might not have to be very complex. Many evolutionary theorists argue that sociability is the "great stimulator"—that our relations with others co-evolved with our cognitive capacities, so that our large brain size and complex cognitive structures are both cause and effect of our social nature (Deacon 1997; Schulkin 2000). John Dewey, responding to allegations by Thomas Huxley that the moral realm and the evolutionary realm are not only not compatible but are actually at odds, notes that our environment of selection is a social environment through and through, and that evolution and ethics are thus not incompatible: "That which was fit among the animals is not fit among human beings, not merely because the animals were nonmoral and man is moral; but because the conditions of life have changed, and because there is no way to define the term 'fit' excepting through these conditions. The environment is now distinctly a social one, and the content of the term 'fit' has to be made with reference to social adaptation. . . . That which would count in the Carboniferous period will not count in the Neozoic. Why should we expect that which counts among the carnivora to count with man—a social animal?" (Dewey 1898, p. 100). These types of arguments amount to a "deep" explanation for sociability and function.

But even a "shallow" explanation for the relationship between sociability and function will do the work we need. Even if the deep story is wrong, it is still the case that *almost all* of our functional needs can be satisfied only by working with others. "Successful intellectual work," Tom Hurka notes (1993, p. 68), "is often communal, and the same holds for many practical pursuits. Games such as chess allow two people to exercise skill together, with the good play of one raising the level of the other's. . . . The acts best for others are also best for oneself, and each can choose rightly by agent-neutral standards, given only agent-relative aims."[27] All I would add to Hurka's account is that even base-level functional needs (e.g., those at the bottom of Abraham Maslow's hierarchy[28]) are best fulfilled by working collectively. Solitary hunter-gatherers simply do not live long.[29]

Thus, the question as to whether the theory is agent relative or agent neutral is a red herring, at least if is posed as a general question. But what about in a *particular* circumstance? What if I know that the ten dollars I am spending to purchase the latest issue of *Behavioral and Brain Sciences* could in fact be better spent, functionally speaking, by feeding the homeless man around the corner? How do I compare his deep need for the basic components necessary for functioning well with my rather shallow need for a journal that is only coincidentally related to personal projects of my own and does not have much to do with functioning well in the larger sense? To answer this question, we must explain how functions "stack," and we must examine whether the account has room for an existential "self-made-function"-style component.

Nesting, Stacking, Re-Equilibration, and Existential Functions

I argue that, except in certain historical circumstances, functions will nest smoothly; it is a historically contingent possibility that, owing to changes in selection pressures in the environment, an organism might come to simultaneously embody functions that have competing ends. First, a hypothetical example. We can imagine creatures (call them "boojums," with apologies to Lewis Carroll) that live in environments where certain types of proteins are readily available for consumption. Boojums come to develop certain organs that enable them to consume these proteins; the organs are specially adapted to eat the protein by sucking it through multiple straw-like appendages. Later, the environment changes, and the proteins accumulate only in balls. Some of the creatures are lucky enough to have straws that are large enough to accommodate the balls; others aren't so lucky. Eventually, selection pressures lead to the evolution of appendages that are nothing like a straw but something more like mouths. Boojums that find themselves with both the old-fashioned straw-style appendages and the new-fashioned stalk mouths will have traits or characters that embody ends in competition. The straw trait will have the end of consuming protein, as will the mouth trait. Owing to the environment, the mouth trait will have a *stronger* modern-history function of consuming proteins; the straw trait will have the same but *weaker* modern-history function, which it simply won't be able to realize.

What can we say of the boojums and their functions? First, their situation is functionally non-optimal. Two traits are competing for the same resources. As a matter of fact, only the mouth trait will satisfy its function. The straw-suckers will poke the protein balls in vain, only occasionally stumbling upon one small enough to actually ingest. In the long run, creatures with mostly or only mouth traits will survive, so the functional problem is at least one of short duration only. But what are the boojums alive now to do? They have three options. First, they can adopt the stoic perspective, accepting their dysfunctional predicament, soldiering on with life as best they can.[30] The boojums may not have any option other than this in many circumstances, alas. But the second option, when they do have it, is preferable: if the boojums are reasonably sophisticated cognitively, they can act together so as to change the selection environment. Perhaps they can build machines that scour the protein fields for balls small enough to fit in even the tiniest straw appendages. The third option consists in changing individual boojums themselves, either by altering their physiognomy or by altering the connection between their physiognomy and their motivational systems (which is actually a proactive variation on stoic acceptance but which has the felicitous side effect of leveraging a creature's general tendency to maximize functional states—boojums who no longer desire straw-harvested protein will not be as dysfunctional as those who both desire protein *and* can't get it through their straws). As functions are things that obtain between organisms and environments, boojums who regulate their affairs intelligently can act to change either aspect of the equation so as to achieve functional re-equilibration. Unless the trait or character in question is a minor one, though, it will probably be the easiest and most efficacious to change the environment, at least in the short term (although in the long term, character development is crucial for proper functioning).[31]

Functions will generally "nest" or "smoothly stack," but owing to the vagaries and contingencies of the environment there will be exceptions. For a real-world case, consider the human vermiform appendix. On the modern-history view, it has the *very* weak function of removing detritus from the digestive system. In animals such as horses, it plays a crucial role, removing and processing from the digestive tract such things as hair and bits of hoof. In humans, however, the appendix has only been very weakly selected for, owing to fairly dramatic changes in our lifestyles and in the types of food we consume. In fact, attenuated appendixes can easily become inflamed, in which case they have to be removed. To maintain functional equilibrium, we must regulate our environment (by removing certain kinds of edibles from it), or regulate our habits (by consuming only certain kinds of food, for example),[32] or regulate our physiognomy (by removing the appendix). The weak function of the appendix is at odds with the functions of the various other traits that collectively constitute the digestive system. But we have reached the point at which intelligent control of means and ends has enabled us to short-circuit what otherwise might have been a very long and laborious process of natural selection against the existence of appendixes.

What are the connections between these scenarios and the case of the man on the corner? First, keeping in mind our social natures, we must examine how best we as human beings can deal with a situation like this. Does it really consist in "hardening our hearts," taking the ersatz stoic option like the first group of boojums—that is, in developing our character in ways such that we come to feel no empathy for those in need? Essentially, this question becomes one of means to an end: how do we best solve the plight of the homeless? Does the solution involve ignoring them, giving them occasional pocket change, instituting government assistance programs, relying on private charities, or something else entirely? Presumably, the option of simply ignoring the plight of those less fortunate than us can be ruled out as dysfunctional (in the naturalized Aristotelian sense)—human beings who are insensitive to the needs of those around them will be dysfunctional in myriad respects: they will not enter into productive social relationships that sustain the acquisition of base-level needs, and they will not partake of a rich and varied diet of social interactions that are (in view of our evolutionary history) valuable in and of themselves. But what happens next seems a less-than-straightforward empirical matter that those with expertise in the policy sciences could best deal with. And in any case, as I will argue in chapter 6, general considerations about epistemic progress in knowing how to function well will lead us to tolerate a Gaussian normal distribution of "experiments in living." Some of those experiments will be at either extreme, and will consist in tolerating those among us who not only refuse to give anything to the person in need, come what may, but also those who dedicate their lives to serving the less fortunate (even to the point of sacrificing every single project that is not other-oriented).

Cases of seeming functional clashes between organisms, human or otherwise, can be dealt with in the same way that functional clashes within organisms are dealt with. That does not, admittedly, lead to a straightforward answer to the question of whether I should forgo all journals so as to help the homeless man on the college campus, but it does at least help us rule out both the option of not acting, and probably also the option of giving him everything I own.[33]

Existential Functions

Might it be the case that some of our actions have no direct impact on lower-level functional concerns such that they are free of moral opprobrium? In other words, what is the role of a "self-given function" in the scheme I have sketched thus far? I think there is room for an existential ethic within this theory. Some things we do and projects we have do not directly impact low-level function concerns. Rather, they are orthogonal to those concerns, not assisting us directly in fulfilling them but not harming their achievement. In these cases, we have libertarian-style freedom to define functions for ourselves. In view of the relative prosperity of many "First World" countries, self-given "existential" functions abound. And, as E. O. Wilson points out in *Sociobiology*, we may succeed in many instances in producing a state of "ecological release" wherein there are only the weakest of selection pressures. Note that in a state of *total* ecological release, after an appropriate period of time, beings in such an environment would *cease* to have functions. All that would be left in that case, perhaps, is an existential ethic. But to be in a state of total ecological release would involve having every functional demand of every organism met indefinitely. Thus, this amounts to saying "In a utopia, you could do whatever you care." This seems like a truism, and, given the variability of our environments, I doubt that we could ever achieve such a total state of release in any case. Moral theorists make much of the fact that certain theories of morality are simply too demanding to be realizable by human beings. "Ought implies can": If a moral system produces obligations upon us that are so severe that we are psychologically incapable of implementing them, then this speaks against the viability of the moral system. Is the functional account too demanding? Fortunately, no. Though it might be a better world if all our personal projects were to deal with the improvement of the human condition, there will nonetheless be ample room in this scheme for hobbies, recreation, and seemingly frivolous pursuits such as philosophy.

Some students of human nature, such as the psychologist and zoologist David Barash, think that *all* evolution can give us is an existential ethic. Consider the following quotation (Barash 2000, p. 1014):

Evolutionists might well look at all living things as playing a vast existential roulette game. No one can ever beat the house. There is no option to cash in one's chips and walk away a winner. The only goal is to keep on playing and, indeed, some genes and phyletic lineages manage to stay in the game longer than others. But where is the meaning in a game whose rules no one has written and which, at best, we can only decipher, and which has no goal except to keep on playing? Moreover, it is a game that can never be won and only, eventually, lost. In short, there is no intrinsic, evolutionary meaning to being alive. We simply are. And so are our genes.

There is a tension in these. comments If there is no intrinsic meaning to being alive, then how does it constitute "a loss" to die, and in what sense can you *fail* to "beat the house"? Implicit in Barash's critique is a reliance on *only* a distal interpretation of an etiological theory of function. Our only function *qua* carriers of genes is to replicate.

Another example of an implicit reliance on distal etiological function comes from a critique of evolutionary ethics proffered by Jan Narveson (2000, p. 269):

Once we have had children . . . evolutionary theory, it seems to me, runs out of whatever gas it may have already had. Evolution, remember, doesn't care whether you survive—it only cares whether your genes do. Most of what you do with the fifty years or so remaining to you after you've reproduced would seem to be a matter of virtually total indifference from the point of view of "evolutionary ethics"—whatever that is, and if it is anything.

This criticism too relies upon an implicit acceptance of the distal etiological theory of functions.[34] But, as we have seen, such a reliance is an extreme interpretation that offers little guidance to either working biologists who wish to fix the functions of traits or to moral theorists who would look to naturalize human functionality. On a modern-history view, human beings have functions, and such functions are rich complexes that bring with them norms whose influence in our lives will very much affect whether we flourish or not. It is not the case that our only function is to reproduce. Our various characters and traits have functions that they can fail to satisfy, even well after our period of reproductive fecundity.

Functions are indicative of norms, and evolutionary explanations must fix functions in such a manner that they have explanatory power. Deep etiological appeals and appeals to the replication of genes do not do full justice to the range of functions encompassed in the biological kind *Homo sapiens*. Any attempt to naturalize ethics that appeals to evolutionary considerations must come to grips with that fact. The tepid reception or outright failure of many attempts to incorporate evolutionary considerations into ethics can be explained, in part, by the absence of such recognition, as a brief examination of some past work that incorporated evolutionary considerations into ethics demonstrates.

The history of attempts to naturalize ethics by way of evolution is long and florid, primarily because of the political sensitivity of issues related to the intermingling of the two fields and secondarily because of the tremendous implications that the latter was thought to have for the former. In the next section, I briefly review some of the most famous attempts at a natural evolutionary ethic so as to highlight similarities and differences between them and the account on offer.[35]

Recent and Not-So-Recent Work in Evolutionary Ethics

Herbert Spencer (1820–1903) articulated a vibrant and original evolutionary ethic. Unfortunately, much of it was based on misinterpretations of Darwin's work, and parts of it espoused a Social Darwinism that most justly find repugnant. Spencer harnessed a theory of evolution that was explicitly teleological to a Lamarckian mechanism for the genetic inheritance of acquired characteristics; this was layered upon a Malthusian conception of population pressures (Richards 1987, pp. 270, 302–315). Thus, on many accounts, Spencer got the facts on which he based his philosophy wrong: "Evolution" as such has no teleology, the Lamarckian mechanism for evolutionary change was incorrect, and some of Malthus's assumptions about population growth have not withstood the test of time. Nonetheless, using this admittedly faulty machinery, Spencer derived an account of morality that is basically utilitarian in nature. The ultimate criterion by which we judge morality is the familiar utilitarian greatest-happiness principle. Owing to the nature of evolution, if we but allow the mechanisms of nature to do their work, there will be "natural social evolution" toward greater freedom, which will in turn lead to the greatest possible amount of happiness. Spencer's theory was widely acclaimed during its time, but by 1900 it was eclipsed, owing in part to its scientific inaccuracies and to attacks upon it by Henry Sidgwick, Thomas Huxley, and G. E. Moore (see Farber, 1994, p. 51).

Though the overall flavor of the philosophy is utilitarian and egalitarian, at his worst Spencer (1873/1961, p. 313) uses the principles purportedly embedded in evolution to generate repugnant norms. For example, here is his reasoning with regard to the "Poor Laws" that were in place in Britain at the time—laws that mandated taxation for the purpose of feeding and housing the impoverished:

Besides an habitual neglect of the fact that the quality of a society is physically lowered by the artificial preservation of its feeblest members, there is an habitual neglect of the fact that the quality of a society is lowered morally and intellectually, by the artificial preservation of those who are least able to take care of themselves. . . . For if the unworthy are helped to increase, by shielding them from that mortality which their unworthiness would naturally entail, the effect is to produce, generation after generation, a greater unworthiness.

Nonetheless, anyone who would spend time thinking about the connections between ethics and the sciences would do well to read Spencer. He serves as a useful inoculation against several tendencies, including our unabashed eagerness to read back into evolution particular ethical views and our lack of humility with regard to the latest science of the day. Caution and fallibilism should be the evolutionary ethicist's watchwords.

The updated Aristotelian account on offer differs from Spencer's in many ways. It acknowledges that evolution has no end (although, of course, the organisms that interact with their environments have ends), that acquired characteristics are not inherited, and that the mechanisms through which we can achieve the goals of cooperative mutual benefit do not have to be cut-throat and *laissez-faire* merely because the mechanism that generated us was thought to be. And the current account, though it has a place for utilitarianism, does not make happiness the *summmum bonum*. Rather, proper function and flourishing serve that purpose (although it may follow as a happy fact that functioning well often will lead to the maximizing of happiness—recall the discussion of this during the summary of Aristotle earlier in this chapter).

Three Contemporary Accounts

It is possible to have a conversation about the relationship between ethics and natural science in which the name of Herbert Spencer is never mentioned. However, such a discussion without a mention of E. O. Wilson would be a real rarity. Wilson, the founder of sociobiology (the study of social behavior from the standpoint of evolution) has done more to popularize the possibility of a biologicized ethic than probably any other figure of the past 100 years. His most famous work, *Sociobiology: A New Synthesis*, was the flagship publication for a burgeoning field of study that attempted to explain (among other things) how it is possible for us to come to have a moral sense within an evolutionary framework.[36] Wilson also addresses questions related to the justification of norms. Though his work on both questions is a model of clarity, he is better at providing an answer to the first question than he is at illuminating the second. His explanations regarding the justification of norms are eliminative in nature, making him a key Eliminative Unionist. For example, in *On Human Nature*, published shortly after *Sociobiology*, Wilson (1978, p. 167) has this to say about the nature of morality:

Can the cultural evolution of higher ethical values gain a direction and momentum of its own and completely replace genetic evolution? I think not. The genes hold culture on a leash. The leash is very long, but inevitably values will be constrained in accordance with their effects on the human gene pool. The brain is a product of evolution. Human behavior—like the deepest capacities for emotional response which drive and guide it—is the circuitous technique by which human genetic material has been and will be kept intact. Morality has no other demonstrable ultimate function.

Manifest in this observation is an implicit commitment to only a distal conception of function. In that sense, then, it is no wonder that the naturalistic ethicist who reads Wilson's corpus either will be disappointed to discover that morality is an "illusion fobbed off on us by our genes" (Ruse and Wilson 1985, p. 51) or will feel that Wilson's work fails to address the justification of norms adequately.[37] His focus on only distal function and his willingness to eliminate moral phenomena serve as contrasts to my account, which takes modern functions seriously and seeks to explain rather than eliminate norms.

James Chisholm offers a competing vision of sociobiology in *Death, Hope and Sex*. Chisholm focuses on developmental facts about human beings, hoping to demonstrate that from these facts and from certain assumptions about cognition a normative basis for security and equality can be established. The argument goes as follows: Human nature amounts to a manifestation of reproductive strategies, and human reproductive strategies are contingent upon the structure of humans' environments. Humans maximize their reproductive chances when they are provided with secure developmental environments, equality, and freedom. Implicit yet again is the notion that only distal functions are genuine functions.[38] Though Chisholm's account is subtle and provocative in the manner in which it mixes developmental concerns with evolutionary ethics, it nonetheless focuses also only on distal functioning, which differentiates it from the account on offer.

Larry Arnhart's 1998 book *Darwinian Natural Right* is an interesting amalgam of Aristotelian and evolutionary ethics, and it is a refreshing change of pace from the literature that focuses solely on distal functions. Arnhart focuses on certain universal desires possessed by all humans, arguing that these desires come as close to constituting an essential human nature as anything. The extent to which an individual flourishes will be determined by the individual's success in satisfying these desires. Some of the evolved desires that Arnhart lists include a complete life, parental care, sexual identity, sexual mating, familial bonding, friendship, social ranking, justice as reciprocity, political rule, war, health, beauty, wealth, speech, practical habituation, practical reasoning, practical arts, aesthetic pleasure, religious understanding and intellectual understanding. Arnhart argues (p. 36) that "these twenty natural desires are universally found in all human societies, that they have evolved by natural selection over four million years of human evolutionary history to become components of the . . . nature of human beings . . . and that they direct and limit the social variability of human beings." Though Arnhart avoids the "only distal functioning counts" trap, he nonetheless offers what is essentially a desire-satisfaction account of morality with an evolutionary twist. However, these accounts have the general problem of conflating the desired with the desirable. Take, for instance, the desire for war. Surely the mere fact that war occurs in all societies does not normatively condone its presence. Though wars well be justified in certain circumstances, Arnhart's account of the universal desire for war does little to motivate its normative acceptance. An additional concern for Arnhart's narrative is that it does not clearly explain the role of desires in an evolutionary scheme. Are they indicators of value? Can they be mistaken? Why should we assume that they point to or constitute value merely because certain desires are universal? Though Arnhart emphasizes the role of prudence and practical reason in reaching an accommodation between the satisfaction of the universally desired and our particular circumstances, he downplays the substantial change in the environment of selection that has occurred in the past hundred thousand years. A modern-history account of functions takes these changes into account, whereas an Arnhartian "the good is the desired" account can leave us stuck in an evolutionary rut (as in "But a million years ago it was functional to hate thy neighbor, and that's why I have this nagging desire to clobber John"). Arnhart's book is sweeping, however, and it does emphasize the serendipitous connections between an Aristotelian approach to ethics and a biologically informed ethic. He is also the only author aside from Wilson discussed thus far who acknowledges the literature in the cognitive sciences that might bear on ethical issues.[39] And Arnhart's analysis of practical issues from an Aristotelian perspective is illuminating and well informed.[40] Nonetheless, the conflation of the desired and the desirable, and an unwillingness to consider that even universally experienced emotions might be dysfunctional on a modern-history story, serve to differentiate Arnhart's approach from mine.[41]

Evolutionarily Informed Aristotelian Proper Functioning: A Summary

In this chapter, using Mackie's error theory as a foil, I outlined the basics of a neo-Aristotelian moral theory that naturalizes human function via a modern-history account of the nature of biological functions. This account coheres well with the wisdom to be found in Aristotle, and can help us make sense of the notion of "proper human function." Using the concept of homeostatic property clusters enables us to rebut Mackie's claims of relativity and queerness and yet still understand how someone might reach such a view. It has the advantage of leveraging our evolved social natures and the social character of the current selection environment so as to explain some of our deeply held moral beliefs. The account successfully finesses the agent neutral/agent centered distinction, leaving certain questions regarding how we ought to treat others open to empirical exploration. Actions that we can take so as to re-equilibrate modern-history functions with the environment include changing our physiognomical traits (extreme), changing our habits (preferred for some circumstances), and changing the environment of selection (preferred for others). The account does not make morality so pervasive as to preclude personal projects, but rather embraces an existential element that can lead to "self-given" functions. It is easily distinguishable from hedonistic (and similar) accounts of morality owing to its account of the evolutionary function of emotion. Though it shares some affinities with other evolutionary ethical systems, it nonetheless distinguishes itself from Spencer's, Wilson's, Chisholm's, and Arnhart's theories, in part because of its willingness to concede that there may be mismatches between what is desired and what is functional and in part because of its willingness to consider modern-history functions rather than merely distal functioning.

According to this picture of morality, certain cognitive traits will be more successful at enabling proper functioning than others. Most basic on this account will be the ability to interact with an environment so as to best fulfill the demands of one's functional nature. Moral skill ("knowing how") will thus be of primary importance. Nonetheless, "knowing that" is still important, especially when moral knowledge is construed as the ability to construct mental models that enable a moral agent to predict functional outcomes.

In the next chapter, I will discuss the two dominant approaches to the nature of cognition, arguing that connectionist accounts can best accommodate the "knowing how" that is most basic to moral engagement with the world in view of our functional natures. Neural nets can also accommodate the aspects of moral reasoning called for by the neo-Aristotelian account of morality I just discussed and Dewey's account of moral judgment covered in chapter 2.

4

Moral Judgment, Learning in Neural Networks, and Connectionist Mental Models

Judgment, Language, and Psychologism: Norms Revisited

Many philosophers have attempted to articulate a robust account of the nature of judgment in a cognizing system. Some of these accounts have been framed with naturalization in mind; that is, they were constructed within a framework that brought to bear the explanatory resources of the natural sciences so as to formulate an explicitly empirical account of what judgment consists in (paradigmatic examples are Hume[1] and Mill). Others have attempted to remain true to the perceived phenomenological features of judgment, shedding empirically oriented naturalism in the process or never bringing it to the "theory construction zone" to begin with (exemplars here are continental thinkers Husserl and Heidegger). One critical argument against those philosophers in the former camp deals with the essential nature of judgment: to engage in judgment consists (in part) of subordinating one's thinking to norms, and norms are by their very definition normative and not subject to the dictates of the empirical sciences. To ignore this difference, conflating logic and psychology in this objectionable way, is to commit the fallacy of psychologism. In contemporary theories of judgment as treated in the cognitive sciences, there are approaches to judgment that have learned from this history, perhaps for the worst—they are sensitive to the essential difference between logic and psychology and do not claim that the laws of thought can be "read off" the laws of psychology. Other approaches, however, either (1) are explicitly psychologistic or (2) think that the overarching framework of rationality as it plays out in the normative component of judgment is wrongheaded.[2] In this chapter, I will briefly (and grossly) characterize contemporary approaches to judgment in the cognitive sciences, using this "science reportage" to frame and explicate a theory of biological judgment that may be able to navigate between the two extremes of psychologism and supernaturality.[3] This notion of judgment will in turn provide insight into the form and nature of our *moral* judgments.

The conclusion of my argument will be that it becomes possible to articulate a conception of judgment that does not rely on a truth-functional analysis. A purely biological notion of judgment is possible; on this view, judgment is the cognitive capacity to skillfully cope with the demands of the environment. Judgments so taken can then best be explained using a connectionist approach. Of course, more advanced forms of judgment might have to take advantage of the benefits of explicit mental modeling. I will discuss the modeling literature as it relates to connectionism. I will detail a spectrum of moral cognitive agents, ranging from those who cope skillfully with the environment using only the first-order tools provided by natural selection (e.g., some insects) to agents who engage in full-blown mental modeling and self-regulated character development and who can have self-defined functions (e.g., humans). I will end by drawing connections between this discussion of naturalized decision making and portions of the Aristotelian and Deweyan corpus discussed in the preceding two chapters.

First I will give a definition of psychologism and a brief recapitulation of the concept's history in philosophy. Then I will survey contemporary work on judgment in the cognitive sciences, grouping experimental and theoretical approaches into camps according to their attitude regarding the relationship between logic and psychology (both broadly construed). Third, I will focus on the revisionist camp in cognitive science, exploring the alternate conception of what cognition (and hence judgment) consists in and how it might be possible to recharacterize the norms to which judgments respond so as to give a naturalistic account of "comportment," the idea being that what really matters from an evolutionary perspective is behavior in an environment.[4] This reformulation will take place within an embodied, natural computational framework. It will entail that animal cognizers make judgments every day, a position that stands at odds with a historical tradition in philosophy that there can be no "mere" animal epistemology. I will address objections to this recharacterization, examining in particular John Haugeland's account of animal "ersatz normativity." Can this biological account really give us what we need to explain the phenomenology of judgment? I will conclude by noting that it is an empirical matter whether naturalized conceptions of cognition will be subtle and fecund enough so as to account for the phenomenology of judgment, and that, conceptually speaking, nothing rules out a biological story *a priori*.

Such a story has the compelling consequence of enabling us to classify moral agents on the basis of a more comprehensive schema; no longer is morality merely the domain of human beings. On the other hand, the most self-aware forms of functional modification are to be found in humans, primarily because humans are excellent mental modelers.

A Foray into the History of Psychologism

The term 'psychologism' was coined by Edmund Husserl in *Logical Investigations* (1967, volume 1, p. 97). The content of Husserl's *Logical Investigations* was dramatically affected by Gottlob Frege's critical review of Husserl's earlier *Philosophy of Arithmetic*. In his review of volume 1 of the *Philosophy of Arithmetic*, Frege accused Husserl of making several critical errors in his attempt to give a psychological analysis of some basic mathematical and logical notions. Logical and mathematical concepts, Frege said, are different from the psychological acts in which they may occur, and to think otherwise is to conflate psychology and logic. Frege successfully converted Husserl to an anti-psychologistic outlook; hence Husserl's use of the term 'anti-psychologism' and his articulation of the commitments that define a psychologism in his *Logical Investigations*. The first volume of *Logical Investigations* makes Husserl's position quite clear: the foundations of logic and mathematics are not to be found in psychology, as psychology is an empirical science, whereas math and logic are *a priori* sciences. A. C. Grayling (1995) summarizes the meaning of psychologism nicely in his entry for it in the *Oxford Companion to Philosophy:* "Acceptance of some or all of the following commitments jointly define a psychologistic outlook: a belief that logical laws are "laws of thought," i.e., psychological laws; a conflation of truth with verification; a belief that the private data of consciousness provide the correct starting-point for epistemology; and belief that the meanings of words are ideas." Frege and Husserl rejected all these commitments. For the purposes of this section, however, I am most interested in the idea that the laws of logic are identical with psychological laws. In view of the constitutive role that logic plays in judgment, this conflation will be the most interesting one to examine when trying to biologize judgment. After all, to argue that judgment answers not to the norms of logic as such but rather to the functional demands of the environment is to identify logical thought with those forms of thought that are empirically functionally effective. This, critics would say, is tantamount to illegitimately co-mingling the normative and the empirical. Raymond Boisvert (1988, p. 47) summarizes: "Both Frege and Husserl like to stress the absolute chasm that separates empirical considerations from logical ones. Investigations dependent on experience exist on one side of the divide. Logical laws, which have *a priori* validity, are situated on the other. There is, according to Husserl, a 'never-to-be-bridged gulf between ideal and real laws.'"

Norms, Good Old-Fashioned Cognition, and Newfangled Cognition

Does psychologism undergird any of the experimental and theoretical approaches to be found in the contemporary empirical study of judgment in the cognitive sciences? Answering this question usefully will require us to make some distinctions that cut across the traditional "departmental" division of labor in the cognitive sciences (the type of description of the composition of cognitive science one gets in almost any college handbook: that it is an interdisciplinary effort to investigate mentality that draws upon work in psychology, neuroscience, philosophy, computer science, anthropology, communication, etc.). In other words, I don't think we can usefully contend, for example, that within cognitive science psychologists "commit psychologism" whereas philosophers don't. A more useful axis upon which to characterize psychologistic leanings has two poles. I will label one pole Good Old-Fashioned Cognition[5] (GOFC) and the other Newfangled Cognition (NFC).[6] The GOFC pole can be characterized as the traditional computational representational theory of thought, the usual components of which are laid out cleanly by Georges Rey (1997, p. 9): " . . . this is the theory that having a mind consists in being structured or organized rather like a modern computer. The theory consists of two main ideas: that mental processes are computational processes defined over syntactically speci-fied entities, and that these entities are representations of the world (i.e., possess semantic content)." Typical GOFC is cast from the Fodorean language-of-thought model, and research in this tradition tends to resemble work done in the classic artificial intelligence tradition. To use Rey's popular analogy, this research emphasizes the software running in the brain over the hardware on which the program runs—to under-stand minds just is in large part to understand the programs that run in our brains.

At the opposite end of the pole, Newfangled Cognition relies on cog-nitive mechanisms that (potentially) de-emphasize the importance of semantic content and make the distinction between "computation" and "representation" a difficult one to maintain. Work in this tradition is biologically friendly, "wet," and concerned with the details of imple-mentation, and it relies on a notion of computation that is more directly tied to our neural hardware. The prototypical approach to NFC is the connectionist or neural-network approach. With this distinction in hand, can we relate typical examples of work in judgment done along this axis to tendencies toward psychologism?[7]

The majority of research in the GOFC tradition does not rely on psy-chologistic principles. There is a healthy respect for the norms of reason and a realization that these norms cannot be derived from psychological knowledge. Much of this work, in fact, is driven by a desire to demon-strate how human reasoning falls short of the rationality mark, or how human reason is characterized by heuristics and biases that often make it fall short of the norm. Dan Kahneman and Amos Tversky's work on judgment in the latter regard (Kahneman et al. 1982; Kahneman and Tversky 2000) is well known. The majority of the work is informed by higher-level psychological concerns but is not involved in the details of implementation. For example, when Lance Rips (1995, chapter 9) devel-ops a miniature general-purpose deduction mechanism, he pays atten-tion to the gross facts about psychology (such as the fact that the human short-term memory store seems to be limited to seven plus or minus two items), but he does not give much consideration to the neuroanatom-ical or neurofunctional details of how this system is implemented in human beings. In the end, any discussion of errors takes place against a background of normativity, as Rips notes (ibid., p. 39): "If current philosophical theories are correct (for example, Davidson 1970), errors like these [when people substitute simple heuristics for proper deduction] are only identifiable against a background of correct reasoning; and so we must balance descriptions of errors with theories of correct judgment." Nonetheless, there are psychologistic holdovers in this research program. For example, a minority maintains that purported errors in human thinking are not really errors at all, and that in fact humans never err when reasoning. A paradigmatic case is the research done by Mary Henle (1978). Mistakes in reasoning, she asserts, occur because people forget the premises of arguments, re-interpret them, or import extraneous material. Henle (ibid., p. 3) goes so far as to claim that she has "never found errors which could unambiguously be attributed to faulty reasoning." The philosopher of cognition L. Jonathan Cohen (1981) reaches the same conclusion, arguing that in every case of "logical" error there is some malfunction of an information-processing mechanism; the mind is furnished with an inborn logic, and if we discover the side constraints that keep us from producing perfectly logical judgments then we can deduce the laws of logic and the laws of thought from empirical data. Although this minority clings to Boolean-style[8] contentions about the laws of thought being the laws of logic, most cognitive scientists working in the GOFC tradition respect differences between norms and empirical data.[9] Though I have no evidence to offer aside from a few anecdotal stories, I suspect that this unwillingness to examine the relationships between norms and facts more closely is informed by an implicit belief in the analytic/synthetic distinction discussed in chapter 2.[10]

In the Newfangled Cognition camp, there is a moderate approach and there is an extreme approach. The moderate approach views NFC as merely a more biologically plausible way to implement GOFC models. In other words, NFC is just an instance of GOFC, and NFC has no claim to being a different approach to cognition. Insofar as NFC aims to deal with cognition, the moderate approach would claim, it must actually be a case of the implementation of a GOFC model.[11] The moderate approach, then, is content to reconstruct judgment as traditionally construed on top of a biologically realistic substrate (or at least a substrate that is more biologically realistic than the digital computer). The extreme NFC approach has garnered most of the press in the last decade, though.

This approach lays claim to territory traditionally claimed by GOFC and presents itself as an alternative; it offers itself as a competitor to and a potential replacement for the computational/representational theory of thought.[12] Steven Pinker (1988, p. 77) discusses the upshot of this extreme approach:

An alternative possibility is that once PDP [Parallel Distributed Processing] network models are fully developed, they will replace symbol-processing models as explanations of cognitive processes. It would be impossible to find a principled mapping between the components of a PDP model and the steps or memory structures implicated by a symbol-processing theory, to find states of the PDP model that correspond to intermediate states of the execution of the program, to observe stages of its growth corresponding to components of the program being put into place, or states of breakdown corresponding to components wiped out through trauma or loss—the structure of the symbolic level would vanish.

If NFC claims to be more than merely a mechanism by which to implement GOFC, then it will definitely have some effect on the perceived ontology of cognition, as Pinker makes clear. And Pinker notes (ibid., p. 77) that the entire operation of the NFC model, "to the extent that it is not a black box, would have to be characterized not in terms of interactions among entities possessing both semantic and physical properties (e.g., different subsets of neurons or states of neurons each of which represent a distinct chunk of knowledge), but in terms of entities that had only physical properties (e.g., the "energy landscape" defined by the activation levels of a large aggregate of interconnected neurons)." Here we see how extreme NFC might offer a plausible way to naturalize cognition, and hence to naturalize the cognitive component of judgment. Whether it does this by throwing the baby out with the bathwater is certainly open to debate. Later I will argue that we lose no babies worth saving when we construe judgment in this potentially deflationary manner.

With regard to psychologism, the moderate NFC camp resembles the GOFC approach. Those who have offered network models of traditional computational representational theories view them as implementations of reasoning that are subject to the norms of logic, just as the majority of traditional modelers do. The extreme NFC camp is difficult to characterize with regard to psychologism. Many researchers are actively seeking new epistemic and ontological structures to support alternate conceptions of cognition and the norms to which cognition responds. For example, here is Paul Churchland's (1989, p. 151) demand for a new conception of cognition that holds at best only a highly derivative relationship to truth: "These considerations do invite a 'constructive' conception of cognitive activity, one in which the notion of truth plays at best a highly derivative role. The formulation of such a conception, adequate to all of our epistemic criteria, is the outstanding task of epistemology. . . . The empirical brain begs unraveling, and we have plenty of time."[13] If we abandon semantics, or at least a truth-theoretic conception of semantics, some of these researchers contend, it may be possible to thoroughly naturalize judgment. Being concerned with the biology of cognition might help boost our sensitivity to a wider variety of more "natural" pragmatic norms to which judgment might respond. This project is promising, as it has the potential of providing us with epistemic standards that will be applicable to a wider variety of cognizing agents than a traditional linguistically oriented truth-tree-making approach.

Language, Learning, and Judgment

Before briefly outlining the conception of judgment proffered by Heidegger, I will do some cognitive "softening up" by blurring some of the distinctions between what we might otherwise think of as different types of cognitive activity. This "softening up" is designed to target two contentions that implicitly inform much GOFC research. The first of the contentions is that to study cognition in general and judgment in particular is just to study the workings of a particular type of language. To judge, this argument goes, one must think in and be able to articulate linguistic statements. The second contention is that, owing in part to the nature of language, such activities are purportedly essentially community activities—judgments and the normative standards to which they respond cannot exist in "splendid isolation," as languages do not exist splendidly isolated.

Pre-theoretically, what would be our motivation for bothering to distinguish between "systems that learn" and "systems that judge"? A first cut, consistent with the preceding paragraph, might be to insist that judging is a community activity, whereas learning is an individual activity. But this would not explain how it is that an organism comes to learn—a feedback mechanism of *some* sort is involved in all learning, after all;[14] an other is required, although this other may not be an intentional system in any usual sense of the phrase. Perhaps that is the distinction: systems that judge do so with respect to other systems that judge, whereas systems that learn do so, at least in some cases, with respect to a system to which the words "learn" and "judge" cannot be applied in any meaningful sense. Judging is *essentially* a community activity, whereas learning is not. Though this distinction can be maintained, it is not (again, pre-theoretically) well motivated. In ordinary language, we have no trouble at all with speaking of the judgments of people in isolation or of the judgments of animals interacting with their environment. If we are to respect ordinary discourse and our pre-theoretic intuitions,[15] the community activity requirement must be framed counterfactually. *If* there were present in our circumstances other cognizing systems that shared our goals and were subordinated to the same norms (in other words, if there were cognizers who shared many of our proper functions), then they too would engage in the same cognitive activity that I am. Just as learning can occur individually, acts of judgment can occur individually. And this has to be so: all systems that learn must be capable of having their judgments changed, because learning *consists in* having the cognitive system that outputs judgments and engages in judging modified by experience.[16]

The critic can immediately reply "But you have changed the subject, as learning is not necessarily a *linguistically mediated* process, whereas judging is." But this is not to argue *against* the tight intuitive connection between learning and judging; rather, it is to restate the assumption that the argument was designed to rebut. Additionally, the seemingly necessary connection between being a member of a community and being a language user is tendentious. After all, judgments issue in action, and non-language-using animals can certainly observe the actions of others; in this sense, it is possible for there to be a community of animals interacting with their environment and observing the actions of others without the use of language.[17] The main point I wish to emphasize is that the cognitive activities that result in the issuance of action, if such activities are modified by the environment in ways that enhance the quality of the organism's interaction with the environment, can usefully be characterized as judgmental activities even if a community of language users is not involved.

Note the implicit requirement here: to biologize judgment, you must be discussing cognitive systems that are capable of being modified by experience; neural plasticity is part and parcel of being a judging system, so the critic of this approach to judgment cannot maintain that it implies (as a *reductio* of it) that, say, insect ethologists are actually studying "insect judgment," as insect nervous systems are in many cases non-plastic and fixed.[18] On the other hand, it is also possible to retort that this is not a *reductio* of the position, as some forms of insect cognition simply are richly judgmental (in my sense of the term). For example, Menzel and Giurfia (2001) discuss the fascinating variety of cognitive activities in which bees routinely engage. In their paper we learn that, although honeybees have small brains (about a cubic millimeter in volume, and compromising approximately 960,000 neurons), they nonetheless have an amazing repertoire of robust cognitive activities.[19] Bees navigate over multi-mile distances using landmarks and celestial cues (including the azimuth of the sun and the pattern of polarized light in the sky); they inspect potential hive sites; they engage in optimization of foraging routes; and they exchange information via the famous waggle dance. If this account of judgment extends far down the phylogenetic scale, then so be it. The explanatory power of this conception should be a plus, not a minus.[20]

The critic can always insist that individual humans and animals do not really learn, but this is a troublesome position. Do we really want to maintain that, for example, Kaspar Hauser, the feral German child, did not learn anything before his introduction to human civilization, or that his learning before his introduction to the German language was "as-if" learning at best?[21] Reflective equilibrium between our theories of what judgment consists in and those cases of activity that we think ought to be characterized as judgment will be necessary as we triangulate on a proper theory of judgment. Nonetheless, the intuition that humans and other animals learn irrespective of whether they are situated in a community and irrespective of whether they possess a language is a powerful one.

To Learn Is to Judge

In the past few pages, I have tried to make the case that the distance between "cognitive systems that learn" and "cognitive systems that judge" is small or non-existent—more precisely, that to learn just is to modify the process by which you judge. Since higher animals and

non-linguistic humans can learn, it follows that judgment is not necessarily either a community oriented or linguistic process.[22] If true, these
arguments go a long way toward supporting the NFC approach to judgment. To understand why this has important consequences for a biological reconstruction of judgment, we must look more closely at
Heidegger's conception of assertoric comportment, which he considers
to be crucial to judgment. Assertions are essentially articulated judgments; Heidegger (1975, pp. 208–210) captures the features of assertion
in the phrase "communicatively determinate dispartative display." But it
is interesting to note that Heidegger quite clearly believes that assertions
as such need not be linguistically articulated. "Assertion," he notes,
"can but need not be uttered in articulate verbal fashion. Language is
at the *Dasein*'s free disposal. . . . " (ibid., p. 208). Thus, although an
account of judgment that focuses on language and community would be
a good account (beings occupy themselves with, among other things,
other beings!), it would not necessarily capture the essence of judgment.
The "significance-contextures" that underlie a being's comportment are
"potentially expressible in words" (ibid.), but this does not mean that
they must be expressed in words. Does the NFC approach have the tools
to explain the phenomena of learning, and to give meaning both to
Heidegger's term "significance-contextures" and the concept of pre-
linguistic judgment?[23] I argue that it does. Making the case for this position will also show how a "biologicized" theory of judgment is possible.

Hill Climbing in Weight Space and Requirements for Judging

Before discussing learning in neural networks, there are seven major
components of connectionist systems that we would do well to keep in
mind: (1) a set of processing units (nodes), (2) a state of activation
defined over the units, (3) an output function for each unit that maps its
activation state onto an output, (4) a pattern of connectivity (with various "weights") among units, (5) an activation rule for combining the
inputs to a unit with its present state to produce a new activation level,
(6) a learning rule that uses experience to modify the pattern of connectivity among the units, and (7) an environment in which the system
functions.[24] Any number of popular treatments of neural networks
are available.[25]

One conception of what it means to learn—learning as "hill climbing in weight space"—is easily captured in a Newfangled approach. Barto (1995, p. 531) notes that "learning involves improving performance with experience" and "artificial learning systems commonly employ a commonsense improvement strategy known as hill-climbing." Hill climbing is the process of finding a better way to transform inputs into outputs by climbing up a fitness "landscape" relative to a fitness function. Thus, for example, if we would like to train a given neural network to discriminate between apples and oranges, we can conceptualize the problem as a hill-climbing problem: In view of the current state of the network, how many apples will it correctly classify as apples, and how many oranges will it correctly classify as oranges? The highest hill the network can climb will be the peak that corresponds to correctly classifying each fruit, and the lowest will correspond to incorrectly classifying each fruit. Intermediate hills will correspond to correctly identifying more apples but fewer oranges, or vice versa, and so forth. Many neural networks use backpropagation of error to perform gradient descent; when the network correctly classifies a fruit, the connections between those nodes in the net responsible for the correct classification are strengthened proportional to the amount of responsibility they share for the output. The opposite takes place when incorrect identifications are made. By slowly changing its weights, the network effectively climbs until it is at the peak of optimal performance (relative to the constraints imposed by the number and connections of nodes in the net, and setting aside for the moment such concerns as local maxima, discontinuities in the state space, and the like). This conception of learning requires a teacher of some kind, be it feedback from the environment or another learner.[26] The former case is the more interesting, as it illuminates how you can give an account of learning that does not require other communities of learners or language—all you need is (1) an environment that makes demands on an organism, (2) a cognizer (e.g. a plastic neural system naturally equipped with a learning algorithm of some kind and embedded in an organism that interacts with the world), and (3) repeated encounters between the environment and the organism.[27]

In this naturalized conception of a learning organism, the environment "forces" itself on the creature—a fitness function relative to which the organism will flourish (or not) is imposed on the creature by virtue of the relationship that obtains between the environment and the organism. The organism need not consent to the relationship for it nonetheless to exist, and the organism need not be aware of the relationship for it to obtain (although, of course, such an awareness might dramatically increase the organism's ability to learn and hence to maximize the value of this relationship).[28] This has obvious import for the debate between the moral cognitivist and the non-cognitivist.

What should we make of this NFC reconstruction of pre-linguistic judgment and Heidegger's notion of "significance-contextures"? First, note that the concept of language does not enter necessarily into a reconstruction of learning. When I speak of a cat's learning to tell the difference between field mice and sewer rats, I need not presuppose that the cat possesses language; however, I must presuppose some neural mechanism that mediates recognition and pursuit of mice but not of rats. This mechanism may contain items we can usefully characterize as proto-concepts, and such proto-concepts may very well issue in "judgmental comportment." I would call these proto-concepts only because the cat's concept of "mouse" is not as richly textured as the concept of "mouse" that you and I possess. Ultimately, however, the difference really is a matter of degree and not of kind (at least by my lights). And, of course, along certain dimensions the cat's conception of "mouse" might be extremely rich relative to ours (e.g., cats probably can distinguish easily and quickly between mice-that-have-been-eating-wheat and mice-that-have-been-eating-cheese).

An NFC-style elaboration of this possibility would go something like this: We can capture the state of the higher cognitive systems that participate in mouse-chasing behavior by visualizing a multi-dimensional space, where the neurons responsible for mediating perception constitute the axes of this space. If we apply certain statistical techniques useful for analyzing these state spaces (primarily Independent and Principal Components Analysis), we can easily distill what might be called a "concept space," where recognition and action are unified, and where recognition/action complexes[29] are clustered according to similarity. Jeffrey Elman's work with neural nets that learn to predict successive words in sentences serves as proof of concept. His artificial neural nets have been trained to predict the grammatical category of the next word that will occur in a sentence, and when the aforementioned analytical tools are applied to the state spaces of these nets a richly structured conceptual space is discovered. The nets have partitioned their state spaces into "verbs" and "nouns," and within the "noun space," the nets have broken up the input into "animate" and "inanimate" objects, with a further subdivision on the animate side between "animals" and "humans."[30]

Moreover, these clusters mediate between input and output for the network. That is, they eventually issue in action (or an analog for action, since most neural nets are simulated on digital computers). In a sufficiently complex neural network—exhibiting sufficient recurrence,[31] coping with our world, and interacting with the environment—"comportmental" behavior would arise naturally.[32] And it does—researchers focusing on embodied cognition have successfully built artificial animals that exhibit animal-like behavior using neural nets connected to the appropriate robot chassis.[33] Of course, this does not mean that we can't draw meaningful distinctions that carve biological neural networks into classes according to their gross abilities to skillfully cope with the environment. And as I will discuss later, there may be rather large cognitive differences between those creatures who can engage in mental modeling— a process wherein inputs are shunted to a recurrently connected but isolated set of nodes so that those nodes can operate on the input in a what-if manner—and those creatures that are unable to take their inputs "off line" for further analysis before action. Though language exactly like this is not used, it undergirds some of the structure that Dennett, Searle, and Haugeland articulate when they attempt to distinguish among computers, animals, and humans along the intentionality dimension.

"As-If" Norms?

Examining Haugeland's position regarding naturalizing normativity will help us determine whether the NFC account I have sketched will have the resources to rebut charges of "ersatz intentionality" against most of the animal kingdom. Briefly, Haugeland's contention is that animals and robots (if they are governed by norms at all) are governed by norms that are external to them rather than self-given. Animal intentionality is exactly like biological teleology. The heart's purpose of pumping blood is biologically teleological, which is to say that it is not *genuinely* teleological in any sense, as it is governed by norms that it cannot grasp and which cannot fail to govern its behavior. "Animals," Haugeland (1998, p. 303) concludes, "do not commit to constitutive standards, hence do not submit themselves to norms, and do not understand anything. . . . It's all ersatz. . . . " Non-human animals simply do not have the cognitive equipment it takes to understand or commit to constitutive standards, those standards submission to which is constitutive of being a player of the "game."[34]

Several fascinating issues are raised here. One important issue stems from the concept of grasping and applying a rule. What does it mean to grasp a rule, and what does it mean to allow it to govern one's behavior? In NFC, one important distinction that is often drawn is between systems that can be rule-described, and systems that are rule-governed. Some proponents of natural computation maintain that, although neural nets can be described as "governed by rules," they are not actually rule-governed systems. They do not "have rules in mind," nor are there explicit representations of rules that the system obeys anywhere in the state space of the net.[35] Rumelhart (1984, p. 60) expresses this sentiment explicitly: "It has seemed to me for some years now that the 'explicit rule' account of language and thought was *wrong*. It has seemed that there must be a *unified* account in which the so-called *rule governed* and *exceptional* cases were dealt with by a unified underlying process—a process which produces rule-like and rule exception behavior through the application of a single process. . . . Both the rule like and non-rule-like behavior is a product of the interaction of a very large number of 'sub-symbolic' processes." It is telling here that connectionist accounts have the most trouble when dealing with processes that can effectively be described as rule governed (e.g., natural language processing, reasoning, inference, etc.). On the other hand, nets that play backgammon to an expert level have been constructed and trained, and neural networks such as NETtalk perform advanced language-processing tasks.[36] Theoretically, there is no given natural function that a net can't be trained to instantiate.[37] But much of this seems to be beside the point—do these systems *really* accede to norms? And if not, how can their ability to "play" backgammon rescue them from charges that any understanding they appear to exhibit is ersatz?

Several options are open: (a) As Searle has done, one could grant that biological neural nets have intrinsic intentionality, understanding, etc., but that artificial computation, insofar as it is construed syntactically (be it GOFC or NFC), does not. (b) With Dennett, one could argue that any appearance of genuine intentionality, understanding, etc., on *our* part is merely (or mildly) an appearance, and that these concepts serve as heuristics that are more or less useful when analyzing cognitive systems, including humans, in general. (c) As the Churchlands have argued, perhaps these ideas have no genuine explanatory power and ought to be eliminated and replaced with more useful neurobiologically sensitive concepts. See, respectively, Searle 1992, Dennett 1987, and P. M. Churchland 1989 for typical arguments for each of these positions. Churchland and Churchland are often set up as "straw figures" against which to joust by ascribing to them extreme positions they don't actually take—so, for example, the concept "judgment" will no doubt be retained in *some* form by a neurocognitively enlightened theory of cognition. Elimination is but one extreme on a continuum of revision. Thus, I plead guilty to the straw-figure charge—or rather, I enter a plea of *nolo contendere* until the results of the completed neurosciences are in and all the necessary conceptual modifications have taken place. Then, perhaps, we'll know how stiff my sentence should be. Churchland and Churchland address this concern in *The Churchlands and Their Critics* (McCauley 1996, p. 298), arguing that "revisionary materialism" would be a better term for their position; they finally settle on "good guy materialism" as the preferred label. Unfortunately, this term has not stuck, and I haven't been able to find any other references to it in the secondary literature.

The Learning-System Option

None of these options taken alone captures a fourth viable position with regard to judgment and learning—this position has lurked under the surface of the discussions thus far. One could admit that there is some qualitative difference between animal judgment and human judgment, arguing that the difference can be accounted for naturally by degrees of recurrence in the brains of these cognitive systems, and that such a difference is just a matter of degree, not of kind. The flexibility of natural computation is great enough that it can serve as an implementation instance of GOFC (insofar as a biological neural net's operations can potentially be rule described and give the appearance of being rule governed). In those limited "mere implementation" instances, the norms of cognition *seem* to be truth functional, and the traditional computational representational game looks like the only game in town; since it is a connectionist reconstruction, though, such "rule-governed-ness" is *apparent* and not basic to the cognitive system. However, the overarching relationship within which both animal and human learning and judgment occur (and whose presence makes the appearance of rules possible to begin with) is not one of "system that learns/judges/can be intentionally characterized/etc." to another "system that learns/judges/can be intentionally characterized/etc." Rather, the essential relationship is one of *embodied cognitive system* (e.g., a system that learns via natural computation so as to act) to *environment* (in most cases, a non-intentional system, but that could potentially include other learners, as is the case with social creatures of sufficient complexity). The relationship between cognitive states and the world can best be characterized in this relationship not as a truth-functional one but rather as a matter of fitness. By fitness, I don't mean a ham-fisted "sheer survival" conception, but rather a subtler pragmatic relation that can perhaps best be captured by the term of art from Greek ethics discussed in chapter 3: *eudaimonia*.[38] Many cognitive systems learn. Those capacities the system has by virtue of being a learning system are judgmental capacities. These capacities are useful not necessarily because their contents are "true," but rather because their contents are richly characterized "action relationships" between the organism and the world. A learning system that is functioning well and is highly adapted makes good judgments (some of which *might* be able to be linguistically captured and assigned a coherent truth value). One that is not makes poor judgments. Any particular judgment may fit "more well" or "less well," functionally speaking, with the environment and the organism.[39] Good comportment is thus not, cognitively speaking, necessarily a truth-functional endeavor.[40]

Unlike Searle's view, this view is not biologically chauvinistic—it can make sense of biological neural nets and their judgmental comportment, but it can also grant that appropriately embodied evolved artificial neural nets can make judgments. Contra Dennett, on this view there is genuine judgmental activity taking place—this is not an instrumentalist position. No matter what your stance, some systems are simply not judging systems (rocks don't make judgments and car drivers do). And unlike the Churchlands', this view is not eliminativist *per se*; the concept of "judgment making" has a direct correlate in our natural (and appropriately "nature-like" artificial) computational machinery. Judgment, albeit in a modified form, is reduced[41] on my view, but not eliminated.

With regard to Haugeland, in the conception of judgment I have developed here, animal judgments are not ersatz judgments. They are full-blooded, modifiable-by-experience, neural-net-mediated "comportments" on par with most of the cognition with which we humans concern ourselves every day. The fact that we have sufficient recurrence and appropriate developmentally engendered structure in our brains to support language and thus linguistic formulation of rules is not a reason to deny to animals the capacity to judge. Moreover, if the connectionists succeed in building and training artificial neural nets that can use language in a robust manner, then we will have little reason to suppose that the underlying cognitive structure that supports linguistic judgment and expression (i.e., linguistic comportment) is itself a language-like structure. In such a case we would not have to presuppose a truth-theoretic semantic conception of cognition at all. The norms to which cognition is ultimately responsive would be pragmatic "fit-functional" norms.[42] Whether this comes to pass is an empirical matter, very much dependent on the state of research into connectionism and Newfangled Cognition in general. I am betting that the connectionists will be able to make good on nearly all of their claims regarding the tractability of language under their paradigm.

Whence Socrates? Moral Dialogue and Connectionism

The classic example of judgmental comportment is the Socratic dialogue, in which you and I have a probing discussion about how we ought to live. We make judgments about the best and worst lives using the via media of conversation and the elenchus.[43] Does the approach I have discussed have the resources to explain these phenomena? The NFC approach may eventually be able to explain the high-level features of a discussion like this, although it doesn't yet have in place the empirical work necessary to claim victory. Thus, to attempt a complete reconstruction using the new framework would be futile. However, I can point out some crucial features of a Socratic dialogue that might otherwise be overlooked so as to motivate the conclusion that non-linguistic non-communal judgmental comportment is nonetheless more basic. If Socratic discussion did not lead to conceptual change in humans—if we did not have a mechanism to translate linguistic statements into the non-linguistic medium of natural computation—then conversation could not change our way of looking at the world. Discussion would never issue in action, and would not result in changes in ourselves that make a difference to the way we behave. If language were not a reflection and distillation of cognitive complexes that mediate action, we would not find Socratic dialogues compelling or useful. Linguistic comportment as such is a crucial portion of human life, but it is crucial because it has the capacity to affect our non-linguistic comportment. We can understand how this is possible only by making comportment in general more basic than linguistic comportment. Language is important *because* we can (already) judge; it is not the case that language lets us make judgments. And in terms of our NFC reconstruction of judgment, the choice seems clear; after all, which would you rather be: a cognitive system that could engage in linguistic comportment *only*, or a cognitive system that could comport well but just couldn't speak?[44]

With regard to the investigation into psychologism that initially motivated this section, then, we can rest easy that the sciences of the mind are themselves mindful of the relationship between empirical cognition and the norms to which it is responsive. But in the case of Newfangled Cognition, it may very well be that the basic form of cognition (and the environment in which it acts) will allow us to formulate a conception of norms and how we respond to them that is *genuinely* naturalistic. Whether this means that "embodied connectionists" plow directly into the norm-elimination extreme, or successfully make both it and the supernaturalism pole disappear, will be an empirical matter that rides on the usefulness and fruitfulness of the work in connectionist modeling of cognition. We would be acting against our better judgment, however, to dismiss the possibility out of hand.

Though judgment proper does not ride on the possession of language, considerations about the differences between the learning capacities of different organisms can lead to fruitful classifications, and examining how these capacities relate to neural-network models of cognition will usefully illuminate the connections between NFC and judgment.

Three Kinds of Moral Functioning, Three Kinds of Complexity

The flexibility an organism has with regard to adapting successfully to its environment is closely correlated with the types of learning it can engage in. In environments that are not perfectly stable and are of moderate complexity, organisms that can learn quickly or in more complex ways will have an adaptive advantage over organisms that learn slowly or in limited ways. Cognitive complexity in a creature directly gains it flexibility in satisfying proximate functions and hence indirectly allows it to fulfill its distal function. Thus, the least cognitively flexible creatures will learn little, and may not learn during the lifetime of the creature at all. Creatures that are hardwired in this sense, that possess some simple sort of cognitive system (broadly construed) but that nonetheless have an extremely limited developmental profile, can be called "minimal moral agents." These minimal moral agents do adapt to environments, but only over evolutionary time. They function more or less well depending on their species' particular history and can take no radically positive individual cognitive action to improve the fit between themselves and their environment. Creatures like this can flourish (or not); moral terms have extensions for them (Lo! A *flourishing* virus!); however, it does not matter, as they have no hope of coming to know this and it makes no difference for the way their lives go. Examples of minimal moral agents include plants, viruses, bacteria, and some insects.[45] These creatures can be objectively evaluated according to their flourishing,[46] but they do not engage in moral judgment—remember that the requirement for a creature to be able to judge is that it be able to learn within its lifetime.

More typical of the cognitive agents we encounter in everyday life are the "standard moral agents." These animals are characterized by learning mechanisms such as classical and operant conditioning, and they can engage in mental modeling (although such modeling might be domain specific and relatively inflexible). Some insects and most other animals fall into this category. Whether they flourish depends in large part on whether they successfully exercise their cognitive systems. These creatures make judgments. They learn or fail to learn, and they enjoy the fruits and failures of their cognitive labor.[47]

"Robust moral agents" learn in all the ways that standard moral agents do and then some. Their modeling systems are much richer and more flexible, and they have the major (some would say singular) advantage of having and using such cognitive aids as language, culture, and complex tools. As far as we know, the only robust moral agents are humans, although there is excellent evidence that we ought perhaps to include dolphins or higher primates (Rendell and Whitehead 2001; Bower 2000; McClintock 2000). One characteristic of robust moral agents is that they often are in situations of environmental release, which enables them to have self-given functions. Having plans, projects, and desires that do not directly relate to the satisfaction of a proximate proper function is, as far as I know, unique to *Homo sapiens*—I would venture to say that possession of numerous such projects is in fact the singular mark of humanity. Another characteristic of robust moral agents is that, because their models are complex and rich, the potential for error in them is ever-present. Moral misperception (this is the "moral error" clause mentioned in chapter 4) can occur because we have constructed a faulty model that does not effectively link the demands of our functional nature to the structure of the world.

Even the most ardent critics of NFC must admit that it has had laudable success in emulating the cognitive characteristics of minimal moral agents and of many standard moral agents. Indeed, one criticism floated against NFC is that it can too easily accommodate classical and operant conditioning; it is often accused of being simply the "new behaviorism," behaviorism having given rise to both of these powerful (albeit not powerful enough to explain many aspects of cognition) conceptions of learning. Critics who make this charge include Pinker and Prince (1988) and Marcus (1998). But what of subtler forms of learning, such as the ability to construct and successfully use a mental model? This seems a crucial capability for many standard moral agents, and surely we need it in order to tell a story about how robust moral agents can internalize their own cognitive aids (e.g., acquire the ability to do a proof in the predicate calculus without a sheet of paper and pencil at hand). How are mental models dealt with in connectionism?

NFC and Mental Models

One of the first suggestions for mental modeling in neural networks occurred in volume 2 of the connectionists' "bible," *Parallel Distributed Processing* (1986), in which David Rumelhart and other members of the PDP Working Group proposed a connectionist reconstruction of mental simulations. Early in chapter 14 of volume 2, Rumelhart et al. discuss connectionist models that bear on the formation of schemata. (Schemata are one popular interpretation of the "molar unit" of thought, discussed by Marvin Minsky as "frames" in 1975 and by Roger Schank and Robert Abelson as "scripts" in 1977.) One problem with networks that are trained to develop schemata (via a process of relaxation) is that they are entirely reactive—the models "can't change without external prodding" (McClelland and Rumelhart et al. 1986, p. 39).[48] The final state of the network after activity values are allowed to settle is ultimately driven only by the environment. The network takes as input environmental cues and produces as output an action. After being trained by the environment enough times, such a relaxation network might produce environmentally appropriate output. However, what are we to make of our capacity to predict the effects our actions would have on the world without actually performing them? Obviously, the proposed model of schema formation needs elaboration if we are to account for our ability to predict the outcomes of actions without actually carrying them out.

The crucial elaborations that Rumelhart et al. suggest consist in adding two features to the network: appropriate recurrence and isolation. Consider adding a second network to the simple model. This network could take as input the output of the first net. After this input passes through the hidden layers, the output of the second net could serve as the input for the first. Thus, the first network takes input from the world and produces actions, while the second takes actions and predicts how the input would change in response (e.g., it predicts what the world would be like if action were taken). This second network amounts to a useful mental model of the world.

Figure 4.1 reproduces a diagram from *Parallel Distributed Processing* (Rumelhart et al. 1986, p. 43) that visually represents the setup.

If events in the world were not really taking place, we could nonetheless use our model to simulate them. We take the output of the mental-model net and use it as input for our action net, taking care to appropriately inhibit the output layer of the latter. We could perform actions internally, judge their consequences, and use such consequences to make further projections about actions and their outcomes. All we need do is isolate an appropriately trained network (the "model of the world") and connect it recurrently to the action network (called the "interpretation network"

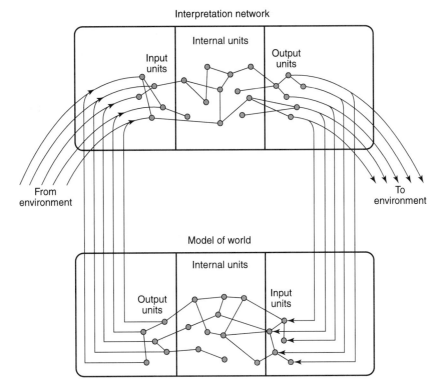

Figure 4.1
A schematic network that models the world. Reprinted with permission from
Rumelhart et al. 1986.

because as a generator of schemata in the example given by Rumelhart et
al. its action is to satisfy the multiple constraints of the input, discovering
the "interpretation" of the world that best fits. In their case, the network
was making guesses about what kinds of room it was in based upon the
features of the room. We can think of the network as saying "Look,
here's a refrigerator, an oven, a sink and a chair. The best interpretation
I can come up with is that this room is a kitchen.").

Modeling a Game of Tic-Tac-Toe

Rumelhart et al. illustrate the practical use of this modeling scheme
by building and training a neural network that mentally simulates playing a game of tic-tac-toe. Two networks are trained. One network,

when given an input pattern representing the state of the game board, relaxes to a solution that is an appropriate move in the game (this is the "action" network). The second network takes as input a board position and the move and settles to a prediction of the opponent's responding move (this is the "mental model of the opponent" network). If the output of the first net is fed as input to the second and the output of the second is fed to the first, the two networks can play a game of tic-tac-toe.[49]

This basic mental-modeling architecture (an action network with a mental-model network connected recurrently to it) can lead to successful simulations of many kinds of cognitive activity aside from that of "naughts and crosses." But, crucially, how is the mental-model network produced? It is trained in the same general manner as the oranges-and-apples "task" network that was mentioned in the "learning as hill climbing" section: by repeated exposure to the environment of action. It is possible to produce decent simulations of mental modeling that rely entirely on biologically realistic Hebbian learning algorithms.[50]

Of course, the network must be constrained in certain ways if it is to model the environment successfully. The network's learning rules must enable it to extract at least the principal components of the input if it is to model the world successfully.[51] If we don't avail ourselves of the backpropagation algorithm, but instead stick to a more biologically realistic Hebbian learning rule, it is still possible for networks to extract principal components if certain other assumptions are made. Those assumptions include that the principal components must be conditionalized (in other words, that the components represent only a subset of the input) and that the network has the property of inhibitory competition (if it is to be self-organizing, there must be inhibitory neurons as well as excitatory ones, and the competition between these two types forces the network to find well-adapted or fit representations). O'Reilly and Munakata (2000, p. 146) summarize: "A simple form of Hebbian learning will perform this principal components analysis, but it must be modified to be fully useful. Most importantly, it must be conditionalized so that individual units represent the principal components of only a subset of all input patterns. . . . Self-organizing learning can be accomplished by the interaction between conditionalized principal components analysis Hebbian learning together with the network property of inhibitory competition . . . and results in distributed representations of statistically informative principal features of the input."

Thus, it is possible to develop a mental model in connectionist terms using only modified Hebbian learning. Such a model can extract the conditional principal components of the input so as to identify the portions of the input that will be useful for developing and deploying fruitful correlations.

In sum: Using only fairly basic techniques, it is possible to train neural networks that can build mental models—these nets develop internal models of the world that mirror important correlations in the environment.[52] Though task learning is much more effective using backpropagation of error (also known as the generalized Delta Rule), these mental models rely solely on neurobiologically realistic assumptions. Of course, if we allow our models slightly more complexity, we can simulate model construction that includes such features as hidden Markov models and Markov decision processes. (Hidden Markov models consist in models that simulate aspects of the world that are hidden from view and hence must be inferred from input, whereas Markov decision processes incorporate different actions that are available to the agent at any given time to give a robust prediction of what the world would be like if a certain course of action were taken. These models are a subset of "Bayesian networks."[53]) But even the basics are enough, and that is all that is needed to get the case for non-linguistic judgment and neural-net mediated effective comportment off the ground.

Language, Diagrams, and Writing

In addition to having the most advanced and complex forms of mental models, robust moral reasoners such as human beings also take advantage of a relatively recent (in evolutionary terms) development: the invention of cognitive crutches and aids such as diagrams, pictorial representation, writing, and language.[54] Although many theorists read the form of our tools back into the basic architecture of our minds (think again of Fodor and the language-of-thought hypothesis), with Edwin Hutchins I prefer to think of these tools as aids that supplement the cognitive limitations of our pattern-recognition and modeling capacities.[55] This is not to say that the aids constitute cognition, nor is it to make the existence of judgment contingent on the existence and use of cognitive aids. Quite the contrary, for Newfangled Cognition can best explain just *why* it is that the aids are valuable (they act as a memory store for models, can serve as a bootstrapping device for enabling us to formulate and reason about very complex models, and can serve as a coordination device for enabling cooperation between groups of modelers). Robust moral agents have come to rely on cognitive aids so as to be able to deal with the functional demands of embodied life.[56] But keep in the mind this warning from chapter 3: Whatever the aids do for us, we should not then think that the demands we place on them should also be placed on our native forms of cognition. Getting around in the world is something that we do very well; external cognitive aids may help us get around even more effectively, but that doesn't mean that to function well we must be responsive to the norms that some our aids are designed to capture. Models fit more or less well with the world, and their ultimate value is given in terms of whether they enable proper functioning. The first-order predicate calculus in its traditional form, binary truth claims and all, does not capture the subtleties of embodied cognitive action, even if it has proven to be a useful cognitive aid.

Summary and Conclusions

My intention in this chapter has been to argue that connectionist systems can save what is worth saving in our traditional conception of moral judgment while also enhancing our understanding of other more basic forms of moral cognition. Using the concept of psychologism as a foil, and the division between old-fashioned cognition and newfangled cognition as a conceptual pickaxe, I have argued for a richer and more basic conception of what it means to be a system that can make moral judgments by demonstrating that neither language nor existence in a community is necessary for judgmental comportment in organisms. Rather, the ability to engage in cognitive modeling is what separates standard and robust moral agents from minimal moral agents. Moreover, robust moral agents can use cognitive aids as an external tool and a bootstrapping device for the most advanced forms of modeling.

Such an understanding of the nature of moral cognition and the norms to which it is responsive will affect other issues in moral psychology aside from the nature of judgment. This gives us good reason to think that NFC approaches have the explanatory power needed to explain gross moral psychology. In view of the account of the nature of morality I sketched in chapter 3 and the reconstruction of judgment I just discussed, these positions become mutually supporting. Taken in isolation they may seem only initially plausible, but taken together they form a powerful and coherent picture. Examining Newfangled Cognition's reconstruction of various moral cognitive phenomena will make the case even more compelling, or so I hope.

5

Connectionism and Moral Cognition: Explaining Moral Psychological Phenomena

Consilience between Theories of Cognition and Moral Psychology

Twentieth-century analytic philosophy has been enriched by a number of successful attempts to make traditional issues in the field responsive to empirical claims and consistent with the natural sciences. As I discussed in chapter 1, this process is called naturalization, and, though one can find naturalized epistemology, naturalized metaphysics,[1] and the like, it remains difficult to find empirically informed work in the area of naturalized moral cognition. There are reasons why moral judgment, development, and reasoning have resisted naturalization, primarily because our conceptions of cognition have not been subtle enough to do justice to moral thinking. With recent advances in our understanding of the neurobiology of cognition and with the re-emergence of connectionism, however, all this is changing. Astute philosophic minds are beginning to place developments in neuroscience and connectionist models of cognition in the same reaction chamber as traditional theories in philosophy that deal with moral matters, and the results thus far are promising. In this chapter, I summarize recent attempts to naturalize moral cognition using some findings of the neurosciences in conjunction with an artificial-neural-net framework; I will extract some of the common themes that unite past work, and I will discuss its strengths and weaknesses. When combined with the general reconstruction of judgment on offer from the preceding chapter, the ability of neural networks to account for many familiar moral cognitive phenomena is yet another reason to think that a naturalized evolutionary ethic and its cognitive demands receive support from, and in turn support, a neurobiologically informed connectionist approach to cognition. As Frans de Waal argues

(1996, p. 217): "Morality is as firmly grounded in neurobiology as anything else we are or do."

More specifically, following Paul Churchland's (1998a) seminal attempt to provide a "cognitive neurobiology of the moral virtues," I will address several key issues in moral cognition, using neural networks to account for them.[2] Concomitantly, I will sketch the relationships between the connectionist reconstructions in question and basic neurobiological facts about human cognitive systems.[3] Making explicit the connections between these levels of analysis will enable me, in the final chapter of this book, to critique moral theory, moral practice, and our moral institutions from the combined perspective of the naturalized ethic and the connectionist approach to cognition that I have advocated.

In this chapter I will discuss moral knowledge, learning, conceptual development, perception, habits, pathologies, systematicity, dramatic rehearsal, motivation, and moral sociability.[4] Following in the footsteps of Paul Churchland (1998a), let us attempt to reconstruct these phenomena in a neural-network paradigm and with reference to the results of the cognitive neurosciences so as to give some bite to this theme.

Levels of Analysis in the Cognitive Sciences

The question regarding at what level we should analyze a cognitive system is really a question about questions: Just what question is it that we are looking to answer? David Marr offered a famous framework for discussing levels of analysis in his 1982 book *Vision*. According to Marr, when discussing cognition we could have one of three questions in mind: We could be wondering just what computational problem a cognitive system is attempting to solve ("the computational task level of analysis"). We could ask what algorithm the system uses to solve the problem or accomplish the computation ("the algorithmic level of analysis"). We could ask what physical parts of the system let it implement the algorithm ("the implementation level of analysis"). An example may help. Consider chisanbop, a method of calculating sums that was popular in the 1970s. Chisanbop allows students to easily perform addition, subtraction, multiplication, and division using a simple algorithm that involves manipulating the fingers. Using Marr's language, we could say that the implementation level of chisanbop would concern itself with the machinery of the hands—the configuration of the fingers and the physiological facts that allow us to move them. The algorithmic level of chisanbop analysis consists in specifying abstractly the particular manipulations that we accomplish so as to (say) add two numbers, which in chisanbop's case involves base-ten representations manipulated according to certain rules (along the lines of "when subtracting fifty, lower your left thumb"). Computational-task analysis is specified in number-theoretic terminology, but it is basically that of addition and subtraction. In other words, we could analyze chisanbop at three purportedly independent levels: the level of task specification (addition), the level of the algorithm (by rule-bound manipulation of digits representing base-ten numbers), and the implementation level (using fingers).[5]

Connectionism Is the Only Approach That Can Sensibly Bridge the Levels

Marr thought these levels of analysis were largely independent—that, for example, one could study the algorithm implemented by a cognitive system without knowing much about exactly how it was implemented. A person's views about the independence of these levels of analysis often correlate strongly with his beliefs about the usefulness of cognitive neuroscientific results. Those who think that implementation-level details can act upwardly in influential and important ways so as to constrain algorithms and computational task specifications will at least keep an eye on the pertinent neuroscience literature; those who think that implementation details are "merely" implementational with no upward effects will be content to stick with algorithms and computations.[6] Still, unless one thinks that the levels of analysis are totally separable, with no upward-facing or downward-facing constraints, there will be a need for a theory that bridges the levels of analysis in a respectable manner. Connectionist approaches to cognition can do just that. Even if in detail they are only neurobiologically approximate, they at least provide us with the machinery we need to move up from implementation-level details to both the algorithmic level of analysis and the computational level of the task. There is another complicating factor: In any given system, at various levels of organization, we can again ask Marr's three questions. Not only will neurons be subject to "levels of analysis," but so will synaptic gaps, groups of neurons, membranes, and molecules. Things get wet and sticky very quickly.[7] Even with these complications, connectionist approaches are the most plausible simulations on offer with regard to being remotely neurobiologically realistic models of cognitive capacity.

For instance, if we are to tell a plausible story about concept formation, our theory of cognition must be able to span the three levels—it must translate implementation-level details (about neural firings and the like) into the language of an algorithm (specified in terms of concept formation and manipulation) and finally into a task specification (for the purpose of, say, identifying faces). In this crucial respect, connectionism is the only game in town. In large part, this chapter will demonstrate the ability of connectionist approaches to unify Marr's three levels of analysis. It will also be an object lesson in the importance of attending to what otherwise might be thought of by critics as trivial neurobiological and neurocomputational details.

Moral Knowledge, Learning, and Conceptual Development

One long-standing issue in moral philosophy revolves around the nature of moral knowledge. What kind of knowledge is moral knowledge? How is it possible, and by what means do we come to have it? Often this debate is cashed out as one of "moral realism" versus "moral irrealism." (See, for example, Sayre-McCord 1988.) Naturalizing moral cognition will have the effect of settling the debate in favor of the moral realist, as I argued in chapter 3—there are facts about the world that we capture with some acts of moral cognition and there are functional facts to which other well-adapted acts of moral cognition respond, and a neural-net framework can help us see how these two things are possible.[8]

Teaching a neural network involves adjusting the weight or strength of the connections between nodes such that collectively they come to embody the desired cognitive function—e.g., so that the inputs are transformed into the desired outputs. The appropriately trained network thus comes to instantiate know-how.[9] In much the same way, a substantial portion of moral cognition is know-how: a morally competent actor has come to embody a set of traits and skills that allow that actor to navigate successfully in the community so as to function well. According to the neural-network conception, such skills are "embodied in a vast configuration of appropriately weighted synaptic connections" (P. M. Churchland 1998a, p. 85). Further, if we construe such a network as coping with or representing the world with a corresponding multitude of activation patterns across a population of nodes and/or neurons, it is possible to construct a higher-dimensional model of the state space of the network. Training a network ultimately consists of partitioning its state space into the appropriately configured volume, with the correct sub-volumes and divisions, such that the network can embody the desired cognitive function. As Churchland points out (ibid., p. 86), "the abstract space of possible neuronal-activation patterns is a simple model for our own conceptual space for moral representation." Moral knowledge becomes the structured higher-dimensional space of possible patterns of activation across our neurons, which space embodies knowledge of the structure of our social environment and how to navigate effectively within it.[10] This is the nature of moral knowledge, and we come to have it (i.e., to have moral learning) by having the appropriate experiences.

Figure 5.1 illustrates a hypothetical moral state space. Points that are closer to each other in the state space are more similar, morally speaking. Of particular interest are points that lie along boundaries in the space—this is where moral disagreement will be most apparent. This diagram (adapted from P. M. Churchland 1998a) is not empirically informed; it is meant as a conceptual aid only. An empirically informed moral state space would be interesting to examine. If we were to accomplish a Principal Components Analysis of the network embodying the space, where would the major axes lie? Would a particular axis correspond to a particular normative moral theory? Substantive moral theory could be informed by the possibilities that might come to light via a thorough analysis of a "moral net." For example, if an artificial neural network were to be trained on a data set corresponding to the responses of moral reasoners at the sixth level of Kohlberg's model of moral development, what would the state space of the network look like? No exploration has been done in this area, although such work would be very fruitful, I believe.

Where in the human brain can we expect to find these elaborately structured state spaces? What neural machinery will be involved in the hyper-dimensional activation patterns that constitute the space of

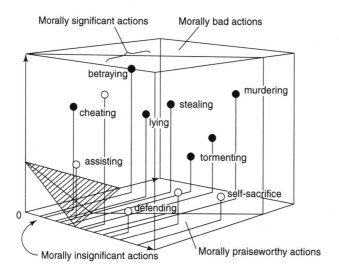

Morally significant actions   Morally bad actions

betraying

murdering

cheating

stealing

lying

assisting

tormenting

self-sacrifice

defending

0

Morally insignificant actions   Morally praiseworthy actions

Figure 5.1
A hypothetical moral state space. Adapted from P. M. Churchland 1998a.

learning and concept development for morality? This is a difficult question, as there are some respects in which the state spaces in question will exist in several locations. For example, for those moral characteristics that have become habits in the pure sense, identification of the presence of certain moral characteristics will lead almost immediately to action; in that case, we might expect these state spaces to exist somewhere in associative cortex, probably in both prefrontal cortex and the posterior association area. In actions that are dissociated from immediate motor action, prefrontal and frontal cortex might play the largest role. In any case, cerebral cortex of some sort will be involved in both situations—almost certainly the frontal lobe's prefrontal cortex, which subserves crucial cognitive functions such as motor planning, language production, and social judgment. Therefore, moral concepts of the type detailed in figure 5.1 probably consist in the activation patterns of groups of neurons in prefrontal cortex and in associative cortex. There is ample evidence that neurons in frontal cortex are continually firing when there are delays in accomplishing tasks or in sequences of task-related actions, indicating that frontal cortex serves as a mediator for tasks that require sustained attention (see, for example, Fuster 1989). This activity could be interpreted as an attractor in the moral state space that keeps the agent involved until the functional task is complete (e.g., "helping the elderly gent cross the street" will require orbiting the "assisting" point in the moral state space of figure 5.1 so that you don't become distracted from the task even when he is walking very slowly).

The famous case of Phineas Gage provides some support for this hypothesis. Late in the nineteenth century, a railroad accident sent a tamping iron through Gage's prefrontal cortex. Most likely, Gage's frontal lobes were all but destroyed. After the accident, Gage was a changed man; he became unreliable at work and eventually became a homeless drifter and alcoholic. Present-day lesion studies also indicate that the frontal lobes play a crucial role in judgment and in long-term planning. For instance, Hanna and Antonio Damasio's patient EVR suffered severe damage to his ability to distinguish between morally functional actions and morally dysfunctional actions after he had a tumor removed from his ventromedial frontal cortex. Before the tumor and the operation, EVR had a functional life as a father, a husband, and an accountant. After the procedure, he exhibited extremely poor moral judgment, becoming financially irresponsible, consorting with a prostitute, and losing his accounting job. He had "generally become incapable of the normal prudence that guides complex planning and intricate social interactions" (P. M. Churchland 1998a, p. 90).[11]

The conceptual dysfunction demonstrated by Phineas Gage and by EVR and similar forms of functional pathology have been modeled using neural networks. For examples, see Hoffman 1992, Hoffman and McGlashan 1993, and Stein and Ludik 1998.

In any case, moral knowledge, learning, and concept development are the key components of moral cognition. Understanding their neurobiological basis will help us diagnose extreme moral pathologies such as those demonstrated by Gage and EVR, and connectionist accounts of cognition have the ability to join brain talk and morality talk within a continuous theoretical framework, as demonstrated by connectionist reconstructions of concept formation in general and by the symptoms associated with moral pathologies in particular.

Moral Perception and Moral Analogy

Another controversial issue in moral philosophy has been the nature of moral perception. How is moral perception possible? Can we explain its characteristics? On the connectionist view, moral perception is of a kind with perception in general. Owing to the nature of prototypical categories embodied in the space of possible activation patterns in the network, moral perception will be sensitive to context. It will be affected by collateral information, and will be subject to priming and masking effects (P. M. Churchland 1998a, p. 87). In much the same way that perception *simpliciter* is subject to perceptual "takes" and gestalt shifts, moral perception will be also.[12]

One early famous connectionist model of a gestalt shift is the Necker-cube "constraint network" constructed and trained by Rumelhart et al. (1986). When the network is given an ambiguous stimulus pattern and then allowed to settle in the manner discussed in chapter 4, it will finally come to rest with an interpretation of the cube (e.g., it is projecting toward the viewer, and to the upper right; or, it is projecting toward the viewer and to the lower left). But until the network has settled on an interpretation, it "experiences" gestalt shifts as it jumps back and forth between solutions to the multiple constraints problem it is facing.[13] For visual gestalt effects, we would expect the connectionist models to find their neurobiological basis somewhere in the interplay of the lateral geniculate nucleus, primary visual cortex (e.g., V1), V2, medial temporal cortex (V5), and probably V4 and infero-temporal cortex, although even visual science textbooks that use the Necker-cube model of Rumelhart et al. (e.g., Palmer 1999) generally do not attempt to correlate the model with the portions of the visual system it is intended to simulate in aggregate.

Moral perception might be closely related to the role of analogy and metaphor in moral reasoning writ large. Moral argument might have a top-down effect, influencing our gestalts of problematic situations and causing us to perceive features of our environment to which we might not otherwise attend.[14] Connectionist models have been very useful in researching the role of metaphor and analogy in argument in general. For example, Hummel and Holyoak (1997) have developed neural-network simulations that use multiple constraint satisfaction so as to simulate analogical mapping and inference. Although their model is a "symbolic-connectionist hybrid," at least it takes a step in the direction of neurobiological plausibility, and it is ultimately intended to model activity in the prefrontal cortex (Holyoak and Hummel 2001, p. 189):

Findings such as these [the results of lesion studies, and fMRI studies of normal patients] strongly suggest that prefrontal cortex must be centrally involved in the kind of working memory that is responsible for relational integration. LISA [Hummel and Holyoak's model] provides an account of why working memory (and in particular, the working memory associated with pre-frontal cortex) is essential for relational reasoning in tasks such as transitive inference . . . in this context, it is tempting to speculate that the 'mapping connections' of LISA may be realized neurally as neurons in the prefrontal cortex. . . .

Forbus and Gentner speculate that commonsense mental modeling, of the type that might be realized in the general manner of the modeling networks mentioned in chapter 4, is perhaps constrained by analogy and metaphor—that is, our everyday simulations will often be qualitative rather than quantitative, and such qualitative simulations can be constrained by analogical and metaphorical forms of inference. (See Forbus 2001, pp. 34–36.) Although Forbus and Gentner's "Phineas" model (which uses structure mapping to learn qualitative mental models of physical domains) is not a full-blown connectionist model, its predecessors, such as the MAC/FAC models that simulated similarity-based retrieval, were. (See Forbus et al. 1995.) Other models that combine memory retrieval with analogical reasoning—e.g., Kokinov and Petrov's (2001) AMBR2—are fully connectionist.

Lest this discussion of analogy and metaphor seem too far removed from moral reasoning, it is helpful to remind ourselves of the essentially metaphorical nature of many of our moral judgments. Mark Johnson (1993, p. 33) elaborates: "Metaphor is one of the principal mechanisms of imaginative cognition. Therefore, we should expect our common moral understanding to be deeply metaphorical, too. *It is* . . . at two basic levels: (1) our most important moral concepts (e.g., will, action, purpose, rights, duties, laws) are defined by systems of metaphors. (2) We understand morally problematic situations via conventional metaphorical mappings."

Some examples of the phenomena Johnson has in mind may help. If I engage in moral reasoning along the lines of "I owe Tom a debt, as he went out of his way to help me move into my new house; perhaps I ought to mow his lawn this weekend to set things right," then I am implicitly using a metaphor that maps *moral interactions* onto *commodity transactions*. "Moral balances" are balances of transactions ("I owe Tom a debt") and "doing moral deeds" is accumulating credit ("I ought to mow his lawn"); "rightness" consists in having a positive moral balance ("to set things right."). This can be useful if the domains between which relations are mapped are *in fact* similar in the pertinent sorts of ways—for example, if functional moral concerns *really are* captured by construing morality as a commodity.

Of course, only the feedback of experience can tell us if the various metaphors we could use to engage in moral reasoning are helpful ones or not. Johnson argues that one particular metaphor, the folk law theory of morality, has come to dominate moral reasoning, much to its detriment. He argues for an alternative that is both Deweyan and Aristotelian, as do I. From one angle, this book could be read as an extended argument for a new and potentially fruitful moral metaphor: that of morality as an essentially ecological evolutionary phenomenon.[15]

Moral Development

The cognitive phenomenon of moral development can also be reconstructed in connectionist terms. Philosophers dealing with moral development have attempted to explain its characteristics and to justify why certain methods of moral development are more effective than others.[16] In much the same way that the contents of the training set are all-important for an artificial neural network, so is the training-set content that we use to configure our moral biological connectionist network. Simply put, your environment counts, and it counts for a lot.[17] When training a network, sensitivity to what function is actually being learned by the net is important—networks can surprise us. For example (in an infamous story that may actually be apocryphal), researchers at the Defense Advanced Research Projects Agency thought they were training an artificial neural net to recognize tanks and classify them as of Soviet or American manufacture. After performing perfectly on the training set, TankNet consistently misidentified Soviet T-72 and American M-1 tanks in test photographs. Later, the researchers realized they had actually trained the net to distinguish between sunny and cloudy days: all the T-72 pictures in the training set had been taken on cloudy days, all the M-1 pictures on sunny days.

Educators involved in character development are (or should be) very sensitive to the importance of the training environment, and a connectionist conception of cognition gives explanatory "oomph" to it.[18] A connectionist conception of moral cognition may explain some of Lawrence

Kohlberg's controversial results regarding the staged nature of moral development. Neural networks can accommodate "tipping phenomena" and via a "less is more" approach can justify transition points between stages in a moral development schema.[19] Of course, we have some reason to believe that Kohlberg's schema does not actually reflect the genuine progress of moral skill. As Flanagan (1996) remarks, "Kohlberg's stage theory . . . is no longer taken seriously as a theory of moral development."[20] Still, Kohlberg has identified sets of trends that hold across moral cognizers, even if those cognitive trends actually turn out not to correlate with the acquisition of moral perception and moral skill. Thus, the ability of networks to accommodate the appearance of stages in a cognitive developmental scheme should not be held against connectionism; quite the contrary, as connectionists must be able to account for appearances as well as bona fide moral mechanisms—they must "save the phenomena" as well as the noumena.

Moral Habits

Some actions we engage in automatically; these actions, if they are well adapted, simply occur in the right environments without any particular overt act of willing on our part. Habits, then, are important components of proper comportment, and having the right sets of habits is critical to living a functional life, as was made clear in the discussion of Aristotle in chapter 3. Habits are rich cognitive processes and should not be disparaged as "merely" a "learned reflex." Rather, the capacity to cultivate what is essentially a skill is a *deep* capacity that involves considerable learning on the part of the organism, be it an owl learning to catch a rat at night or a human learning to navigate a social space. Traditionally, habits are often thought of as procedural knowledge—they are "knowing how" rather than "knowing that." Neural networks are exceedingly good at implementing the cognitive functions that one must have in order to engage in skill-based coping in a given environment. To their credit, they capture know-how in a very natural and fluid manner. And owing to our ability to probe the mechanics of a connectionist system, as well as our growing ability to do the same to a biological neural net, we have confirmed one intuition that informed this project, namely that cognition is so much more than moving symbols around according to rules.

Deeply ingrained habits are richly structured cognitive acts that we can't help but engage in. Automaticity is part and parcel of the ontology of habits. Before discussing the neural structures that mediate action-oriented habits, however, I should briefly review some of the skills that connectionist networks have managed to emulate. This list should include, but is by no means limited to, the following: pattern recognition, pattern completion, mental modeling, analogical inference, Bayesian inference, abduction, deduction, hypothesis generation, vector calculations of all sorts, image compression, principal components analysis, feature discovery, independent components analysis, computing the arguments of logical operators, linear regression, non-linear regression, multiple regression, classification, autoregressions on time-series analysis, fuzzy inferences, function approximation, parallel combinatorics, multiple-constraint satisfaction, combinatorial optimization, cascade correlation, object identification, content-addressable memory implementation, and universal function approximation. Bluntly, the appropriately structured nets demonstrate Turing-equivalence computational ability. Admittedly, I mix levels of computational analysis in this list (e.g., vector calculations are what *enable* neural networks to complete patterns); and, of course, just listing Turing equivalence is enough. However, I am relatively unashamed, as I think it often necessary to remind ourselves just how powerful this approach to cognition can be, especially when confronting arguments such as "Connectionism is nothing but associationism."[21]

In more practical terms, these skills have translated into (again, among others) the following real-world abilities: nets can play games, read aloud, do proofs, add numbers in base 10, learn the past tenses of words, model lexical development in humans, solve the balance beam problem, simulate deep dyslexia, model deficits in semantic memory, model schizophrenia, model memory formation, steer automobiles, recognize speech, make robots walk, scuttle around like cockroaches, swim like fish, daydream, translate languages, process sentences, recognize faces, recognize emotions, identify enemy tanks, forecast the weather, detect cancer, identify patients at risk for heart disease, emulate the scratch reflex, grab objects, act like leeches and crayfish, and sort good apples from bad ones. Unfortunately, there are no nets yet (aside from natural biological ones) that can write books. Again, only slight apologies for mixing levels of task analysis. For confirmation of both these lists, consult most any of the works in the bibliography that have the word "neural net" or "connectionism" in the title, as the capacities and projects mentioned span multiple books and articles.

In accordance with chapter 3, the types of learned skills that would be particularly valuable for proper functioning, morally speaking, include all of the basic motor skills; lower-level cognitive processing skills such as perception, memory, etc.; and higher-level skills such as the ability to engage in robust mental modeling, the ability to articulate a theory of mind, the ability to use cognitive aids, etc. Although it is true that ontogeny does not *exactly* recapitulate phylogeny, it is nonetheless not mere coincidence that we can view individual developmental trajectories as historical recapitulations of proper functions. These trajectories, to an approximation, *do* resemble an evolutionary unfolding of the history of our nested proper functions—this reflects the fact that proper functions accrete over evolutionary time. Thus, blastoids merely reproduce, fetuses develop organs and systems, babies develop sensory-motor skills, children develop social skills, and adults enable the system to maintain itself, often leaving room for the development of self-given projects and life pursuits, the most fruitful of which will cultivate the very environment that allows all these functions to exist.[22]

Needless to say, this amounts to saying both "look to the brain for the seat of skill acquisition," and "look to the general theory of learning implemented in neural networks for explanations of such acquisition." Thus, the comprehensive neural-network literature just cited serves as proof of concept that the theory of learning embodied in neural nets is capable of mediating action in the world and modeling all sorts of cognitive skills embodied in animals. Some of those skills are ones that we normally think of as "uniquely moral" (e.g., some forms of empathetic imagination, the ability to navigate social spaces, the ability to model outcomes universally just as though all other agents were acting on the same principle, etc.); others are often not considered to be "moral" skills at all (e.g., prudential skills like knowing when to brush your teeth, knowing how to plant a good crop, the complex of abilities you need to run a business, etc.), but all of them nonetheless undergird proper functioning. Some are more "prototypically moral" than others, but all that are of use are ultimately useful only because they enable us to flourish as human beings.

Are there systematic relationships between the objects of these various cognitive functions? Can we articulate a moral theory that systematizes our moral judgments and highlights the connections between those judgments and the myriad cognitive capacities just listed? Moral systematicity and the existence of moral theory can also be discussed in neural-network terms.

Moral Systematicity and Moral Theory

Many of the milestones in the history of ideas include theories and research programs that unified previously disparate phenomena. The great scientific theories are ones that conjoined various unconnected realms into one glorious singular package, identifying the principles that explain the structure of the merged sub-realms. Thus it is for moral theories. Paul Churchland (1998a, p. 93) points out that moral theories amount to attempts at conceptual unification. Successful moral theories unify our moral prohibitions and obligations, pointing out what features unite the lists. To a first approximation, Kantians view moral prohibitions as stemming uniformly from the demands of the categorical imperative. Utilitarians view moral prohibitions and obligations as functions of the amount of pleasure produced (and pain prevented) by acting on them. Virtue theorists view morality as a matter of embodying the appropriate states of character so as to function well and achieve *eudaimonia*. Churchland (ibid.) also points out that moral theories are thus superordinate prototypes, assembling together the subordinate moral concepts embedded in particular moral obligations. An equally useful way of construing the traditional moral theories is as the various principal components of the higher-order moral state space under examination. To frame yet another way of viewing this book, it has amounted to a long argument for a naturalized virtue theory as the largest single principal component, and possibly the only significant component at all, in the state space of moral representation. Insofar as the other theories are useful, they will either be reducible to a virtue theory or will constitute only extremely minor and negligible secondary and tertiary principal components of that state space.[23]

As Paul Churchland (1998a, p. 93) reminds us, we should not think that axiomatization of state spaces via *linguistically articulated* principal components is the only way to discuss such spaces: "The preceding is a neural-network description of what happens when, for example, our scattered knowledge in some area gets *axiomatized*. But axiomatization, in the linguaformal guise typically displayed in textbooks, is but one minor instance of this much more general process, a process that embraces the many forms of *non*discursive knowledge as well, a process that embraces science and ethics alike." Thus, it may very well be that there are some aspects of morality that have not yet been axiomatized and hence which can only currently be "pointed to," or for which we will have to invent entirely new terminology. The articulation of a vocabulary for those things toward which we can only now gesture (or whose existence we wouldn't even suspect until we do some of the empirical work I call for in the conclusion of the book) is an exciting prospect for moral theory. Perhaps the principal components and unifying concepts of morality really are captured by the "big three" moral theories discussed in this book . . . or perhaps not. Moral progress will consist in the continued exploration of this question, using the feedback of moral functional experience as our pragmatic guide. Progress in exploring moral systematicity will be judged by the fruits of such unification, and we should be prepared to admit the existence of discontinuities, catastrophic cusps, asymptotes and other "state-space shenanigans" into moral theory . . . *if* experience so demands.

The current debate between moral particularists and moral universalists can be thought of as a debate about the existence of principal components in our moral state spaces. Moral particularists urge that our moral state spaces will be fragmented, disunified, and geometrically misshapen. Moral universalists hold out hope that our moral theories can safely unify disparate moral phenomena and that we will find useful principal components and unifying concepts in our moral state spaces. For entry into this literature, I recommend the collection *Moral Particularism* (2000), edited by Brad Hooker and Margaret Olivia Little.

Moral Dramatic Rehearsal

Moral modeling requires not just that we be able to predict the consequences that will occur when particular means are used for the aim of achieving particular ends. If it is to be truly effective modeling, it requires that such rehearsals draw on the full range of experience in our repertoire so that we can predict both objectively observable and subjectively experienced results. Moral modeling is, as Dewey pointed out, a form of dramatic rehearsal. Advanced moral modeling of the type that humans engage in will thus be a very complex cognitive achievement.

It will therefore likely take place at a high level of organization, drawing not only on resources in cerebral cortex (e.g., that of the ventromedial frontal cortex, which cognitively modulates emotions, and the neural basis of judgment in prefrontal cortex) but also on more primitive brain structures such as those in the amygdala (which plays a crucial role in the experience of emotions such as fear), the hippocampus (which is critical for memory) and the hypothalamus (which coordinates the peripheral expression of emotion). The lateral orbitofrontal circuit of the basal ganglia subserves empathetic emotional responses and will probably be involved in effective moral dramatic rehearsal as well.

Damage to those portions of the brain in the right hemisphere that mirror those on the left involved in processing language causes problems with comprehending the emotional qualities of language. Thus, depending on what action is being rehearsed—suppose I am trying to decide whether I ought to have a conversation with my spouse about my dissatisfaction with the distribution of child-care duties[24]—certain portions of right temporal and right frontal cortex might be involved. This goes across the board for all the sense modalities and their associated processing centers. For example, visual imagination activates some of the same portions of the brain involved in processing incoming visual stimuli.[25]

The connectionist models that deal with advanced moral modeling will thus aggregate together disparate information and modes of cognition, using them to adjudge both objective and subjective consequences. Little integrative modeling has been done in this area.[26] However, Paul Thagard has modeled a process of "ethical coherence," and that work could be extended to meet these demands with only minor modifications.[27] Although the constraint networks that Thagard works with examine four different kinds of coherence demands and how they interact—namely, deductive (fit between principles and judgments), explanatory (fit of principles and judgments with empirical hypotheses), deliberative (fit of judgments with goals), and analogical (fit of judgments with other judgments in similar cases) coherence—they could easily be extended to include the types of affective and conative concerns I just mentioned. For instance, projections from the amygdala to prefrontal cortex could be construed as entirely filtering out the impact of certain principles and judgments while modulating the cognitive impact of others. These effects are easily modeled using the inhibitory and excitatory connections standard in most connectionist models.

Recall EVR, Hanna and Antonio Damasio's patient who had damage to the ventromedial frontal cortex. Crucially, the connections between EVR's amygdala and his ventromedial frontal cortex were completely severed.[28] As a result, EVR's visceral somatic responses to certain judgments, principles, and beliefs had no impact on his practical reason, in stark contrast to normal individuals. For example, before his surgery, EVR might have had a "gut" reaction to the belief that he ought to falsify accounting documents in his firm—this is something that just wasn't done, and no one wasted their time deliberating about the possibility of doing so. EVR lost the ability to have his gut reaction affect his practical deliberation. As a result, he became an irresponsible accountant and was fired from his work. The Damasios postulate that "somatic markers" (gut feelings, visceral emotional reactions) are *crucial* parts of effective and functional practical reasoning. In other words, good practical reasoning is good dramatic rehearsal, as Dewey pointed out.

Thagard has used his somatic-marker-less constraint models to simulate ethical deliberation about capital punishment. Without these crucial connections, though, Thagard is begging the question slightly, as he is probably *already* using his native somatic marker system to condition the judgments, principles and beliefs that the coherence networks are *given* as inputs and to *initially fix* the connection strengths between them. Thagard (2000, p. 162) asserts that his multicoherence account of coherence "provides a much fuller account of ethical inference than is found in recent naturalistic accounts that emphasize either perception-like neural networks (P. M. Churchland 1995; Flanagan 1996) or metaphor (Johnson 1993, 1996; Lakoff 1996). These accounts capture aspects of conceptual and analogical coherence, but neglect the contributions of deductive and deliberative coherence to ethical judgments." This observation is somewhat disingenuous for two reasons. First, although the accounts proffered by both Churchland and Flanagan do de-emphasize deductive and deliberative coherence, this is only because such skills are not primary on their account of what good moral cognition consists in. Second, both Churchland and Flanagan go to great lengths to stress the interconnectedness of deliberative practical reason with other cognitive faculties not traditionally thought to be legitimate partners in practical reason, such as our somatic marker capacity. To argue that Churchland and Flanagan fail to provide an account of deductive and deliberative coherence and that simultaneously they fail to discuss other important constraints on models of ethical coherence is not entirely consistent. These quibbles and remarks notwithstanding, Thagard has accomplished excellent connectionist modeling work that can fruitfully be extended into the realm of neurobiological plausibility and comprehensiveness.

Further extension of these models will require not only augmenting them with somatic marker auxiliaries but also clarifying the nature of the relationship between the principles, judgments, and beliefs across which coherence is computed. Are these items of folk psychology where the real action is, morally speaking? To answer this question will require, in part, a painstaking dissection of pre-frontal cortex function, and ultimately of cerebral cortex in general. When Golden Age neuroscience has arrived, we might be able to answer this question with more confidence and assess the modifications that we might have to make to traditional canons of moral reasoning so as to naturalize moral cognition and make it consistent with the neurobiological facts on the ground.[29] Chapter 4 was an argument for softening up some of the traditional demands that we place on the ontology of moral cognition, but only further work will enable us to co-evolve our moral cognitive language and our moral neurobiological models.

To bother engaging in dramatic deliberation, one has to be motivated to do so in individual cases, or motivated to take the necessary steps to cultivate its automatic operation. How do connectionists reconstruct moral motivation?

Moral Motivation

The issue of moral motivation is critical to moral psychology. When asked, ethicists will often admit that in the classroom they would be happiest to have undergraduates leave an ethics course strongly motivated so as to act morally—the rest (cognitive sophistication, a workmanlike grasp of the traditional moral theories, and so on) will naturally follow if the students just *care* about being moral to begin with. Moral motivation thus has two aspects. On the one hand, we want our students to care to come to know the good; on the other, we want them to act on the good when they know it. Both of these capacities are, most likely, learned capacities.

Greek philosophers had a term for those who know the good but nonetheless do not do it: *akrasia*. Explaining akrasia and akratic action has been problematic for many theories of practical reasoning. After all, if one believes that it is really and truly not in one's best enlightened interest to (say) tell a lie, then why do we ever tell lies? Most theories advert to "weakness of the will" to answer this question, or to the overpowering influence of emotions or some other factor that temporarily disables our moral agency.

Connectionists can take two general approaches to moral motivation. They can explain those aspects of moral motivation that need explaining by modeling them and linking them to the appropriate brain mechanisms, or they can point out the divergences between some of the theoretical constructs used by connectionist moral cognition and the traditional posits of moral theory. These are not necessarily contradictory goals for the reasons I alluded to in chapter 4 regarding the need to save the phenomena.

With regard to the first approach, it is relatively straightforward to construct a higher-order model in which emotional systems act as inhibitors or gatekeepers for decisions to act; in many respects, this modeling would resemble that discussed in the summary of Thagard's work in the preceding section. However, a search of the secondary literature reveals no work that lays claim to models of moral motivation as such. There are, though, more general attempts to link together motivation, decision, and action, some of which involve neural-network modeling. (For a summary of neuroscience's burgeoning literature on decision making and some of the associated modeling efforts, see Schall 2001.)

With regard to the second approach, when some reliably functional cognitive acts are ingrained in the complex of skills and habits one needs to live well, issues of moral motivation become less important; either the skills are low-level enough that the organism achieves automaticity in that cognitive domain (common-sense examples: think of those people you know who can't help but be charming, or who can't help but take into consideration the feelings of others when arguing), or the issue becomes one of ensuring that the cognizer comprehends the *relationship* between the advanced modeling demanded by morality and more pressing and immediate functional concerns. This is not a dodge—the first amounts to a call for proper habituation ("virtue of character"), and the second amounts to a call for good moral education ("virtue of thought"). And it also falls in line with the traditional Aristotelian account of moral motivation: to know the good is not *necessarily* to do the good, as you may be poorly habituated. Moreover, the high-level models that mediate moral deliberation and dramatic rehearsal may not necessarily be appropriately connected to those brain centers that subserve reactions of aversiveness. For example, with appropriate limbic lesions, it is possible to create human beings who recognize the smell of rotting meat but who no longer find it aversive. They know that rotting meat smells horribly but they are not motivated to do anything about the fact that it is in front of their nose. Similarly, data from lesion studies and from opiate application indicate that the "painfulness" of pain can be dissociated from the feeling of pain. Patients can say things such as "My pain still *feels* the same as it did before the operation [to lesion the basolateral amygdala], but now I no longer find the pain objectionable." Still, run-of-the-mill akrasia is probably explained by bad conditioning of the links between basic centers of motivation and high-order mental modeling complexes rather than something as severe as basolateral amygdala tumors.

Think again of the analytic/synthetic distinction. Some analytic philosophers would argue that by its very definition pain motivates one to want it to cease. A painful stimulus that is not accompanied by the desire to be rid of it is not painful, they would say. However, the studies cited in this section indicate that for many types of pain it *is* possible to dissociate pain from the desire to be rid of it. Our concept of pain has undergone revision under scientific tutelage—it is not an "analytic truth" that pain and the suffering aspect that accompanies it are inseparable, though introspection in normal cases might tell us otherwise.[30]

Ronald de Sousa (1990, p. 16) summarizes the connection between emotions and rationality:

This point of view will also yield a solution to the problem of actions done intentionally but "against one's better judgment"—the problem of *akrasia*, or "weak will." Akrasia has seemed paradoxical to many philosophers since Socrates. An akratic action is done for a reason: therefore, it is rational. But it is also irrational, for it flouts the best or "strongest" reason. But how can one follow reason, yet not follow the best reason? The answer is . . . emotions affect the relative saliency of the two arguments. One form taken by the ambiguous connection between emotions and rationality, then, could be summed up like this: The power to break the ties of reason, like other forms of power, can be abused.[31]

I would only add that the power to break the ties of reason, or to influence even unequal ties, like other forms of power, is necessary if one is to take effective action at all. Abuse is the "flip side" of efficacy.

Most of us develop the ability to achieve some amount of skill in the social world relatively early in life before the problem of moral motivation becomes directly pertinent in our day-to-day affairs. What of human sociability? Can the connectionist framework reconstruct both our impulse toward sociability and the mechanisms we use to infer the states of mind of others?

Moral Sociability

By moral sociability, I mean both our basic desire to be with other human beings and our ability to skillfully infer what others are thinking so as to engage in social cooperative action. The former is captured by adverting to those facts of neurobiological development that can be captured in neural nets. The latter is captured by arguing for a friendly combination of the simulation theory and the theory-theory of other minds, one that hitches both implicit theories of the behavior of others with the results of first-person simulations of the behavior of others. Although the second topic in particular merits a book in itself, I do hope to at least make the case for détente between the simulation theory and the theory-theory plausible on face in a few paragraphs.

Our primal and basic wish to be with others (and not merely because their presence is instrumental to the satisfaction of almost all our functional needs) is present almost from birth. Almost immediately after birth, infants attend preferentially to faces and face-like objects. They are able to imitate facial expressions made by others, and cry when left alone. The tendency of infants to attach to others is not unique to humans. Konrad Lorenz's classic work on imprinting in animals introduced us to the inherent sociability of many organisms. Birds, for instance, become attached ("imprinted") to their parent (or any other large moving object for that matter).[32] This capacity must have a neural basis and will probably best be explained and simulated by a constructivist developmental model, one that explains how new cognitive abilities arise as the result of interactions between appropriately timed environmental input and ontogenetic neural development. I will discuss this more in chapter 6 when I talk about the importance of timing in "training up" a neural net and briefly review Elman's arguments for the "importance of starting small."

The second capacity, our ability to theorize about other's minds, expresses itself sometime between the ages of 3 and 5 years.[33] Considerable cognitive development in interaction with a fair amount of worldly experience is necessary for us to begin to recognize that others have minds and before we begin to theorize about their contents. The two major competing explanations for just how it is that we come to have such knowledge are simulation theory and theory-theory. Theory-theory reigned supreme as orthodoxy until simulation theory was introduced by Robert Gordon and Jane Heal independently in 1986, and there has been fierce competition between the two paradigms since.

Theory-theorists believe that we have full-blown theories about the mental states of others. We reason about their states of mind using these theories, in much the same way that we reason about the locations of the planets in the solar system using theories about celestial mechanics. Although details differ dramatically from theorist to theorist (e.g., all the traditional divisions in cognitive science recapitulate themselves here—you can think "theory-of-mind" theories are innate vs. learned, explicitly represented vs. implicitly represented, domain general vs. domain specific, modular vs. distributed, etc.), theory-theorists are united in maintaining that our knowledge of the states of minds of others is essentially theoretical.[34] Simulation theorists such as Robert Gordon and Alvin Goldman, on the other hand, argue that our ability to project ourselves imaginatively into another person's shoes by simulating their activity is what enables us to possess a theory of mind.[35]

Hybrid positions are available, and I think the case for moral cognition that I have made thus far pushes us somewhat in that ecumenical direction. For example, Josef Perner argues that a hybrid model can gain us explanatory power by acknowledging the strengths and weaknesses of each form of explanation relevant to the pertinent experimental data from children. Though his argument is complex in execution, its gist is fairly straightforward: any theory use involves some elements of simulation, and simulations alone cannot account for the empirical data, so the future lies with hybrid models (Carruthers and Smith 1996, p. 103). The process of imaginative deliberation discussed earlier will very much depend on both theories and simulations—theories (in the connectionist sense of the term[36]) must be *merged* with the results of simulation, as simulations are what will provide the affective component of our knowledge of other's minds (as in: it literally pains me to know that my child is hungry). Connectionist models can merge theories with simulations using the common currency of weight spaces and activation vectors. The models would resemble those discussed in the moral dramatic rehearsal section, and would have to (at the very least) aggregate neural activity in the orbito-frontal cortex, the medial structures of the amygdala, and the superior temporal sulcus.[37] This has the explanatory plus of being consistent with the theory-of-mind data from autistic individuals, and is consistent with what we know of primate cognition (there is evidence that, for example, chimpanzees possess a theory of mind, and yet they do not possess linguaform theories).[38]

(Very) Brief Objections and Rejoinders

There are numerous objections that can be offered to the reconstructions discussed in this chapter. Having dealt with some specific and empirical objections while discussing the mechanisms of reconstruction, I will conclude by examining the more general far-reaching arguments that might deflate my explanatory ambitions.

First, moral reasoning seems to be a very high-level form of cognition and reasoning, and neural nets often have more difficulty instantiating higher-level functions than other more traditional conceptions of cognition.[39] Marvin Minsky and Seymour Papert made this objection in their influential 1969 paper ("Our purpose is to explain why there is little chance of much good coming from giving a high-order problem to a quasi-universal perception . . . ," p. 167); their work set the connectionist agenda back many years. Nonetheless, the neural-net research program continues to advance—Minsky and Papert's criticism, for example, applies only to single-layer networks and not to multi-layer networks—and has empirically accomplished tasks that skeptics predicted would be both theoretically and practically impossible. To insist *a priori* that there are certain things neural networks (artificial or biological) can never accomplish, especially in view of their theoretical capacity to serve as universal Turing machines, is to sin on several fronts. Such an insistence ignores the empirical work cited in this chapter's section on moral skill, and it smuggles in the analytic/synthetic distinction that was discussed and rebutted in chapter 2.

Second (and in a related vein), if neural networks really are "just" pattern detectors, then how do we ever expect to capture moral reasoning with them? Moral reasoning seems to be much more complex than this. In response, though, proponents can emphasize the large part of morality that does seem to consist of know-how with regard to detection and manipulation of morally relevant properties, and can point to the success of networks at capturing other higher cognitive functions. (A related objection might go: "If nets are just pattern detectors, how do we *ever* expect them to be able to read?" We should direct the objector to Jeff Elman or Terry Sejnowski.)

Third, Jerry Fodor and Zenon Pylyshyn would insist that neural networks are just implementation-level devices.[40] The real action in moral reasoning, they would argue, is still taking place at the algorithmic level and is still best captured by a traditional computational/representational theory of thought. Space considerations keep me from addressing this concern in any more depth than I have in the preceding chapter on judgment; others have done it very well.[41] Suffice it to say, though, that results in moral cognition that are informed and constrained by progress in connectionism may very well stand or fall with connectionism. And, as was discussed in chapter 4, neural networks can accommodate model-theoretic accounts of cognition without necessarily "lapsing into linguaform."[42]

Conclusion

Even with these concerns in mind, however, the marriage of connectionism and other neurobiologically realistic models of cognition with traditional issues in moral cognition promises to be a watershed event in the field of ethics. It will help settle some long-standing issues in the field, and will bring to bear empirical evidence pertinent to adjudicating between competing conceptions of moral knowledge. It will affect how we construe the nature of moral cognition, it will allow us to search the state space of possible ways to parse morality, and it may also help us in the search for realistic normative moral theories. Paul Churchland (1996a, p. 107) sums this up nicely: "This novel perspective on the nature of human cognition, both scientific and moral, comes to us from two disciplines—cognitive neuroscience and connectionist artificial intelligence—that had no prior interest in or connection with either the philosophy of science or moral theory. And yet the impact on both these philosophical disciplines is destined to be revolutionary."

Researchers in moral philosophy would do well to re-approach some of the traditional issues in the field from an interdisciplinary perspective that is informed by a connectionist conception of cognition and that takes neurobiology seriously. The results from this liaison, if preliminary research is any indication, should be provocative, interesting, and (most important) useful to us as we learn how not just to live but to live well.

The particular capacities discussed in this chapter are just the tip of the iceberg, as many other cognitive moral phenomena can probably be reconstructed in connectionist terms. Such reconstructions have initial plausibility and excellent explanatory power. By my lights, however, this form of reconstruction is less provocative than the impact that connectionism can have on our normative ethical theories. It is no coincidence that this will also be the area of inquiry where attempts at naturalization are perceived as being least useful (and simultaneously most threatening to traditional moral inquiry) by those who oppose an empirically informed conception of morality. In part, this reaction may be a result of previous rather heavy-handed attempts to naturalize morality (e.g., some forms of pop sociobiology, simplistic evolutionary ethics). Hopefully, this account has acknowledged and avoided some of the shortfalls that attended other naturalistic projects.

Given a connectionist conception of cognition, what can we say regarding what we *ought* to do and how we *ought* to live? In the next chapter, I examine the consequences that the combined forces of the naturalized ethical theory and connectionist account of moral cognition I offer might have for moral theory, moral practice, and moral institutions.

6

Applications and Critique: Moral Theory, Moral Practice, Moral Institutions

Consistent with the overall pragmatic tone of this book, many of the points covered would be irrelevant if they didn't promise to inform intelligently the way we live our lives. The modern-history theory of evolutionary ethical function that I articulated in the first three chapters, and the neurobiologically informed connectionist accounts of judgment, modeling, and moral cognition that I discussed in the subsequent two chapters, have the potential to fruitfully affect several areas of human experience. First, they promise to provide some tentative answers to long-standing issues in moral theory, one of the crucial tools we use in moral thought and discourse. Debates about the purview of moral theory, and about the psychological plausibility of certain forms of moral reasoning can be viewed from a new perspective. Second, they shed new light on what kinds of people we ought to *be,* and what kinds of things we ought to *do,* given the general features of the environments in which we find ourselves; they also provide us with some general guidance regarding how we should structure large-scale regulatory institutions such as government and the law. Finally, they provide some advice regarding how we should structure our moral institutions so that they are as *effective* in encouraging moral learning as they can possibly be. Our character-development institutions—our colleges, our schools, our homes, and our spiritual centers—can all benefit from carefully considering both the nature of a naturalized ethic and the emerging picture of moral cognition discussed in this book. Though opinions and asides about these issues have been inserted at various portions of the book thus far, in this chapter I propose to examine these issues explicitly and in slightly more detail.

Recap and Extension of Chapter 2's Coda

First, let me turn to the implications that these positions have for normative moral theory. I will briefly recap chapter 2's coda, which notes that you do not have to believe the case for appropriately informed integration of facts and norms that I make in that chapter in order to think that these results can usefully constrain moral theory.

Recall one skeptical position about the relationship between norms and facts: the facts of evolution or cognition would not have any impact on normative moral theory. As I noted, this is usually supported by referencing either G. E. Moore's "open-question argument" (which states that any attempt to define an ethical norm in non-ethical, natural terms is to make "natural" something that is patently not "naturalizable"), or David Hume's 'is'/'ought' distinction (which states that it is impossible to deductively derive an 'ought' statement from a set of premises that contain only 'is' statements).[1] For example, Virginia Held (1996, p. 69) has a clear position regarding the utility of cognitive science as it relates to ethics: " . . . cognitive science has rather little to offer ethics, and that what it has should be subordinate rather than determinative of the agenda of moral philosophy." I have already argued extensively in chapter 2 that there is no *theoretical* reason to isolate ethics from the sciences, so any such isolation will be the result of the empirical failures of naturalized moral theories. But for the moment, let us assume that Hume, Moore, and others are right. What effect would this have on the project?

Although these arguments have some *prima facie* force, they ignore the palpable contributions that empirical knowledge can make to a normative theory even given an 'is'/'ought' barrier. For many moral philosophers, 'ought' implies 'can'—in other words, if your normative theory asks the impossible of you as a moral agent, it is not a very useful normative theory. On this view, we should examine what constraints the nature of our cognitive faculties places on our ability to reason morally. Owen Flanagan (1991, p. 32) takes an even stronger position. His "principle of minimal psychological realism" maintains that almost *all* traditions of ethical thought are committed to a minimal sort of psychological realism:

PRINCIPLE OF MINIMAL PSYCHOLOGICAL REALISM: Make sure when constructing a moral theory or projecting a moral ideal that the character, decision processing, and behavior prescribed are possible, or are perceived to be possible, for creatures like us.

If we accept Flanagan's principle, then neurobiology and connectionism might constrain normative moral theory as well. We have good reason to accept such a principle—a telling criticism against any moral theory is that it asks of us the impossible. This amounts to committing a "non-naturalistic fallacy," and it results from not attending to the proper relationships between norms and facts. Even if we accept a similar principle of what we might call "minimal neurobiological realism," we might find an interesting interplay between concepts that play key roles in our traditional moral theories and their neurobiological implementations.[2]

A Critique of Pure Reason: Kantian Ethics, Virtues, and the Structure of Cognition

Paul and Patricia Churchland, Owen Flanagan, Antonio Damasio, and Mark Johnson have all done work in this area. Johnson, for example, contends that any plausible conception of cognition doesn't have room for "pure reason" of the kind called for in a Kantian moral psychology. Ergo, traditional versions of Kantian moral theory (ones that don't have room for Deweyan moral dramatic rehearsal and moral imagination— see chapter 1 of Johnson 1993) must be rejected.[3] Though Johnson never mentions connectionism, the connectionist's ability to accommodate metaphor is a notable improvement over theories of reason that make sentential/deductive-nomological-style claims.[4] Patricia Churchland rejects a Kantian approach to morality on account of its neurobiological implausibility,[5] and Paul Churchland is explicit in his endorsement of virtue theory as being most strongly accommodated by connectionist-style cognition. This is a direct result of construing moral knowledge as a set of skills allowing one to navigate in a community, where such navigation, I argue, has the purpose of satisfying the functional demands of one's evolutionarily semi-fixed nature. "A morally knowledgeable adult," Paul Churchland notes (1998a, p. 85), "has acquired a complex set of behavioral and manipulational skills, which skills make possible his successful social and moral interaction with others in his community. According to the model of cognition here being explored, the skills at issue are embodied in a vast configuration of appropriately weighted synaptic connections." On the account I have detailed, this amounts to being able to work with others in a way that enables you to satisfy the demands of your biological nature; humans are social animals, and sociality is both an end in itself and a means to satisfying other biological functional demands.

Morality, then, consists in large part not of mastery of a set of propositions but of mastery of a set of skills. Recall my discussions in chapters 4 and 5 of the difference between "knowing how" and "knowing that." Neural nets can clearly accommodate "knowing how" and may even make it the basis upon which "knowing that" is built.[6] As it turns out, the 2,000-plus-year-old research tradition in virtue ethics becomes germane when virtue theorists emphasize the importance of *praxis* over *theoria*. Contemporary virtue theorists such as Alasdaire MacIntyre and James Wallace can find support in a connectionist framework. For example, the opening paragraph of Wallace 1996 sounds like it was written by a moral theorist who was informed by artificial neural nets:

Practical knowledge is obviously the result of people's cumulative experience in coping with the particular problems they encounter. We learn from others how to do things, we seek and cultivate better and more effective ways of doing them, and we transmit this knowledge to others. Know-how and practical norms—standards of better and worse ways of doing things—are in this sense human creations based upon our experience. The norms that originate in this way derive their authority from the activities they constitute and from their role in facilitating the purposes the activities serve. The aim of this book is to present an account of ethics that emphasizes the similarities between moral and other kinds of practical knowledge. Morality is presented as a collection of disparate items of practical knowledge that have their origin and authority in the learned activities that are the substance of our lives. The result is a naturalistic account of ethics that understands moral knowledge as straightforwardly empirical.

A skills-based conception of moral coping such as this one differs radically in aim from a more traditional Kantian conception, and it demands very different things of us as cognizers. The Kantian conception of morality requires, if our actions are to be truly morally praiseworthy, that they arise from a faculty of reason that is not tainted by affective concerns. In order to be praiseworthy, our actions must stem from and be motivated solely by respect for the categorical imperative. We must do our duties for duty's sake, and not for any other reason.

For Kant, morality makes categorical demands on us. Morality can be boiled down to this categorical imperative. The other imperatives we act on are hypothetical; that is, they are of the form "If you desire x, then you ought to do y." Thus, many of our actions are Humean, in the sense that reason serves as an instrument to tell us how we should act so as to satisfy our desires. As Hume contends, reason is and ought to be the "slave of the passions." Kant thinks, contra Hume, that the formulation and the satisfaction of hypothetical imperatives are morally irrelevant. The distinguishing feature of moral actions is that they are not driven by an ulterior or hidden motive; rather, they are motivated purely by respect for the moral law as it is deduced from pure reason.

Kant's is thus a non-consequential ethic (in the technical sense of the term). It does not rely on consequences so as to distinguish the goodness and badness of actions. Rather, we can look to the state of mind of the moral agent to make our moral evaluations. Our maxims and intentions are what counts, not the outcomes of our actions.

The categorical imperative itself serves as a test through which we filter the maxims of our actions so as to determine whether they are morally permissible. There are several formulations of the categorical imperative—according to Kant, they are all equivalent at root, as there is technically only one true categorical imperative.[7] Kant (1786/1964, p. 88) states succinctly "Act only on that maxim through which you can at the same time will that it should become a universal law." From this, we can derive several other imperatives, such as "Act in such a way that you always treat humanity, whether in your own person or in the person of any other, never simply as a means, but always at the same time as an end" (also from the *Groundwork*, p. 96). The categorical imperative and some of the practical imperatives to which it gives rise serve as filters through which we strain the maxims that guide our actions. If the maxim passes the "categorical-imperative test," it is permissible to formulate that maxim and act on it; if not, it is prohibited. In this sense, although Kant's ethic is very demanding (the categorical imperative issues in absolute and universal prohibitions such as "never lie," "never murder," and "never break a promise"), it is also very liberal. If your maxim passes the categorical-imperative test, formulating and acting on the maxim is morally permissible: do as you will, pursue your own projects, and otherwise live as you choose, just so long as you do not formulate maxims that violate the demands of the categorical imperative. The perfect duties generated by the categorical imperative are thus "side constraints," to use Robert Nozick's term. They tell us what we cannot do as we pursue our life projects.

Kant's system of ethics, his epistemology, and his metaphysics are all tightly woven together, so that to understand any one of them you must grasp the basics of them all. For present purposes, a brief discussion regarding why Kant thought the categorical imperative was so important will have to suffice. Kant thought that morality makes sense only in a world inhabited by rational and autonomous creatures—organisms who have a will that can be conditioned by the faculty of reason, and who can act freely on that will. To respect morality, then, we must begin by respecting the conditions that enable it to exist. Respect for reason and autonomy are thus the bulwarks of morality. The categorical-imperative test is how we ensure that our intentions respect the very conditions that make talk of morality possible. In a world where creatures are incapable of reasoning, such creatures would have no reason to talk of what they ought to do and what they ought not do (non-contradiction is the most fundamental tenet of reason, so the link between this and the first "universalizability" formulation of the categorical imperative should be clear). In much the same way, in a world where creatures are not free, moral talk would serve no purpose, as maxims and actions could not be other than what they are. (Respecting the freedom of others by using them to achieve your ends only when they consent is captured by the "mere means" formulation of the categorical imperative.)

Here is an example of a derivation of a moral law using the categorical imperative. Suppose I wish to deceive someone for the purpose of gain. The maxim that underlies my action goes something like this: It is acceptable for me to lie to someone in order to achieve an end I desire. Can I universalize this maxim consistently? Can I will that it become a universal law of nature? Kant says that I cannot. When made universal, the maxim contains the seeds of its own destruction. If all free and rational creatures were to deceive others when it was in their interest to do so, deception would be impossible, as we would all suspect that others were not telling the truth in those circumstances, and thus deception itself would become a practical impossibility. We could not will that this maxim become a universal law; rather, we want it merely to apply only to ourselves, hoping that everyone else will continue to follow a different universal law that would prohibit deception. This is not something that we must experiment with in order to determine. We need not go out and "test" the imperative by lying several times and observing the results. The problem with the imperative is discoverable *a priori,* using reason alone.

What kind of cognitive faculties are posited by the Kantian system? The ability to reason "purely," for one. Exactly what this capacity consists in is difficult to determine. At the very least, however, it involves formulating language-like maxims that are then checked for consistency. If emotion or affect tags or marks the maxims and the logical processing that is accomplished over them, then the reason is not pure; either we will fail to respect reason as such owing to bad advice from our limbic system, or our maxim will become tainted with the inappropriate motivation even if we "do the right thing." (Remember, we should respect reason—do our duty—for duty's sake alone.) Kant is forthcoming and admits that this is an epistemically impossible standard. One can never be sure whether one acted out of respect for duty and not *merely* in accordance with it, and the same can be said of the actions of others.

Apologists have managed to soften up some of these requirements. (See, for example, O'Neill 1989.) Nonetheless, there is a tension between the things that Kantian pure reason demands and the things of which we are actually capable. Indeed, we have reason to think that agents who reason *without* allowing their maxims to be influenced by emotions and affective concerns will form poor maxims and act inappropriately. As Patricia Churchland points out (1996, as reprinted in Churchland and Churchland 1998), "the perfect moral agent, Kant seems to suggest, is one whose decisions are perfectly rational and are detached entirely from emotion and feeling."[8] Yet our examples of people who have achieved total detachment from affect are filled with moral pathology and immoral action. Recall EVR, the Damasios' patient who had crucial portions of his affective system disconnected from the portions of his brain responsible for judgment and decision making. EVR was morally dysfunctional because he could no longer use visceral emotional cues to help him sort out which options were conducive to flourishing in his life and which were not.

Given the normal course of brain ontogeny, moreover, we have good reason to believe that Kant's ideal is simply not achievable by any moral cognizer, aside from those with injuries and severe developmental problems. There are two strikes against Kant, then: First, we have empirical reason to believe that his ideal form of moral reasoning is not as fruitful as one might initially think. Second, we have reason to believe that his ideal form of moral reasoning is not achievable by anyone with a normally functioning cognitive system.[9] These are both problematic conclusions for anyone who would support the aboriginal Kantian theory. Many of the crucial skills we need in order to interact with others would not be available to us if we were to take that theory seriously as an ideal.

Salvaging Kantian Reasoning: Simulating Dissimulation

The preceding conclusion should not be too surprising in view of the naturalistic constraints with which we began this investigation in chapter 2. Transcendental argument, rampant thought experiment, and armchair *a priori* reasoning were all discounted as potential sources of error. The types of reasoning called for in a Kantian ethical system violate all three of these constraints.

At root, Kant's thought is transcendental—it derives conclusions about necessary conditions for morality and experience not by testing theories against experience but rather by arguing for what conditions must be the case to account for the phenomena in question. Thus, for example, the type of radical autonomy that Kant requires of us in his ethical system is based not on a thorough examination of the seat of choice in the brain, but rather on library reflection about the seemingly necessary conditions for the existence of freedom. Such transcendental moves are not consistent with a thoroughgoing naturalism.

In the same way, Kant relies on ill-constrained thought experiments to drive home his reasoning about the demands of the categorical imperative. A famous flaw with the categorical-imperative test is that it fails to establish at what *generality* the maxims that we test ought to be pitched. For example, the maxim I act under when lying might be something more like this: it is permissible for anyone who is exactly 6 feet and 2.88 inches tall (my height) to deceive others for gain. If so, the maxim can be universalized without contradiction, for I am probably the only moral agent in the universe who is exactly that tall. This particular example is a bit contrived, of course, but the general point should be plain. We have no clear guidance regarding at what level of generality maxims should be tested. Similarly, we have no guidance regarding when the categorical-imperative test becomes pertinent to us cognitively. Do I filter every single maxim through the categorical imperative every single time I act? Doing so would consume almost all of my cognitive resources, especially if I were diligent, in which case I would probably never even get around to acting. Kantian reasoning becomes subject to a frame-problem-style objection: how do I know what maxims to bother testing?[10] Some theorists have suggested supplementing the categorical imperative with general "rules of moral salience" that tell us when the test becomes pertinent.[11] This seems like an excellent addendum, although it is derived from experience and cognitive labor in the real "empirical" world.

Relatedly, Kantian moral reasoning has a critical *a priori* component. Insofar as naturalists generally disdain armchair morality as much as they disdain armchair metaphysics, this is reason for worry. Testing of imperatives against experience is not part of the procedure; though Kant argues that in fact we do have genuine experience of some of the phenomena to which he points (e.g., he thinks we have the experience of being motivated purely out of respect for the moral law), such arguments are really beside the point. The categorical-imperative test is not an experiment; rather, it is an *a priori* logical test. This *a priori* element is antithetical to the experimental spirit that would probably inform any naturalistic morality.

Of course, Kant is refreshingly straightforward on these matters. He admits that his moral system really makes sense only if three assumptions are made that we can never hope to prove, in view of our cognitive limitations: that God exists, that there is an afterlife, and that we are absolutely free. Indeed, given the current state of the sciences, we have reason to suspect all three of these claims. (See P. S. Churchland 2002.) It should also be mentioned that Kant was a very good scientist. His philosophical system was formulated primarily to defend science against the ravages of David Hume's arguments against the possibility of science (as in "causes do not exist . . . only constant conjunctions," which argument roused Kant from his "dogmatic slumbers"). Kant contributed to many fields of science; notably, he formulated the first scholarly version of a plausible theory detailing the formation of the solar system (that the planets accreted from a dust disk that surrounded the sun). Perhaps it is an uninteresting biographical fact about me, but I have difficulty being too hard on Kant, in part for these reasons.

Despite its limitations, Kant's system is a beautiful achievement—it does capture, in many cases, our intuitions about what is permissible and what is not. But it does so by eviscerating the very features of morality that many of us find critical, which is why it has provoked a backlash from ethicists who are more concerned with an "ethic of care" and less concerned with the "formal" aspects of morality on which Kant seemed to focus almost exclusively.[12] Can we accommodate some of Kant's concerns within the evolutionary connectionist framework artic-ulated here? We can. Though Kant's methodology may be problematic, he is on to something important: there are certain conditions that just as a matter of fact must be met if we are to sustain large-scale cooperative enterprises. This social aspect of Kant's thought can be recapitulated within the modern-history framework. Also, the categorical-imperative test, if connected to our emotive faculties and allowed full play via simu-lations and dramatic rehearsals, might very well confirm some of his moral edicts, although not in the absolutist sense in which he intended them ("Though the heavens may fall, never lie . . . ," etc.).[13]

The categorical imperative captures important aspects of those insti-tutions that enable cooperative behavior to exist. Owing to the facts of our evolutionary history, sociability and cooperative engagement with the world are both ends in themselves and means of achieving just about any other important end we care to mention. Thus, any well-formed evolutionary ethic is going to support some of the same prohibitions that Kant's categorical-imperative test does. A crucial difference, how-ever, is that an evolutionary ethic would test these venerable institutions against their actual success in the long run. Thus, if it were ever to be the case that social institutions and cooperative effort could actually be *enabled* by lying (all other things being equal), there might be room for this type of behavior; such an intuition might underlie our feelings about the social acceptability of things such as white lies ("Grandmother, your pot roast was wonderful" or "My, what a beautiful Spandex neon-pink floral dress you are wearing").

Paul Grice's rules governing conversation are a good example. (See his 1989 book *Studies in the Ways of Words.*) Speech is eminently useful as a tool for coordination. If Grice's rules governing conversation were ignored often (if we didn't communicate mostly relevant information, if we didn't communicate mostly truthful information, and so on), then the institution of speech would come to lose its function. Those parts of us that evolved so as to be able to deal with speech effectively would slowly lose their modern-history function of enabling cooperative action, and this institution would decay into the dustbin with other evolutionary relics, along with most of the fruitful social results such speech acts enable us to achieve.

The categorical-imperative test does allow us a certain amount of leverage upon these prediction problems. A reformulated categorical imperative that was experimental in nature, and that allowed affect and emotion to play their appropriate regulative roles, would start to look very much like the connectionist simulations and moral dramatic rehearsals discussed in chapters 2, 4, and 5. Reconstructing the categorical imperative in this manner would also allow us to extend the "sociomoral ladder" down the phylogenetic scale in appropriate ways. Kant would not allow that social primates, wolf packs, or dolphins and whales were capable of reasoning in the manner required by his ethic, but we can certainly see how these creatures take full advantage of both simulation and dramatic rehearsal to regulate their affairs in ways conducive to their flourishing. For example, Frans de Waal (1996) has documented extensively the ability of chimpanzees and capuchin monkeys to engage in social reasoning and cooperative activities such as tool use and food sharing. Dolphins engage in cooperative hunting that seems to be characterized by extensive vocal coordination.[14] Such aspects of the behavior of various animals surely warrant explanation and incorporation into our nascent naturalistic moral theory.

A functional evolutionary ethic, and the neurobiological connectionist capacities that fit hand in glove with it, can save the important parts of Kant's theories while remaining true to the neurobiology of moral cognition and the empirical facts about successful ways to produce human flourishing. It can also be extended down the phylogenetic tree in a way that a Kantian account cannot.

Moreover, the functional theory has more flexibility with regard to the extension of norms to other living creatures that may have life cycles very different from ours. Our ontogeny is relatively boring compared to that of other creatures that go through radical changes in form and structure over the course of their life history. We should prefer a moral theory that can speak to the norms that obtain over all phases of a diverse life history over one that limits itself to the autonomy and rationality we possess for only a limited span of even our lives. A functional account can make sense of the norms that apply to all phases of *any* evolved creature's life span (even those, like the parasitic trematode *Quinqueserialis quinqueserialis,* that experience radical changes in bauplan and in cognitive capacity over the course of development; these creatures go through six distinct developmental stages, each quite different from the other).[15]

The Opportunistic Nature of "Opportunity-Driven" Ethical Theories

The ability of the functional account to capture what is good and true about Kantian ethics is demonstrative of the opportunistic nature of the theory. In much the same way that the Darwinian search algorithm for bauplans can effectively and fruitfully explore the boundaries of body-design space so as to produce well-adapted organisms, so can a functional evolutionary ethic take advantage of our attempts to explore the state space of possible moral theories by latching on to those aspects of the theory that have proven useful. This pragmatic aspect of the modern-history reconstruction is a notable strength of the theory. This should also allay the fears of those who think that admitting such a theory into the space of possible theories amounts to giving up *entirely* on the research programs established by the more traditional moral approaches. Far from it; as I will discuss later, a modern-history theory of function, in keeping with its pragmatic nature, mandates that the doors of inquiry be kept open and calls for toleration of a Gaussian normal distribution of viewpoints about the moral life.[16]

The existence of ethical theories, even competing ethical theories, can be explained by the modern-history approach. Moral theories can be viewed as tools. For some creatures in some environments, one tool will prove more useful than another. When the environment changes, or when the creatures change, other tools might prove yet more useful. This does not make the tools any less useful objectively—they succeed, after all, because they fit the needs of both the environment and the creature. For example, if the tip of your screwdriver does not fit well with the environment (say, if all you have is a Philips-head screwdriver in a world of slotted screws), your screwdriver will not be effective. On the other hand, if your screwdriver does not have a properly designed handle (say, if you have a screwdriver that was made to be used with a drill, which you do not own, rather than one made to be used by a human hand), it doesn't matter how well adapted the tip is to the world. Tools are functional bridges between creatures and environments, and useful tools are well adapted to both.

Moral theories are just like tools on this account. Though the account on offer lobbies for the essential truth of a neo-Aristotelian moral theory, it nonetheless has an instrumental place for any moral theory that proves useful for changing the environment or changing ourselves in ways that enhance our functioning. And this is how it should be.[17]

The Limits of Theory and the Virtues of a Neo-Aristotelian Virtue Theory

The nature of this approach also explains just why there are limits on how useful any particular normative theory will be in helping us deal with actual situations. Tools make assumptions about both the environment and the creature that may or may not hold across time and space. The more adapted the tool is to general conditions, the less useful it will often prove to be in any particular situation, as generality is gained only by abstracting away from the details of particular environments and particular organisms. Virtue theories are particularly adept at explaining this feature of morality, which is another reason to think that the account of morality on offer is best considered a pragmatic virtue theory.

This does *not* mean that morality cannot be a canonical science. As I have argued, it can be, although, as Georgios Anagnostopoulos has pointed out, even a modified Aristotelian approach may not be able to achieve the precision and explanatory depth of other more basic sciences. Anagnostopoulos (1996, pp. 64–65) explains:

. . . Aristotle in his remarks on the inexactness of ethics does not assume that ethics is nondemonstrative. He rather holds a broad view of demonstration which accompanies both the more exact and the less exact disciplines and within which he tries to fit ethics and any other discipline that happens to suffer from similar kinds of inexactness (e.g., biology). Given this broad conception of demonstration, the supposed inexactness that Aristotle attributes to ethics does not necessarily imply that ethics is altogether nondemonstrative. Ethics for him is a less exact science and not something which is not a science at all. Similarly, the practical nature of ethics does not deprive ethics of all cognitive goals, consign it to being a discipline concerned wholly with particulars, or eliminate the need for any form or degree of rigor in the discipline.

This is as it should be in view of the picture of ethics I have pushed in this book. Those who argue for an extreme form of moral particularism, or for moral anti-theory,[18] do not do justice to the nature of theories as tools.

Using the language I have articulated in this section, it would be a mistake to think that there is a single tool that is perfect for every job. But this does not mean that we have to build a new tool for every particular situation. Rather, there are certain constants in both the environment and the creatures that live in it, and the tools that rely more on those constants than others do will have more general applicability. Of course, if the situation changes, our tools may have to change as well.

Getting Down to Brass Tacks: Some Particular Advice

With these caveats about the usefulness and limits of theory in place, can we articulate some particular advice that the approach has for those dealing with morally problematic situations? We can. In chapter 3, I discussed briefly what the theory might have to say about my obligation to forgo buying a journal so as to donate money to the homeless person on the corner. Though my answer might have been unsatisfactory (avoid the extremes and consider this a practical question about the best cooperative methods to prevent homelessness), it did have some content, and if I were well versed in the public policy analysis of the housing situation, the structure of the theory might very well have supported a particular answer. I would like to examine two more situations, one dealing with action at the individual level and one dealing with institutional action, to see if I can import more content into the functional account. Rather than deal with some of the obvious issues I have discussed in the last few sections (e.g., whether the evolutionary account can derive familiar norms, such as the obligation to be truthful in conversation), I will focus on more offbeat issues.

Developing Deep Friendships

John moves from city to city fairly often. His contracting work requires that every few years he leave his settled home and relocate with his family to a new domicile in another state. John has a choice about how he can spend his free time: he can cultivate many friendships that are all fairly shallow, or he can focus on cultivating a few deep friendships that might stand the test of time and the stress of relocation. What is John to do when it comes to friendship? His problem is a genuine, felt, lived problem; he often wonders whether he is doing the right thing when he accepts social invitations to events that he knows will bear no fruit in terms of deep friendships but will nonetheless keep him in contact with people whose company he generally enjoys, and who generally enjoy his presence. What should John do? Should he accept these invitations at the expense of spending time with only a few people with whom he might be able to develop long-term relationships? He will have to move soon anyhow; perhaps it is for the better in terms of the pain and suffering of separation that he not cultivate "deep" friendships.

To answer this question, we would have to establish the modern-history function of some of the biological and mental capacities that mediate sociability. The evidence from archaeology indicates that, in general, over the course of evolutionary history, humans were in intimate contact with a fairly small group of others (close relatives and kin, primarily), and that their social circles were fairly small. Some of the social capacity that we have probably has the proper function of enabling us to develop deep and intimate friendships. As David Buss (2000) notes, being deprived of close kin and deep friendships often leads to depression in modern environments, in part because there is a mismatch between the evolutionary environment of adaptation and modern social conditions.[19] Many of our social capacities and inclinations, and the mechanisms mentioned in the preceding chapter that subserve such capacities, probably have a fairly strong modern-history function that is best fulfilled by increasing both the closeness of extended kin and by developing several deep and lasting friendships.

Having a wide but very shallow social network will not give John the opportunity to satisfy these deep biological demands. In addition, seeing more people more infrequently, particularly when they do not have a stake in his welfare, will deprive him of valuable sources of feedback for character development that are essential for flourishing. Recall my discussion in chapter 3 about the importance of friendships; Aristotle devoted a goodly portion of the *Nicomachean Ethics* to the imperative that people cultivate close, deep bonds with those who share their interests. Bonds such as these are ends in themselves, for modern-history reasons. They are also means to other important functional ends: by having relationships such as these, we come to know facts about ourselves and our natures more directly, and we receive important feedback from those who can make informed judgments about the course of our lives with respect to our proper functioning.

Although John should spend some time experimenting, he has at least a defeasible modern-history function argument that says that he should focus on cultivating several deep and lasting friendships, even if this means more pain and frustration upon his leaving than would otherwise be the case if his social network were more shallow. There is convergence between the ancient advice offered by Aristotle and the modern-history theory of moral functions.

Other Advice for John

This same form of reasoning could underlie several types of advice for John regarding how he should regulate his close social relations. For instance, Buss (2000, pp. 15–23) offers these pieces of wisdom, which are based on an evolutionary understanding of our functional nature: increase the closeness of your extended kin, select a mate who is similar so as to reduce jealousy and infidelity, understand the cognitive differences that underlie the tendency to treat events differently on the basis of sex, and manage evolved competitive mechanisms sagely. This list is primarily focused on those things that John can do to make his environment more closely match the complex of modern-history functions that constitutes his soft nature, but it could just as easily have suggested things that John do to change himself so that he will be better adapted to the conditions of modern life. In most cases, this process will probably be co-evolutionary, although experience will be the crucial feedback mechanism regarding which method leads to success in any individual's case.[20]

Advice on a Larger Scale: Structuring Our Institutions

The functional account can also provide us with some general direction regarding the form and structure of our social institutions. In large part, such direction will be provided by the watchwords that inform evolution and science, both of them verbs: "experiment" and "inquire." The pragmatist Charles S. Peirce states eloquently and forcefully: "Upon this first, and in one sense this sole, rule of reason, that in order to learn you must desire to learn and in so desiring not be satisfied with what you already incline to think, there follows one corollary which itself deserves to be inscribed upon every wall of the city of philosophy, **Do not block the way of inquiry.**"[21] In other words, a society that seeks to maximize the proper functioning of all of its members will allow, within the general bounds set by past experience, a spirit of inquiry to flourish. A normal distribution of traits will be a feature of life in such a society, as those who are more daring experiment with different ways of life, odd means relative to various extremes, and unusual habits and modes of interaction. Exploring "function space" in this manner will enable a society to experiment with ways of life that might turn out to be more closely related to modern-history proper functioning than the status quo. It will also result in a wider distribution of newly developing proper functions so that the society does not stagnate and face loss of cohesion if there are sudden changes in the environments in which they are situated.

In other words, a modern-history theory of function, and the theory of neurobiologically informed learning that accompanies it, will give default to something like a liberal democratic approach to social organization. In addition to the benefits mentioned in the preceding paragraph, this conception of social organization fits well with what we know of primate evolution; for a large part of our recent evolutionary history, we have been subject to selection pressures that have fixed modern-history functions in such a way as to enable flourishing in environments that assure us of autonomy, freedom, and choice. The sociologists Alexandra Maryanski and Jonathan Turner (1992, p. 169) explain: " . . . our review of the evidence . . . suggests that a society which allows choice and restricts inequality and power is more compatible with human nature than the ones it succeeded, as that nature evolved in the primate order over the last 60 million years . . . the goal should be to recreate . . . a system that enables people to stay out of highly restrictive and oppressive cages." Maryanski and Turner, based on a review of the probable environmental pressures that obtained during our evolution, and also on an examination of modern day primates, conclude that this optimal form of organization would be "politically democratic; it would give people choices in open and free markets; it would let them maintain a sense of personal identity; it would reduce inequalities; and it would hold back . . . the cage of power."

The epistemological requirements for good inquiry into proper functioning and the actual history of our species thus coincide: do not block the way of inquiry by overly restricting personal freedom, and give people a say in how their lives are structured by the very institutions in which they participate. This is a happy accident for us. We flourish best in those same environments that also allow us to best conduct inquiries about ways to flourish. The perfectionist Tom Hurka (1993, pp. 155–156) reaches the same conclusions in chapter 11 of his book, using similar reasoning albeit with slightly different Aristotelian perfectionism language: "Government interference with self-regarding action reduces citizens' autonomy and especially their deliberated autonomy. At the same time, it rarely succeeds in promoting their other perfections and can work in several ways to diminish them, by removing routes to excellence, including less valuable motives, and weakening self-direction. Although its elements are all *prima facie,* the case as a whole is impressive . . . it can affirm a fairly strong version of the liberty principle."

This is not a trivial result. The epistemology of discovering proper functions is essentially scientific—it requires experimentation and a toleration of a certain diversity of approaches, as well as a communitarian commitment to constant criticism and improvement. This inquiry-based epistemology fits in well with our softly fixed natures, as our forms of organization from the past several million years of our evolutionary history have fixed in us proper functions that can only be satisfied in conditions of liberty and autonomy.

Of course, both these results (cultivate deep friendships, structure your societies democratically) are under-specified insofar as there are tensions within each that are not resolved, and many specific issues that must be addressed if either piece of advice is to be followed fruitfully.

I do not pretend to have worked out the details; on the other hand, no one can say that the position is empty of content as these are both very substantial outcomes.

Structuring Our Character-Development Institutions

The institutions with which we are affiliated as we develop can have a large impact on our capacity to flourish. Certain traits are required if we are to live fully functional lives, and it will be to our advantage to structure character-development institutions such as schools and colleges in certain ways. The form of these institutions can be loosely specified on the basis of evolutionary functional facts and what we know about how our brains come to embody their complexes of skills and traits. Connectionist neurobiology can change some of our pedagogical practices for the better.

The account on offer restores an emphasis on habituation and mindfulness that our institutions would do well to attend to. Moral development and character education can best be accomplished by emphasizing a narrative-driven case study approach to moral education, a solid grounding in the biological and sociological dimensions of the human situation, and by carefully tending the institutional environment in which character development occurs. Our institutions would also do well to have built in to them a flexibility that lets them adapt rules and regulations to situations in a manner that promotes flourishing. Nothing teaches like experience, and so the proper environment for moral experience must be carefully cultivated and maintained.

Narrative-driven "case studies in moral functionality" are valuable for several reasons. First, they are ecologically valid. They situate moral concerns in the activities of day-to-day life and force the students considering them to be sensitive to moral ecologies—to the interaction between moral agents and the structure of their environments. In addition, moral instruction in the form of probing stories is more amenable to the native forms of cognition used by our moral cognitive systems. Simulations and dramatic rehearsals are essentially narratives; they are embedded histories that are built up in an organism by repeated encounters with the environment. Moral stories that involve the students in an engrossing real-life situation help them engage their native simulation and rehearsal capacities. Alicia Juarrero (1999, pp. 227–228) makes the case that dynamical systems (such as connectionist neurobiologies) are more adept at dealing with stories than with deductive-nomological-style arguments: "Explaining why the agent took this path rather than that after forming the prior intention will require reconstructing the agent's background, circumstances, particular frame of mind, and reasoning . . . reconstructing the mental attractor that constrained Sutton's [a bank robber] behavior requires accounting for the particular behavioral trajectory by situating it in its full historical, social, physical, and psychological context and showing how interaction with that context changed that particular alternative's prior probability." Although the case of Willie Sutton is not merely a narrative-driven case study (rather, it is an actual case facing a jury in a courtroom), Juarrero's point is nonetheless well taken. If students are to get "inside the head" of those pursuing dysfunctional lives of crime, realize why they are dysfunctional, and avoid such behavior themselves, they must understand the rich context of the real-life character in the story. Genuine moral cognition is not language-like, "nomological-deductive linguaform." Rather, it is ecological, contextual, simulated, and dramatized. Thinking of trajectories in state spaces is not just a nice metaphor but rather captures something genuine about the contexts in which moral concerns are genuinely felt. Juarrero (ibid., p. 230) concludes, quite sensibly, that "instead of trying to force judgments about human actions into an argument-like mold to which they do not belong, the solution must come from improved skills in *phronesis:* practical wisdom. Interpretation, however, can be taught only through example and practice. Children must be educated so that they develop a nurtured sensibility to context and circumstances. Only through habituation can the requisite interaction and dependencies between children and their environment be established."

In a related vein, Jeffrey Elman's work in the timing and development of neural networks sheds light on why it is important that we start character development and moral education early. Again, this demonstrates that taking into account the native form of human cognition can usefully influence the structure of our character-development programs.

In his 1992 essay "Learning, development, and evolution in neural networks: The importance of starting small," Elman examines the learning properties of connectionist networks. These include (1) the fact that networks rely on the representativeness of their data sets for efficacious learning, (2) that they are most sensitive during the early period of training, and (3) that gradient descent styles of learning make it difficult for a network to make dramatic changes in its hypotheses later. Elman derives two morals from these facts: that this may explain why we have a long period of cognitive immaturity, as such immaturity may actually help us overcome some of these disadvantages, and that we can respond to these facts by (perversely) either "starting small" with the net by feeding it limited data or "starting big" by feeding it a wildly divergent data set.

Elman's results are instructive; we wouldn't have thought of learning in this manner if we had been stuck in the sentential mode. But consider character development from this angle. First, we must be very careful what data we feed to our children—a bad training set can put them onto a poor developmental trajectory from which they may not be able to recover. Second, character development should start early. Parents have known this for a long time, but it is nonetheless comforting to see it confirmed by theoretical results from the cognitive sciences. Finally, the content of that first training set should probably stick to one of the extremes; it should be either very focused or widely divergent, as either of these will prevent nets from getting forced onto poor developmental trajectories.[22]

Manfred Spitzer (1999, pp. 312–313) offers similar advice; he notes that "understanding the function of neural networks changes the way we see ourselves" by reminding us that when teaching children we should "provide examples, not rules," give children structure, start with the basics, and watch their "mental diet." Though these lessons aren't as revisionary as some of the others, they are healthy affirmations of the essential correctness of some of our conventional wisdom about moral education and character development.

Taking into account the functional nature of evolutionary ethics and the native form of cognition in our brain will make a difference with regard to the way we approach moral education in our character-development institutions. We should focus more on narrative-driven real-world case studies and less on particular theoretical points, attend closely to the environment in which learning occurs so that the students are actually learning what we think they are learning, provide a variety of positive and negative moral exemplars (or else provide a tight grouping of only positive exemplars, depending on whether we want to start big or start small), and seek to cultivate *phronesis* (practical wisdom) in our students. The traditional moral tool kits are useful, but should be layered on top of this firm real-world practical groundwork.

These comments are consistent with the approach to "moral coping" advocated by Dreyfus and Dreyfus ("What Is Morality?" in Rasmussen 1990).[23] Their phenomenological account of the development of ethical expertise postulates five stages of moral reasoning capability, ranging from novice to expert. The important thing to note is that, if we attend to actual moral experience, we discover that moral experts see what must be done, decide how to do it, and respond almost immediately and intuitively to each situation. Recall the discussion in the preceding chapter about "moral skill" and automaticity, reflect on the nature of the advice offered in this section about moral development, and the consilience between their account of moral expertise and the pedagogical recommendations that stem from taking connectionism seriously should then be happily apparent.

7

Objections and Conclusions: Nature and Norms

Let's Not Get Ahead of Ourselves—At Least, Not Yet

Although evolutionary ethics and connectionism may very well impact normative moral theory and the structure of our institutions, we would do well to pay more than passing attention to the warnings of Hume and Moore with which we began this project. There are drawbacks and difficulties associated with a research program conjoining connectionism, neuroscience, evolutionary biology and moral philosophy. Here is a grab bag of them and my rejoinders.

Objection 1: Don't Forget Hume and Moore

The naturalistic fallacy and the 'is'/'ought' distinction loom large (perhaps more so in the minds of critics than in the minds of friends of this kind of work). We should carefully examine our rationale for drawing lines such as these before allowing a set of empirical facts to run roughshod over our normative theories. And even though I have undermined the *a priori* case for isolating these areas of inquiry, that doesn't mean that "any old fact" will interact fruitfully with "any old norm." This said, though, I still think connectionism lends support to normative moral theories that focus on morality as skills and practical knowledge; a pragmatic neo-Aristotelian virtue theory serves as the "big tent," and other moral theories serve as tools to help us achieve human flourishing. And it would be just as foolhardy to allow normative theories to stand pristine and untainted by considerations regarding how cognition really works with respect to neurobiology. It might very well be the case that the 'is'/'ought' distinction itself is fallacious and, pragmatically speaking, an unproductive way of dissecting moral cognition, as I argued in chapter 2. We should not pre-judge the issue by ruling naturalization out across the board and before trying it on for size.

Objection 2: Evolution Is Anti-Essentialist, So There Can Be No Useful Complex of Modern-History Functions for *Homo sapiens*

Even if a modern-history theory of function can help us naturalize morality, a biologically sophisticated critic might argue that any moral theory we get out of this picture will be so threadbare as to be useless. In part, the critic says, this is because the neo-Darwinian synthesis demonstrates that particular species simply have no essence. In addition to being contrary to outmoded Aristotelian assumptions about a species being characterized by a particular function, this also makes it difficult to formulate any useful general statements about moral functionality. Kitcher (1999) makes several arguments that are rooted in concerns like these in an attack on Hurka's perfectionism. Kitcher has two targets in mind in his review article: one is the neo-Aristotelian method that Hurka uses to fix the human essence. I am sympathetic with the crux of several of these arguments. However, Kitcher also targets any attempt to use more biologically informed evolutionary considerations to fix human functions. Fortunately for this project, Kitcher's second target, at least as exemplified in this book, survives unscathed. In the next few pages, I will briefly discuss the relevant portions of Kitcher's arguments, agreeing with some of his points but disputing his conclusion that he has "scotch[ed] any thought that evolutionary considerations might aid an objectivist's search for some conception of our species essence that might ground a notion of the human good" (p. 78).

Kitcher rightly notes the presence of a fairly stable orthodoxy among biologists and philosophers of biology regarding what constitutes the essence of a species. "Population thinking" is part and parcel of the neo-Darwinian synthesis; variation among population of species members is something to be expected and something that the modern synthesis successfully explains. On the other hand, Aristotelian biology relied on a "natural state model" in which organisms were considered to all share a peculiar essence. If they did not, it was because there were interfering forces that prevented the proper development of that particular member of the species (see p. 62 of Kitcher 1999). Though modern genetics has exposed the inadequacies of the Aristotelian conception of species, a neo-Aristotelian mode of explanation that adverts to the "normal" course of development that occurs during the life cycle of an organism still persists. Kitcher explodes any hope of relying on this notion to fix the human essence, however, by noting that it smuggles in assumptions about what is valuable (e.g., we think of certain environments as normal *just because* they are environments that are good for the organism). It was the notion of value that was to be explained in the first place by essences, so there is a damaging circularity here. Kitcher thinks that appealing to the property of fitness enhancement (something that Hurka does not do) to explicate "normal" falls prey to the same objection. After all, "we don't accept the value of success-promoting capacities either in the human ancestral environment or in any environment that would maximize human reproduction; rather, we try to change the environment so as to promote the capacities we antecedently take to be valuable" (ibid., p. 78).

Recall now some of the details of the modern-history function account of flourishing that I offered in chapter 3. First, my approach is "softly" (and expansively) essential—it accepts population thinking, admitting that modern-history proper functions for human beings as a group may overlap dramatically among conspecifics but that they may nonetheless not be exactly the same across all members of our species. Moreover, the account also welcomes the fact that some of our functions overlap with functions of the other evolving denizens of this planet (bacteria, bobcats, bears, etc.). In this sense, it isn't Aristotelian, as it does not leverage a "unique" account of the human function.

Note, however, that this does not preclude us from saying that we are the best tool users on the planet, or the species with the most advanced language, or the population with the most highly developed mental modeling system. Arguing that the complex of functions that constitutes our essence admits of overlap with other evolved creatures does not imply that we can't draw distinctions between the types of capacities that will develop for the average member of a species in the average developmental environment, nor does it mean that every functional capacity we have is shared by every other living creature. Frogs do not use tools; humans do. Providing young children with the stimulating environments they will need to become excellent users and producers of tools will enhance their ability to function properly. The same cannot be said of the average frog—it has been and will be subject to different selective pressures, and hence will have different modern-history functions, than the average child.

My account differs from Hurka's scheme too on this count, which is why Kitcher's finding that many humans "fail to be rational" (pp. 71–76) is not threatening to it (to which I would add that many animals often succeed at being rational, in the sense of chapter 4).[1] Second, recall that the proper subjects of reductive analysis in a functional account will often be Boyd-style homeostatic property clusters such as "healthy"; these property clusters can act as intermediaries between fitness and the details of anatomy, and as long as they share generally reliable upward connections with proper functioning (and, only distally, reproductive success), and downward connections with the physiological and physiognomic details of biology, Kitcher's objections that there can be no "useful" level of evolutionary analysis for discovering the human good find no purchase. Third, Kitcher's focus on reproductive success as the major contender for how evolution could fix the human essence lopsidedly concentrates on only one endpoint of the norm-fixing processes of nature that I discussed; there is more to proper functioning than distal proper functioning, as I argued extensively in chapter 3. Fourth, recall the discussions in chapters 3 and 6 regarding how functions are relationships between (a) the character complexes that constitute organisms and (b) environments; in this sense, it is functional to change the environment if changing the organism is not practical; this is why we often change our surroundings so as to promote capacities that are purportedly justified as valuable "only antecedently." And in any case, it is not as though we are ignoring our functional essences when we do this, as the standards by which we will adjudge it proper to change the environment in any particular case will themselves be based on other functional concerns.[2] The functional account does not reverse the order of explanation, seeking justification for values that we had already picked out in advance; rather, in my theory, to be shown that a modification to our habits or to our environment is, all things considered, more functional, is to be given a reason to think it valuable.[3]

Note that this entails that we begin to criticize adjustments to our nature (even the possibly radical change foreseen in certain forms of genetic engineering) from the perspective of where we are now, functionally speaking. We criticize existing environments (including other evolved life forms, such as a virulent bacterium) from the standpoint of our extant functions. This isn't to say that we *can't* change our nature; rather, it is to say that any change we do care to make should be made with respect to some existing function that is part of our functional complex.

Having briefly discussed and rebutted Kitcher's arguments, I still have to acknowledge the kernel of truth that lies at the heart of the critic's objections: If we accept population thinking, we have reason to think there might be some variation in proper functioning across humans. But in response, let me point out that such variability will not be so widespread as to preclude general law-like conclusions regarding what will enable functionality for human beings (recall the conclusions of the earlier portions of this chapter), and let me note that this observation on the part of the critic has a pleasant epistemological upshot. It is consistent with my discussion of the nature of inquiry, and it mandates some tolerance for and some variation in the pursuit of the functional life. These are welcome entailments. Rather than argue that in principle the approach cannot generate any morally useful theoretical conclusions, the helpful critic should begin by attacking the particular substantive derivations I discussed in chapters 3 and 6.

Objection 3: This Account Gives Us Only "Wimpy Normativity"

For some ethicists, a moral theory that fails to generate conclusions that are certainly true, and that are known with certainty to be so, is a failed moral theory. These critics would argue that the types of non-apodictic and non-"absolute" moral conclusions that fall out of a functional approach are too "wimpy" to be genuinely normative. To take the sting out of charges of "wimpy normativity," I will first re-emphasize the fallibilistic epistemology that undergirds my approach. Second, I will argue that our intuitions that the only genuine norms are apodictic and absolute are based on interesting analogies with scientific theories like those in basic physics; drawing out the bona fide consequences of taking such analogies seriously will help us see how the functional approach is actually palatable on that score. Finally, I will note that taking demands for apodictic morality too seriously can lead to some of the very problems that this book was designed to address. Needless to say, in this discussion I am glossing over or sidestepping *numerous* issues in philosophy of science. My purpose is to make the position seem plausible, not to explain and rigorously defend the philosophy of science that it coheres with best.

First, regarding the fallibilism that informs this book, although it might not seem initially appealing to admit that "certain" knowledge is difficult to come by, and that even things we think we know apodictically can be revised in the light of experience, such an epistemology can nonetheless be appealing. It offers us a realistic assessment of our cognitive capacities; we are embodied creatures coping with our environment, not oracles and founts of eternal knowledge. There is a very genuine sense in which we are all at sea together in Otto Neurath's boat[4]—our moral theories are the planks of the ship, which we replace as necessary so as to stay functionally afloat. Though it is true that nothing but the sea is holding the boat up, the particular planks that we stand on, even though they might be replaced in the future, are nonetheless solid. If constructed carefully and integrated well with the rest of the ship, they will serve us properly by getting us to our destination. Asking more of the ship—that it survive forever, that it sail in every possible sea, and that its individual planks never need replacement—is not only unrealistic but also unnecessary (although these goals might admittedly serve well as regulative norms that we realize will never actually be met by any extant theory or plank, except perhaps at the hypothetical end of inquiry).

Second, apodictic demands are often informed on analogy with physics. The laws of physics (e.g., the second law of thermodynamics) are true across all of space and time, this argument goes, and if our moral science is to be a science it should strive for the same epistemic status. However, this is to confuse a nearly completed science with one that is still fledgling. In the moral functional case, there *are* hard and fast facts to be discovered (for a given creature with a given history in a given environment, there are optimal ways to act), although our moral concepts might still have to play a bit of catch-up to mirror this situation accurately. Admittedly, there are additional complications presented by the fact that evolutionary life histories will often be unique, making the application of general principles to particular circumstances difficult, but this can't be helped. Of course, some would insist that hitching our moral theories to such historically contingent evolutionary facts is a mistake—after all, we could have evolved differently, in which case morality would demand different things of us. But this is not really an objection, as it holds even for basic physics (the basic laws of the universe "could have" been different, in which case the second law of thermodynamics "might not" have held); ultimately, it doesn't amount to saying much more than "the universe would have been different if it had been different" (which seems correct, not something we should deny).

Finally, demands for absolute and timeless moral dictates can mislead us about the nature of moral inquiry. Rather than encourage the epistemic attitudes that are necessary for flourishing, such demands can often stifle inquiry and be used as an excuse to indoctrinate students involved with our character-development institutions rather than to teach them. For our long-term moral health, it would behoove us to instruct and educate our children, not brainwash them.[5]

Objection 4: The "Noble Lie"—Even If All This Were True, We Would Do Harm to Ourselves to Believe It

In *The Republic*, Plato famously counsels that tall tales and instructive legends should be used to shape the character of certain classes of people living in his ideal society.[6] Such stories might be technically incorrect or untrue; however, their telling has a therapeutic effect on the population, encouraging proper character development and serving to motivate action in a useful way. The "Platonic noble lie" is thus a lie told with good intention and to good effect; it is for our own good that we believe such a noble lie. A critic might argue that we are in a parallel situation with morality in this case. Although the narrative I have constructed might in fact be correct, it would be corrosive to our moral institutions if we were to come to acknowledge its truth. Rather than take action to propagate the truth, we should nod respectfully in its direction but nonetheless continue to disseminate moral advice that is given backbone by a more easily respected source of norms (perhaps some competing ethical theory, or some supernatural source). The situation resembles that during the early days of Darwinian theory: Upon learning of

Darwin's findings, Barash reports (2000, p. 1013), the wife of the Bishop of Worcester remarked: "My gracious, let us hope it isn't true. But if it is true, let us hope it doesn't become widely known." Why did she react this way? There are usually three arguments offered to support the telling of a noble lie. First, if a moral theory has entailments that seem contrary to those of the accepted tenets of moral wisdom, we might not wish to propagate the theory even if we think it has considerable cognitive support. Second, we might think that even if the moral theory does not actually have such entailments, we fear that many people would nonetheless believe it to have them. Finally, if the metaphysics of a certain moral theory has the effect of undermining the psychological plausibility of individual consent to normative governance, we might well be tempted to install a noble lie in the theory's place. In other words, telling people about the actual wellsprings of morality might have the effect of making them much less likely to act morally in day-to-day life.

Setting aside the somewhat repugnant paternalism that informs these considerations, there are several responses we can make to the critic. With regard to the first reason, we can point out that the functional theory actually reaffirms much of our received moral wisdom. Aristotle's virtues are in fact virtuous—as he was at pains to tell us, they help us live a fully functional life. Though the view has considerable constructive critical heft, it does not dispense wholesale with the received moral wisdom of many of our ethical traditions. Finally, we can also point out that intuitions regarding what is moral must be capable of being modified by theories that are informed by moral functional experience, as such intuitions might be based on a poor moral theory or a scant understanding of the components of a good human life.

The second consideration can be rebutted by pointing out that the potential for misunderstanding does not justify a noble lie; rather, it justifies improving our educational system, allowing the findings and assumptions of a naturalistic ethic to slowly percolate into our character-development institutions. If someone thinks that an evolutionary ethic justifies "acting like an animal" (in the pejorative sense of the phrase, presumably), then we should educate that person about the actual entailments of a well-formulated naturalistic ethic. Lest this seem like a straw man, recall the remarks of Arkansas legislators during a recent debate about evolutionary theory in the biology classroom, wherein one of the supposed entailments of the theory was that it justified "acting like monkeys" (generously, perhaps Representative Denny Altes had something like the type of behavior that characterizes bonobo society in mind, although he didn't mention this species by name; see the *Los Angeles Times* of March 22 and 26, 2001).

As was discussed in chapter 3, the theory on offer does not suffer from some of the tensions that attend other evolutionary ethical systems, so we can in good faith tell such a person that the norms of morality are not an illusion but are in fact genuine and that such norms do not include (say) acting indiscriminately violent, if that is what acting like an animal means.

The third argument can be rebutted in much the same way; any inability on our part to abide by functional norms can be redressed with education, unless such an inability is based on deep psychological facts about people. Oddly, this point is usually used to support a cognitivist view of morality; telling someone that morality is "illusory" or "merely a matter of emotional state" but arguing that he should nonetheless behave morally is a position replete with considerable psychological tension. Since the functional account is objectivist and realist about morality, it does not suffer from this tension. If anything, it actually helps defuse it. As Marcel Lieberman explains (1998, p. 24), non-cognitivist theories of morality, and error theories like that offered by Mackie, are the types of theories that actually undermine our ability to genuinely commit to norms: "Clearly, error theories in ethics fail this constraint. First, they endow individuals with beliefs, for example, beliefs in the existence of moral facts, that the theories themselves declare false. Second . . . if the agents become aware of the (non-cognitive, antirealist) model and used it in their deliberations, their behavior would radically change; such models are . . . self-destructive."[7]

One of the virtues of the functional account is that it makes clear, in a way consistent with the best theories of our natural sciences, just how it is that genuine norms can exist in a natural world. Thus, the third argument for a noble lie is not just rebutted, it is actually turned so as to *support* the integration of an explicitly acknowledged naturalized morality with our moral institutions. Ultimately, making moral progress involves recognizing and coming to grips with moral reality. We will live better lives by using a naturalized ethic to improve the human condition.

Objection 5: You Didn't Achieve Your Explanatory Goals

The final objection I consider is not really an objection as such; it is an invitation to recapitulate the findings of the book as they relate to the desiderata from the introduction. The exasperated critic might finally question whether the project has in fact successfully addressed the issues raised in the introduction about the possibility of a naturalized reductive ethic.

Recall Kitcher's list of the four possible relationships between the sciences and ethics that I discussed at the end of chapter 1. The initial two relationships were (relatively) unproblematic. First, the sciences could have the task of explaining how people come to acquire ethical concepts, formulate ethical principles and make ethical judgments. The leading science here is cognitive science, and in large part this was the point of chapters 2, 4, and 5. People acquire ethical concepts by having their biological neural net's weight spaces sculpted appropriately by experience, and by having their neuronal activation levels nudged into the regions of an appropriately structured activation state space such that the organism engages in modern-history functional activity. Ethical principles and the theories that organize them are tools that we use to dissect the structure of the habits that enable us to realize the demands of our functional natures; they may very well be principal components of the high-order state spaces discussed in chapter 5. Ethical judgment consists primarily in "knowing how" to act, although "knowing that" certain actions and the habits that constitute them will be functional is also valuable and is a matter of possessing comprehensive and well-informed mental models that are subserved by a healthy imaginative and empathetic capacity. These considerations fell out of a discussion of developments primarily in the sciences of cognition and secondarily in the sciences of life.

The second relationship (that the sciences can teach us facts that, when combined with moral principles we already accept, can be used to derive new normative principles we hadn't yet appreciated) was also consummated. This was the task of parts of chapters 3–6. Even if the neo-Aristotelian functional account is not persuasive, a straightforward virtue-theoretic conception of morality could make use of the findings of the cognitive sciences to argue for a psychologically realistic conception of the relationship between reason and the passions, and for a rich conception of cognitive habit that would help us appreciate how to best develop character. Even if one does not appreciate the "new wave" virtue theory on offer, one can find the approach to have useful normative import when it is combined with traditional moral theory.

The third more problematic relationship consisted in demonstrating how the sciences can help us settle metaethical issues. This was the explanatory task of chapters 2 and 3. Taking the collapse of the analytic/synthetic distinction seriously, and coming to grips with our nature as evolved biological organisms, helped us address and rebut non-cognitivism and error theory in metaethics. Since Hume's and Moore's arguments were undermined by the dissolution of the analytic/synthetic distinction, by taking Dewey's conception of moral reasoning to heart our moral ontologies could finally be explored using scientific tools. Modern-history functions on loan from evolutionary biology can successfully naturalize Aristotle's virtue theory. Chapters 2 and 3 thus serve as existence proofs that we can make progress on metaethical issues using the sciences.

The fourth relation, and the most controversial, is that the sciences can be used to derive new fundamental norms. Chapters 3 and 6 are primary here. Some of the norms discussed and derived from a modern-history account include developing deep friendships, acting in some manner so as to alleviate the suffering of others, structuring social organizations liberally and democratically, being well rounded, supporting instruments (such as truth telling) that maintain sociability, and tolerating some variability in experiments in living. Most of these norms receive support from other moral theories, but in view of the opportunistic nature of a functional conception of morality this should not be surprising. Perhaps the critic will dig in at this point and demand more than these vacuous, trivial, unimportant norms and goods; that, however, would be an unsympathetic reaction, as the norms discussed are not flaccid, and the research program is relatively young. Even the more traditional virtue theories have only recently experienced a resurgence of interest.

Of course, none of these goals has been achieved with certainty or axiomatic proof. But such is the nature of empirically informed inquiry, and the history of past attempts to relate the sciences and ethics reminds us that we ought to be epistemically humble when approaching the subject matter. I do not claim to have rebutted all the arguments against the enterprise of naturalizing ethics via evolutionary biology and cognitive science, nor do I claim to have articulated the countless details that will be necessary to make the account compelling. However, I do hope to have shown that such an enterprise is not philosophically wrong-headed, to have demonstrated that it has great potential to enhance our lives, and to have suggested the general shape that one very promising approach to naturalization would take.

A Research Program

In this concluding section, I will very briefly discuss some areas that are in need of further research if this approach is to reach fruition. First, although connectionist models proliferate, there are relatively few neuro-biologically sensitive models that address moral cognition in either theoretical or practical terms. Given the value of pursuing the analysis of cognition at several levels at once, connectionists should act so as to fill this gap and thus demonstrate the continued importance of their research program for higher-order cognition. Applied moral cognitive psychology is also relatively understudied, and most of the work has used theoretical structures that predate the cognitive revolution. Innovations here that are informed by the cognitive sciences would be welcome. Second, research that makes use of the accumulated moral experience of humans in various social and cultural environmental milieus is still vital; "moral anthropology" is currently a piecemeal affair, and the theoretical integrity the functional approach offers would go far toward organizing what research there is and spurring further investigation. Third, the neurobiology of moral cognition remains woefully unexplored. While cover stories about "neuro-theology" abound in the major newsweeklies,[8] no one has yet synthesized "neuro-morality" or "neuro-ethics" comprehensively, but as chapter 5 made clear, we are finally reaching the point where such a synthesis is thinkable. Finally, other approaches to norm development that are naturalistic can interact in interesting ways with the functional account. For example, biologically informed game-theoretic approaches to skillful coping can help us understand the evolution of social structures and their usefulness.[9] As that research program grows, it will no doubt usefully interact with the more basic account offered here.[10] Other more traditional topics in philosophy also warrant further exploration, ranging from the normative role of emotion in moral reasoning to continued articulation of alternatives to a simple-correspondence account of cognition. It is an exciting time to be working in any of these research areas, especially if one is willing to pay attention to developments in the sciences that offer us new vantage points on older issues in philosophical discourse.

A pragmatic ethic informed by biology and neurobiology holds the most hope for being the unifying procedural glue that can successfully hold together otherwise disparate and possibly mutually antagonistic approaches to the moral life. Although moral progress using the approach articulated by Aristotle and Dewey and given a scientific burnish by me is not a certainty, progress will best be made by integrating moral theory with the rest of human knowledge, not by segregating it. I am optimistic that this effort will improve the human condition and will help us to reconcile the de facto separation that has been developing between the sciences and the humanities, particularly in the past few centuries.

We would do well not to ignore these issues; after all, nothing rides on them except whether we will live fruitful lives, which is to say that much of importance is contingent on settling them intelligently and with the best epistemic tools we have. Consistent with the actual nature of ethics, those tools will be scientific—they will be informed by our best theories in evolutionary biology, cognitive science, and naturalistic ethics, and they will succeed or fail according to how well they accommodate functional experience. Living well depends on reweaving our ethical theories into the warp and woof of our scientific heritage, attending to the myriad manifest consequences such a project will have for the way we live our lives and the manner in which we structure our collective moral institutions.

Notes

Chapter 1

1. I argue for this position, which I call "soft essentialism," in chapter 6.

2. See, e.g., Kim 1998, wherein it is argued that supervenience relations in the philosophy of mind do just that.

3. There are no important differences between the Natural Method and the "co-evolutionary strategy" articulated by Patricia Smith Churchland; see especially pp. 373–376 of her 1986 book *Neurophilosophy*. Flanagan (2000, p. 14) explicitly acknowledges the affinity.

4. I say "provisionally" because all good science is rooted in assumptions of fallibilism. I take this to be an implicit methodological canon of the natural sciences. Following the American pragmatist Charles S. Peirce, the only non-fallible science is *final* science—all that is fated to be agreed upon by those who investigate until the end of inquiry. But this hypothetical final is merely a regulative ideal, and we shouldn't expect to achieve it anytime soon, if ever. See "The Fixation of Belief" in Peirce 1877.

5. Exemplars, past and present: John Stuart Mill, Peter Singer.

6. Exemplars: Immanuel Kant, Christine Korsgaard.

7. Exemplars: Aristotle, Michael Slote.

8. See e.g. Williams 1985, pp. 6–9.

9. See e.g. John Deigh's entry "Ethics" in *The Cambridge Dictionary of Philosophy* (Audi 1995, p. 244).

10. Wilson cannot be faulted for not being an expert in metaethics or normative ethics. As Kitcher well knows, interdisciplinary work is difficult. Although Wilson may have been unclear and overstepped his bounds at times, his expertise in entomology and population genetics, combined with the breadth of his vision and his underlying humanism and compassion, makes his system well worth examining (and sociobiology's progeny, evolutionary psychology, does offer much promise and, in many cases, has evolved enough to sidestep some of the pop objections to their research program). In any case, we should not let the failures and shortcomings of some forms of sociobiology prevent us from pursuing equally naturalistic evolutionary projects.

11. Kitcher himself notes that A and B are possible and relatively unproblematic. C and D, though, are beyond the pale, at least, he argues, for Wilson's sociobiology program.

Chapter 2

1. I set aside for the moment questions about the pragmatic efficacy of truth claims. Later, I argue that we do not necessarily have to treat the content of moral claims as being either merely true or merely false—they must be useful for helping us deal with the demands of our functional nature, and for this, they must be good *models*. Reconstructing moral cognition as being concerned with matters of "fit" rather than focusing upon a falsely polarizing demand for binary truth claims will help us better understand just how a naturalization of morality is possible. Reduction is possible without insisting that moral cognition must be of the strict correspondence variety. For some, this might mean that the approach is no longer cognitivist in nature. But that would be a misleading inference, as I think we can reconstruct truth-functionality from the right sorts of models. And in any case, I think that there are objective correlates to moral claims, so if (for our erstwhile sentential correspondence theorist) cognition must be sentential through and through, then the sentences *will* have truth values.

2. So called because it reduces ethical discourse to the mere exchange of "Boo!" ("I don't like what you are doing!") and "Hurrah!" ("I like what you are doing!").

3. For interesting and intelligent exceptions, see the non-cognitivist approaches advocated by Allan Gibbard (1990) and Simon Blackburn (1998).

4. I ignore for the moment an "error theory" alternative like that championed by John Mackie wherein moral judgments are truth evaluable but are nonetheless globally false. The next question tends to be: Are the things we morally cognize reducible to the natural or not? I will address Mackie's arguments for an error theory in the next chapter.

5. See e.g. Quine's paper "Two Dogmas of Empiricism" (reprinted in Margolis and Laurence 1999) and Dewey's book *The Quest for Certainty* (1929).

6. William Rottschaefer (1997) defines *three* versions of the naturalistic fallacy: a deductive, a genetic, and an open-question version. The first corresponds to the Humean argument; the last is the Moorean argument. The "genetic form" is simply the traditional genetic fallacy, wherein one invalidly makes judgments about justification for claims based on their origin. I think a reliabilist, externalist approach to epistemology adequately deals with the "genetic version" of the naturalistic fallacy; however, this is a subject for a later publication, and I will discuss it only in passing in chapter 4.

7. Book III, part I, section I (p. 469 of the Selby-Bigge edition, listed in my bibliography as Hume 1739).

8. For a contrary reading, see Capaldi 1966. Capaldi argues that most philosophers misinterpret Hume's argument. It is perceived to be an argument for the

invalidity of reasoning from an 'is' to an 'ought.' However, it is actually intended by Hume to be an argument against the existence of any peculiar *normative* entities. Hume's ethical theory is empirical *through and through,* with no place in it for normative language—ethics is simply an empirical science, and as no other sciences use 'ought' phrases, neither should our moral science. On this reading, Hume is a radical eliminativist about most of our traditional moral language. Though this approach is interesting, it is a minority view in the secondary literature about Hume.

9. One famous attempt to derive an 'ought' from an 'is' takes place in John Searle's 1964 article "How to Derive 'Ought' from 'Is'." Here is the structure of Searle's argument (ibid., p. 44): "(1) Jones uttered the words 'I hereby promise to pay you, Smith, five dollars.' (2) Jones promised to pay Smith five dollars. (3) Jones placed himself under (undertook) an obligation to pay Smith five dollars. (4) Jones is under an obligation to pay Smith five dollars. (5) Jones ought to pay Smith five dollars." A slew of critics quickly pointed out that Searle was helping himself to hidden institutional norms—we have an institution of promise keeping that generates norms, and the crucial normative question that can't be addressed by listing empirical statements is "Ought we to have the institution of promise keeping?" Searle's derivation helps itself to hidden normative premises, they contended. This question confronts us only because we have a *choice* as to whether to partake of the promising institution; but we do not "choose" to participate in evolution. Rather, we are part of this institution by dint of being biological creatures of the right sort. This might have very interesting implications for the critic's otherwise quite reasonable response to Searle. But that is a project for another book.

10. See Pigden 1993, pp. 426–427. Pigden makes an interesting argument, stating that the "semantic autonomy" that Moore demonstrates goes nowhere toward proving the ontological autonomy of goodness. In addition, as a logical argument, it has no particular upshot, because *all* logical arguments must be supplemented with definitions, and definitions are beyond the purview of logic (narrowly construed). The definition of morality should be thrown open to pragmatic investigation—if logic is construed as the process of inquiry (e.g., in the wider Deweyan and Quinean sense), then definitions will be the subject of scientific investigation, and Moore's argument will have been defeated on all fronts. On this picture, using Pigden's language, the "logical autonomy" of ethics is trivially true but unimportant for naturalization, the "semantic autonomy" of ethics is true only by begging the question against the naturalist, and the "ontological autonomy" of ethics is exactly what remains to be investigated using the methods of the natural sciences. This is an attractive set of arguments, none of which I am inclined to dispute.

11. See e.g. Goodman 1979; White, "The Analytic and the Synthetic: An Untenable Dualism," in Hook 1950.

12. This is not to say that the empirical methods we use to gather normative information will be simple or straightforward. The sciences are intricate, and, although Ockham's Razor–style parsimony is a worthwhile goal, staying true to the subject matter may require theories of considerable subtlety (e.g., theories of

protein folding are enormously complex) and may call for ample epistemologi-cal humility (e.g., as far as we know, I can never hope to simultaneously know both the position and momentum of a particle). So it goes for the moral sciences—whether they will exhibit the same levels of complexity and epistemo-logical humility is an open, empirical question. Insofar as I think there will be reductive relationships between moral facts and facts about evolutionary biol-ogy, and insofar as the biological sciences are notorious for not producing law-like statements in the manner of physics, it is likely that our moral judgments will be fraught with both complexity and epistemic constraint. Nonetheless, we will still be better off attempting the integration, as what success we do have will be contingent on our recognition of moral reality, and such a recognition requires a theory of natural morality.

13. See Farber's (2000) articulation of domain integration.

14. This "confirmatory holism" led Quine to remark that when it comes to con-fronting experience the "unit of empirical significance is the whole of science" (1953, p. 166). Quine later realized that this statement was too strong, and admitted that there could be smaller units of confrontation; see his 1980 fore-word to his collection *From a Logical Point of View,* where he agrees that "practically the relevant cluster is indeed never the whole of science; there is a grading off."

15. See e.g. Kornblith 1993.

16. Despite the cogency of Quine's arguments, there is a secondary literature on the existence of the analytic/synthetic distinction. One of the best recent defenses of it is found in Boghossian 1996; however, Harman (1999) does an admirable job of dismantling that defense. Harman notes that the nonexistence of the analytic/synthetic distinction is a generally accepted result, but that nonetheless there are a few holdouts, such as Frank Jackson. Harman (ibid., p. 140) summa-rizes: "In my view, the [analytic/synthetic] distinction was conclusively under-mined at least 30 years ago. I am surprised that this fact has not been universally appreciated."

17. For a general characterization of this process, see Dewey's *Ethics* (both the 1908 and 1932 versions), *Human Nature and Conduct* (1922), and *Logic: The Theory of Inquiry* (1938).

18. Dewey was one of the first philosophers to systematically examine the effect that evolutionary theory would have on general issues in philosophy. See *The Influence of Darwin on Philosophy and Other Essays in Contemporary Thought* (1910).

19. Indeed, Vicedo argues that turn-of-the-century population geneticists who dabbled in ethics used Dewey's work to provide substantive backbone for their theories.

20. For interesting explorations of Dewey's views on moral imagination, see Johnson 1993; Fesmire 1995, 1999; Alexander 1993.

21. Dewey (1922, p. 228) once remarked: "Were it not for one consideration, this volume [*Human Nature and Conduct*] might be said to be an essay in con-tinuing the tradition of David Hume."

Chapter 3

1. Mackie is a cognitivist about moral judgments; he thinks such judgments are truth evaluable. As a matter of fact, however, he thinks they are all false as they are all in error. There is no such thing as objective morality. Hence, this approach is called an "error theory."

2. By "moral realism" I mean (roughly) something like the position that Boyd (1988, p. 105) outlines: "(1) Moral statements are the sorts of statements which are . . . true or false. . . . (2) The truth or falsity . . . of moral statements is largely independent of our moral opinions. . . . (3) Ordinary canons of moral reasoning—together with ordinary canons of scientific and everyday factual reasoning—constitute, under many circumstances at least, a reliable method for obtaining and improving (approximate) moral knowledge."

3. Of course, this is an empirical matter. Depending on your optimism about human reason and moral motivation, you might think that many people have excellent moral perception but are purposely acting immorally.

4. This seems to stack the deck against the realist about values, as Platonic forms are notoriously spooky and strange. This is why I later argue for an Aristotelian conception of value and for the naturalization of the notion of value in general. Mackie (1977, p. 41) acknowledges this: "It may be thought that the argument from queerness is given an unfair start if we thus relate it to what are admittedly among the wilder products of philosophic fancy—Platonic forms, non-natural qualities . . . and the like."

5. Following most other scholars in the field, I will treat the *Nicomachean Ethics* as the primary source text. The *Eudemian Ethics,* though valuable, is thought by most scholars to be an earlier work than the *NE* and not as full an expression of Aristotle's mature thought. Three chapters of the two books overlap in any case, so some of the material is redundant.

6. See *Politics,* book 1, chapter 2 (1253) (p. 509 in Ackrill 1987): " . . . man is by nature a political animal. . . . Man is a political animal in a sense in which a bee is not, or any other gregarious animal."

7. Myriad fascinating issues are implicit in this paragraph. For example, would virtue of character be enough for flourishing if the environment were simple enough or if our needs were relatively banal? Is virtue of thought only important insofar as it leads to the acquisition of subtle and flexible character-based habits or is it really a good in and of itself *no matter what the environment is like?* Can you possess the relevant virtue of tooth brushing without knowing how brushing your teeth relates to other equally pressing functional demands? Does this mean that if you have one virtue (e.g., if you *really do know* when it is appropriate to brush your teeth—say, that it is proper to skip brushing your teeth in order to rush someone to the hospital) that you must thereby possess them all (the "unity of the virtues" thesis)? For treatments of these topics, see Crisp and Slote 1997 and Statman 1997.

8. If you have a rare gum disease that requires frequent brushing, the mean relative to you may be much higher.

9. Also, Aristotle notes that some things do not admit of excess or deficiency as they are already either means or extremes themselves. For example, it would not do to say "to kill unjustly only one person today is one extreme, while to kill unjustly ten people is the other. . . . I will strive for the golden mean and kill unjustly only five people." Unjust killing, or murder, is itself already an extreme relative to the taking of life.

10. For more on this, see Solomon 1995.

11. Anagnostopoulos (1994, p. 10) writes: "I argue here that, contrary to claims by some recent philosophers, Aristotle does not eliminate the role of universality or truth in ethical theory. Ethical theory must aim at the universal and at truth, but it must also, because of its ultimate practical goals, reach down to the particular and recognize that its propositions are not as true as the propositions in some other domains presumably are." Dewey and Aristotle diverge on their stance regarding a truth-theoretic account of moral judgment, but we can successfully reconstruct Aristotle's position using Dewey, some assumptions about the nature of representation, and the pertinent connectionist mental-modeling literature.

12. "We do have an organ for understanding and recognizing moral facts," Paul Churchland (1989, p. 303) points out. "It is called the brain."

13. This account of the relational nature of moral motivation does not seem to be present in the secondary literature, aside from an account of moral functionalism offered by Frank Jackson and Philip Pettit that varies considerably from the account I am offering here. See Jackson and Pettit 1995. See also Jackson 2000. I don't mean to imply that there isn't a lively secondary literature regarding whether the case I have just made is true—Aristotle scholars disagree on the finer points of interpretation. But it does at least, on the face of things, effectively deal with Mackie's contentions. For more, see Rorty 1980 and Heinaman 1995.

14. My thanks to Patricia Churchland for pointing this out (personal communication, 2000): "In biology, it is increasingly obvious that pattern recognition is inextricably connected with a do-this aspect. From an evolutionary point of view, of course this makes sense. . . . In sum, what is queer is not the recognition/feeling complex in animals—that is the fundamental way things are done."

15. See Wright's 1973 paper "Functions," reprinted in Allen et al. 1998.

16. Of course, there are many differences between Wright and Millikan, but they are nonetheless roughly of the same family. In a cladistics diagram, they would share a common branch point.

17. For the most part, in evolutionary biology the objects of functional terms are called characters, which is a nice dovetailing of terms with Dewey and Aristotle's ethical theories. To my knowledge, this interesting consilience has not been noticed before. For enlightening essays on characters in biology, see Wagner 2000. Humans can be viewed as *sets* of characters; this opens the possibility that, owing to the accidents of history, we might embody conflicting functions. Fortunately, there will be pressures for these conflicts to be minimized or reduced over time, all other things being equal. It is also interesting to note that

professional biologists and cladistics experts tend to use the term 'characters' whereas philosophers of biology generally use the more common term 'traits'.

18. Though the list has grown over the years, everyone is in agreement that at *least* these three things are necessary for evolutionary adaptation to occur: phenotypic variation, differential fitness, and heritability, all of which are subsumed by reproduction insofar as it is reproduction makes them all possible. See e.g. Sterelny and Griffiths 1999.

19. As we will see later, this no doubt accounts for the deflationary language of Darwinists like Dawkins and Wilson, who are (in)famous for saying things like "Ultimately, we are just lumbering robots whose purpose is to reproduce our genes." See e.g. Dawkins 1986; Wilson 1978.

20. In Greek mythology, Scylla was a nymph changed into a sea monster that antagonized sailors in the Straits of Messina (in the Peloponnesian Islands), and Charybdis was a whirlpool off the coast of Sicily that was also personified as a female monster. My suggested analogy at least preserves the geographic relationships in both the source and target domains, although the sex of the philosophers is unfortunately not conserved in the mapping.

21. For more on this, see Bechtel and Mundale 1999; McCauley and Bechtel 1999.

22. See P. M. Churchland 1998a and the papers collected in May et al. 1996.

23. For provocative virtue-theoretic work that is sensitive to these developments, see McKinnon 1999.

24. Although there are interesting parallels to the visual system. For example, in the perfect world, I would feel emotionally compelled to do what is functional, perhaps in the same way I am compelled to believe there are red objects when I see red objects.

25. Damasio draws a distinction between states of the body (emotions) and our self-representation of such states (feelings). My concerns are orthogonal to details such as these. I will have a more detailed discussion of emotion and moral reasoning in chapter 5.

26. Again, nothing in particular rides on the form given to a theory of the emotions as long as it has room for the states of being discussed by hedonists, utilitarians, and the like. Thus, I would be happy with a theory like that offered by Ekman, Johnson-Laird and Oatley, or even Darwin, as discussed in Elster 1999.

27. 'Perfectionism' is the name for the moral theory that there is such a thing as human nature and that it ought to be perfected. Aristotle is usually considered a perfectionist. Hurka is an excellent exemplar of modern-day perfectionism, and the moral theory articulated in his 1993 book *Perfectionism* bears many similarities to my functional account.

28. Maslow's hierarchy of needs ranged from base-level needs to higher psychological needs. In order from base-level to pyramid-top they are: physical, security, belongingness, esteem, self-actualization. See Maslow 1998.

29. Nietzsche's advice to "live alone so that you *can* live for yourself" (*Ecce Homo*, p. 234) seems disingenuous. What Nietzsche really means is something

like "*pretend* to live alone, all the while taking advantage of the fruits of the actions of groups of others." Even Zarathustra uses a language; unless he invented a language of his own and intends for no one else to hear his remarks, he is merely being disingenuous (or, more strongly, hypocritical).

30. By 'stoic' here, I mean to connote only the typical meaning that an English speaker has in mind when they use the word. The Stoic philosophers (e.g., Epictetus and Marcus Aurelius) have very interesting and subtle ethical systems on offer whose content is not done justice by modern definitions of 'stoic'.

31. A more real-world example that is not as entertaining as thinking about boojums is the tension that exists between the parts of our nature that are sociable and those parts that demand autonomy and isolation from others.

32. Note again how this process is one of character development. Dewey notes (1898, p. 104) notes: " . . . just because the acts of which the promptings and impulses are the survival, were the fittest for by-gone days they are not the fittest now. The struggle comes, not in suppressing them nor in substituting something else for them; but in reconstituting them, in adapting them, so that they will function with reference to the existing situation."

33. Indeed, we should probably be *fearful* of any normative theory that has such a *direct* entailment for a particular set of environmentally complex, context-laden, agent-contingent circumstances. I will discuss this issue more in chapter 5 when I deal with the role of moral theory in this scheme.

34. Berys Gaut (1997, p. 186) summarizes nicely the position that there will be lots of norms that derive from the functions of traits and characters in organisms: "The notion of a function possesses a certain kind of normativity (things can malfunction), and for familiar reasons has evaluative implications (if A has the function of f-ing, we know what a good A is, and what is good for A.) Further, a complete biological explanation needs to state why the parts or behaviour of an organism have the function of f-ing rather than y-ing, and such explanations have at some point to appeal to the fact the organism needs to rather than y in order to live a certain kind of life (the life characteristic of its kind). Similar remarks apply to evolutionary explanations, which are also incomplete without appeal to the function of the parts and behaviour of organisms."

35. Quine himself provided a provocative discussion of just what ethics would look like in a world devoid of the analytic/synthetic distinction that I mentioned in chapter 2. His conclusions were primarily eliminative and skeptical, provoking a response from Flanagan. I omit Quine from this review of evolutionary ethicists, in part for that reason and in part because the discussion between him and Flanagan covers any ground I would care to discuss. For the beginning of this debate, see Quine 1979 and Flanagan 1982.

36. Indeed, this is often taken to be one of the two key questions that any naturalized evolutionary ethic must answer: How did we come to have a moral sense? The other key question is the one I am addressing in this chapter: What is the relationship between evolution and the justification of norms? Moral issues aside, *Sociobiology* is wonderfully researched and informative.

37. On the other hand, the general approach that Wilson brings to bear on ethics is an extremely fruitful one; it is non-transcendent, naturalistic, and informed by the sciences of life and mind. One could have far worse models.

38. As Chisholm says (1999, p. 25), "to effect our purpose in life is to foster reproduction." The first two chapters of Chisholm's book are a nice summary of arguments against the naturalistic fallacy that others (notably Dennett and Petrinovich) have made.

39. Arnhart (1998, pp. 48–49) cites Owen Flanagan and Paul Churchland (among others) as providing support from the cognitive side of the sciences for the primacy of Aristotelian practical reason.

40. Anyone interested in evolutionary ethics should spend a great deal of time with Arnhart's book, and especially with its detailed case studies.

41. In correspondence, Arnhart has suggested that the ample case studies he covers in his book demonstrate that all that is universally desired is not actually desirable. I think there is a tension between some of these conclusions and the theoretical setup for the book. However, if that tension can be successfully resolved, my program and Arnhart's approach will agree in many important respects. I look forward to seeing him develop his theory further, as it is a promising approach to naturalized ethics; his writings on the topic are not to be missed.

Chapter 4

1. Hume was perhaps an "armchair naturalist" at best, at least by modern standards (keeping in mind that standards regarding what constitute the "natural sciences" and the "natural approach" vary across time). Of course, Hume's arguments regarding the nature of cause and effect had an admittedly debilitating effect on the philosophical foundations of science; nonetheless, in the secondary literature Hume is often cited as a well-known proponent of a naturalistic psychology. See e.g. Robinson 1982.

2. This characterization needs tremendous unpacking to be intelligible, of course—such unpacking will be the hidden agenda of this chapter.

3. From some perspectives, this characterization of the nature of the two threats is unfair. Some will be happy veering to one extreme—there never was such a thing as normativity and there never will be . . . and if there is ersatz normativity, it had best be scientifically tractable and non-spooky. I would characterize this attitude as "scientistic," and it is not one I would condone. As I made clear in chapters 2 and 3, there can be useful and illuminating relationships between "is's and oughts," but it is not the case that norms are illusions, nor is it the case that "any old science of norms" will do. On the other hand, others will be happy careening to the other side—the *a priori* is sanctified, the empirical sciences are vilified, and most of the work going on at contemporary universities can safely be ignored, as it is unimportant to the genuine concerns of philosophy and life as lived. This "super-duper-anti-naturalism" strikes me as equally cavalier.

4. Lest this language seem strange, Webster (1987, p. 270) has the following to say about comportment: "comport: . . . to be fitting . . . to behave in a manner conformable to what is . . . proper."

5. Apologies to Haugeland (1985, p. 112) and his distinction between Good Old-Fashioned Artificial Intelligence (GOFAI) and alternate (non-traditional computational, non-traditional representational) approaches to AI.

6. The two poles correspond very roughly to the (in)famous East Pole/West Pole distinction in cognitive philosophies.

7. It is difficult to find an explicit definition of judgment even in that research that claims to be about human judgment. When a definition is given, it tends to be non-specialized—for example, Arkes and Hammond (1986) cite *Webster's Dictionary* in their introduction. When a technical definition is offered, it tends to resemble this one (ibid., p. 7): " . . . judgment is a cognitive or intellectual process in which a person draws a conclusion, or an inference (Ys), about something (Y_e), which *cannot* be seen, on the basis of data (X_i), which *can* be seen. In other words, judgments are made from tangible data, which serve as cues to intangible events and circumstances." Even more interesting is the fact that most of the research in the field of judgment research does not make a distinction between judging and deciding (although for an exception, see Hammond, McClelland, and Mumpower 1980, pp. 55–58). This provides an important clue regarding in what context judgment must be situated if it is to be ecologically valid. Judgments count when they issue in action, so the focus should be on the components of cognition that result in action in the world. This will become important later.

8. Among those who make reference to George Boole's position identifying the laws of logic with the laws of thought are Johnson-Laird (1998, p. 30) and Heath (1967, p. 347). According to Heath, "Boole believed that the parallels between his class calculus and ordinary algebra were due to their common subservience to a 'higher logic,' which he identified with the 'laws of thought.' " Boole's title for his 1854 work is suggestive even without interpretation: *An Investigation of the Laws of Thought on which are Founded the Mathematical Theories of Logic and Probabilities.*

9. For a summary of work done in rational judgment and decision making that bears on the larger philosophical issue of the status of human rationality, see Stein 1996.

10. For instance, nativism about concepts—popular in GOFC camps—seems in part to be driven by a desire to cordon off meaning from both the world and theory change.

11. For concise statements of this view, see Fodor and Pylyshyn 1988 and Pinker and Prince 1988.

12. I should acknowledge a subconscious debt to Georges Rey (1997, pp. 224–226), who makes a distinction between Liberal Connectionism and Radical Connectionism that exactly mirrors the cut I make between Moderate and Extreme NFC.

13. For more on Paul Churchland's positive proposal and Livingston's criticisms of it, see Livingston 1996. For a book-length assault against the pragmatic proposals of Churchland (and Steve Stich), see Miscevic 2000.

14. Even self-organizing systems (for example, Kohonen networks) organize with respect to environmental input (although there is admittedly no "teaching signal" akin to backpropagation of error in such nets).

15. I am not ready to argue that we must respect either of these things. This is merely a "softening up." Both ordinary discourse and our untutored intuitions might have to be revised in light of scientific tutelage.

16. As Russell noted, "judgment" has a dual sense—on the one hand, it refers to the products of a process, and on the other it refers to the process that has that product. For the purposes of this analysis, I will traffic in both senses. However, I think we can usefully diagnose one source of entrenched intuitions regarding the conditions for judgment: overemphasizing the conception of "judgment as product" while underemphasizing "judgment as process" can lead to an unhealthy infatuation with language as a constitutive part (if not the whole) of judgment.

17. There is a healthy theory-of-mind literature with regard to the higher primates that testifies to this fact. For a summary, see Schulkin 2000.

18. Thus, for example, the spider wasp's cleaning of its nest before inserting anaesthetized prey cannot be unlearned or modified by experience. Even if we simply immediately repetitively remove the prey, forcing the wasp to reinsert it, the wasp still laboriously checks the nest to ensure that there isn't something already there. For more on insect learning (or lack thereof), see Papaj and Lewis 1993. For certain species of insects, learning seems to take place primarily on an evolutionary time scale, not within the confines of an individual insect's life.

19. Bees have clusters of neurons that function as "value systems" for the bees; these value systems are modality specific (there is one for the olfactory system, one for the visual system, and so on) and are thought to correlate with the presence of food. See Hammer 1993.

20. To show my hand here, and engage in some polemics, this section (indeed, this chapter) constitutes a "softening up" of the traditional reason-based Kantian picture of morality, which basically buys into a Fodorian Language of Thought structure, relegates the higher primate—not to mention the rest of the animal kingdom—to the moral backwater, and sets up innumerable tensions between pragmatic action, emotion-driven moral behavior, and the categorical demands of a "pure reasoning" faculty that probably doesn't actually exist.

21. For instructive defenses of this position, see Haugeland 1998, p. 303. Haugeland insists that there is some very weak sense in which animals can be described as learning, but that such learning is not genuine. Note also that the example of Kaspar Hauser avoids any entanglement with past community experience in a way that a Robinson Crusoe–style thought experiment does not.

22. This is not to say that it cannot be improved by using a linguistic tool or engaging in community discourse—quite the contrary. For arguments regarding

the relative importance of language-like rules in moral deliberation, see Andy Clark's "Word and Action: Reconciling Rules and Know-How in Moral Cognition," Paul Churchland's "Rules, Know-How, and the Future of Moral Cognition," and Clark's response to Churchland, all published in the supplement to the *Canadian Journal of Philosophy* titled *Moral Epistemology Naturalized* (Campbell and Hunter 2000). This volume also includes other papers pertinent to the issues dealt with in chapters 1–3.

23. Hubert Dreyfus (1992) was one of the first philosophers to discuss the affinity between some aspects of the Continental approach to cognition and action and neural-network reconstructions of cognition.

24. For a discussion of these characteristics, see David Rumelhart, "The Architecture of Mind: A Connectionist Approach," in Thagard 1998b. The list is adapted from Rumelhart's.

25. I recommend especially P. M. Churchland 1996c and Spitzer 1999. If this paragraph makes no sense to you, these books would be an excellent starting point for bringing yourself up to speed on the generic structure and function of connectionist neural networks.

26. The learning algorithms in neural networks can be divided into two classes: supervised and unsupervised learning. Supervised learning algorithms can be further divided into corrective learning algorithms and reinforcement learning algorithms. Supervised learning, or learning with a teacher, occurs when the output of a network is observed and the deviation from the correct or expected answer is measured, at which point the weights of the network are adjusted according to the calculations of the requisite learning algorithm (for example, by backpropagation of error). Unsupervised learning occurs when we do not have an *a priori* output expectation against which the performance of the network is measured. For supervised learning, corrective learning uses both the magnitude of the error and the input vector to determine the amount of change to the weights, whereas reinforcement learning is used when we only have feedback of a binary sort (as in a simple, "Yes, your answer is right" or "No, your answer is wrong"). For further discussion, see Rojas 1996, p. 78.

27. This example should not be taken to imply that the backpropagation algorithm is itself biologically realistic—arguably, it is not. More plausible learning algorithms include those governed by Hebbian rules, which are explicitly derived from data regarding how real neurons come to change their firing propensities.

28. I hope to articulate a middle way between the view that judgment in general and moral judgment in particular are linguistic through and through and the view that language plays no role in moral cognition.

29. These "recognition/action" complexes resemble Millikan's account of pushmi-pullyu representations in May et al. 1996.

30. And so on, down to the level of particulars. For a rich illustration of this method, see either Elman's original 1990 paper or page 96 of Elman et al. 1996.

31. Recurrent neural networks are ones in which the hidden layers are connected recursively to (usually) the input layer—this gives the network the ability

to engage in a form of temporal reasoning. Recurrent layers have been called "context layers" for this reason. For a complete typology of recurrent networks, see the entry on "Recurrent Networks" in Wilson and Keil 1999.

32. For a series of thought experiments demonstrating the conceptual plausibility of this claim, see Braitenberg 1984.

33. See chapters 9 and 10 of Pfeifer and Scheier 1999 (probably the first textbook on embodied cognition in cognitive science).

34. This is an admittedly bastardized summary. For elaboration, see "Understanding: Dennett and Searle" in Haugeland 1998.

35. For example, Rumelhart and McClelland's *Parent* series of nets learns to convert regular verbs to their past tense forms. According to Bechtel and Abrahamsen (1991, pp. 202–203): "On their view, the linkage between regular verb stems and their past tense forms is *described* using just a few general rules, but is *governed* by a mechanism that does not use explicit rules."

36. On backgammon nets, see Tesauro 1990; for NETtalk information, see Sejnowski and Rosenberg 1986.

37. Within some reasonable computational limits. See e.g. Clark and Thornton 1997.

38. By this I mean "functioning well" or "living well," *not* "happiness" (in a shallow modern construal) or "affectively satisfied." See 1097a15–b21 in Aristotle's *Nicomachean Ethics* for a good operational definition of eudaimonia, and recall my discussion in chapter 3 about emotion and function.

39. There might be a link between judgment making and model making—a particular map may be more or less accurate or useful but isn't necessarily "true" or "false" itself, just like judgments. Giere (1999, pp. 118–146) has some instructive statements about visual models that may have direct correlates in this approach to judgment. This is probably not mere coincidence, insofar as Giere's main project in that book is to sketch a naturalistic account of scientific cognition.

40. I am not sure if there is friction between this statement and received opinion in the arena of naturalized epistemology. It may seem to provide additional evidence for Alvin Plantinga's arguments against the possibility of naturalized epistemology (regarding how evolution may not produce cognitive systems that possess beliefs that are generally true). I am uncomfortable with this conclusion, as Plantinga seems to have in mind a traditional sentential conception of belief, whereas the account I am sketching is intended to be much broader and to subsume a GOFC approach.

41. In a loose sense of the term. I have no particular conception of reduction in mind, although my approach may very well require a certain one. I do find John Bickle's (1998) model-theoretic conception of reduction attractive. Furthermore, these remarks should be taken modulo this chapter's comments about elimination and about golden-age neuroscience as it pertains to characterizing the Churchlands' positions.

42. Even the "laws of logic" would be servants to the pragmatic norms of global excellence. This could be made sense of in a Quinean picture where the

analytic/synthetic distinction is not a player and where experience and the demands of embodied cognition could result in a modification of what we would otherwise consider to be the most fundamental tenets of logic. Recall chapter 2 to see how this plays out using moral rather than logical concepts. The same goes for any field of study, *mutatis mutandis*.

43. The Socratic elenchus is a form of argument—a cross-examination that attempts to show that a speaker holds inconsistent opinions. In Plato's dialogues, especially the early ones, Socrates often engages in an elenchus so as to demonstrate the ignorance of his opponents and build up a reasonable position on which to advance the positive Platonic account.

44. Kathleen Akins (1996b) sees the problem of linking up our ontological framework with the sensory-motor framework as the outstanding "gap" that needs to be filled in the cognitive sciences. I think connectionist explanations have the resources to bridge these gaps. For more, see Casebeer 2000 and Hubbard 2000.

45. There is an ample and fascinating recent literature on learning in bacteria and protozoa; for a summary and a review, see Crespi 2001. As the paucity of this list shows, nearly every living creature has at least some cognitive capacity.

46. This should not sound strange. MacIntyre (1999, p. 79) rightly points out: "Whatever it means to say of some particular members of some particular species that it is flourishing, that it is achieving its good, or that this or that is good for it, in that it conduces to its flourishing—assertions that we can make about thistles and cabbages, donkeys and dolphins, in the same sense of 'flourishing' and the same sense of 'good'—it is difficult to suppose either that in making such assertions we are ascribing some nonnatural property or that we are expressing an attitude, an emotion, or an endorsement." As you can tell, MacIntyre is an unrepentant Aristotelian when it comes to moral realism, much as I am in chapter 3.

47. Bruce Waller (1997) concurs with this extension of moral agency to the animal kingdom: "Philosophical tradition demands rational reflection as a condition for genuine moral acts. But the grounds for that requirement are untenable, and when the requirement is dropped morality comes into clearer view as a naturally developing phenomenon that is not confined to human beings and does not require higher-level rational reflective processes . . . morality cannot transcend its biological roots."

48. Relaxation networks are interactive networks in which the net "settles" to a stable state that minimizes error and maximizes constraint satisfaction. Hopfield nets and Boltzmann machines are examples of relaxation networks. For an easily digestible summary, see pp. 40–45 of Bechtel and Abrahamsen 1991.

49. This should also provide a hint as to how neural networks can engage in Socratic-discussion-style linguistic comportment. Rumelhart et al. (1986, p. 43) explain: "Imagine a situation in which we had a relaxation network which would take as input a sentence and produce an interpretation of that sentence as well as the specifications for a response to that input. It is possible to imagine how two individuals each with such a network could carry out a conversation.

Perhaps, under appropriate circumstances they could even carry out a logical argument. Now, suppose that we don't actually have another participant, but instead have a mental model of the other individual. In that case, we could image carrying out a conversation with someone else. We could hold an imaginary argument with someone else and perhaps even be convinced by it!"

50. Recall that Hebbian learning, at its most basic, consists in postulating that connections between neurons increase in efficiency in proportion to the degree of correlation between pre- and post-synaptic activity. If one neurons synapses on another, and both fire, then it will be more likely next time that the two will fire concurrently. This is called long-term potentiation.

51. In the case of a neural network, principal components are those hyperplanes within the activation space of the hidden layers of the network that are most active in coding the features of the world.

52. Other forms of connectionist mental models exist as well, including promising "generative models" that are self-organizing and that can learn on the basis of the difference between the predictions of the internal model and what is actually perceived. For more on these models, see Hertz et al. 1991. See also Hinton and Sejnowski 1999.

53. See Pearl's entry on Bayesian networks and MacKay's article "Bayesian Methods for Supervised Neural Networks" in Arbib 1995.

54. Dewey (1925, p. 134) characterized language as the "tool of tools."

55. See in particular Hutchins 1995, especially chapter 9.

56. For an interesting debate about the importance of "rules" as cognitive aids in moral judgment, see the exchange between Paul Churchland and Andy Clark in Campbell and Hunter 2000.

Chapter 5

1. Indeed, to the chagrin of some, most present-day professional philosophers are committed to a metaphysics that is thoroughly naturalistic.

2. In structure and tenor, this chapter owes much to P. M. Churchland 1998a.

3. With regard to the neurobiology and cognitive science of moral cognition, my summary will necessarily be simplistic to the professional eye. In my defense, I would point out that the literature on the neurobiology of moral cognition is scant—mostly, what one finds is passing references in works that have other larger fish to fry about phenomena that might be important in moral cognition. To my knowledge, there are few professional articles that focus on the cognitive neurobiology of moral judgment exclusively and no general book-length treatises on the subject (although Damasio 1994 comes close). For a more comprehensive review of the present literature, see Casebeer and Churchland 2003.

4. Paul Churchland (1998a, p. 83) thinks that we can sketch in neural-network terms the following phenomena: "moral knowledge, learning, perception, ambiguity, conflict, argument, virtues, character, pathology, correction, diversity, progress, realism and unification."

5. For more on chisanbop, see Lieberthal 1983.

6. It is no coincidence that GOFC approaches are usually dry whereas NFC approaches are wet; the latter at least can lay some claim to being neurobiologically realistic.

7. For a discussion of these complications, see Churchland and Sejnowski 1992, pp. 18–23.

8. I don't mean to pretend that this is the only conclusion we could draw. It would be disputed. Nonetheless, it is a reasonable position to take with respect to realism if naturalization is successful.

9. At least, the obvious interpretation is that networks embody knowing how rather than knowing that. See Bechtel and Abrahamsen 1991, pp. 151–155; Ryle 1949, p. 48. "Knowledge that" probably resides in our capacities for mental modeling (chapter 4). In a connectionist conception of cognition, it may well be that "knowing that" is less basic, and is parasitic on, "knowing how." Chapter 4 was essentially an argument for this position. This may have important implications for ethics and metaethics, as I will discuss in chapter 6.

10. I don't mean to gloss over the considerable difficulties with a state-space conception of semantics. This issue isn't yet settled—see e.g. Fodor and Lepore 1992. However, Churchland's 1998 response, which relies in part on Laakso and Cottrell 2000, satisfies any doubts I had.

11. EVR also had damage to the connections from frontal cortex to the amygdala. I will discuss the importance of these connections later when I examine moral motivation. For more detail, see Damasio 1994; Damasio et al. 1991; Adolphs et al. 1996.

12. For interesting work in this area, see DesAutel 1996; Gilligan 1987, 1988; Flanagan 1990.

13. Systems like these will often find a local maximum when satisfying multiple constraints. This can be prevented by adding stochastic elements to the net or by using simulated annealing. (For more on this, see "Simulated Annealing" in Arbib 1995.) For an alternative analysis of the Necker-cube phenomena that nonetheless makes use of the same principles at stake in the model of Rumelhart et al., see Feldman 1981. Of course, Rumelhart et al. recognize that the processes underlying actual Necker-cube gestalt shifts are more complex than their model allows for. They intended for the model to serve primarily as a demonstration of the characteristics of a constraint satisfaction network, and only secondarily as a model of actual Necker-cube effects in human beings. For more biologically realistic models, see Grossberg and Mingolla's 1985 work, which also relies on a relaxation network. See also the entry on gestalts in Wilson and Keil 1999.

14. Indeed, some moral theorists highlight moral "vision" and "perception" as the crucial elements of moral development—see e.g. Blum 1994. As Paul Churchland notes (1998a, p. 88), moral argument is often a matter of getting your interlocutor to see the world using a different frame of reference—rather than, for example, thinking of the fetus as a *collection of cells,* we might think

of it as a *miniature human being*. This perhaps amounts to being nudged into a different conceptual trajectory in moral state space.

15. For related readings, see Johnson 1993; Flanagan 1996b.

16. See e.g. Flanagan 1991a.

17. This is an ancient view, espoused mostly by virtue theorists such as Aristotle and Plato. For a paradigmatic example, see Aristotle's *Nicomachean Ethics*.

18. One example: at the U.S. Air Force Academy (a public institution whose charter explicitly involves developing the character of the students), educators are sensitive to concerns that, though we may think we are teaching one thing when we promulgate an honor code with a strict enforcement regime, we may actually be teaching another. In other words, if we are not careful, we may think we are teaching cadets to never lie, steal, or cheat, but what we may actually be teaching them is that they must always *only appear* to never lie, steal, or cheat. If the pessimistic view is true, then we are actually doing damage to the character of the students. Fortunately, at least at that institution, the pessimistic view is false, I think. More on this in chapter 6.

19. For more on Kohlberg's three-level, six-stage model of moral development, see Kohlberg 1981. For criticism, see Gilligan 1982.

20. For alternative perspectives, see Rest 1986, 1991.

21. For a discussion of connectionism and Turing machines, see Eduardo Sontag, "Automata and Neural Networks," in Arbib 1995.

22. For a classic study of the history of ontogeny's recapitulating phylogeny (or, rather, *not* recapitulating it), see Gould 1977.

23. I swallow hard while saying this, as this is ultimately an empirical question, and the empirically informed ethical sciences are still fledgling and nascent.

24. This is, of course, *purely* hypothetical.

25. For a summary of the literature, see pp. 612–613 of Palmer 1999.

26. This is for good reason, as making progress in neurobiological modeling requires dealing with *tractable* problems. However, we should be attacking all cognitive levels simultaneously so as to seek co-evolution between the assumptions that inform the various levels. We are finally reaching the point where it is feasible to talk about large scale integrative models in general, and models of moral cognition in particular. For a summary, see Casebeer and Churchland 2003.

27. See Thagard 1998a. For a fuller account, see Thagard 2000. The four types of coherence listed are from page 126 of the latter.

28. Technically, they were only functionally "completely" severed, as it is notoriously difficult to remove *every* projection from any brain part to any other.

29. For more on folk psychology and its relationship to the cognitive neurosciences, see the first four essays in Churchland and Churchland 1998.

30. My thanks to Patricia Churchland for pointing this out. For more, see Schulteis et al. 2000, Schall 2001, Kandel et al. 2000, and the "emotions"

section of Gazzaniga 1995. On the subject of severe moral pathology and more common failures of moral socialization, see pp. 89–90 of P. M. Churchland 1998a. Joan Stiles (personal communication, 2000) has made some excellent recommendations regarding the need to compile databases of lesion studies that look across populations of subjects with abnormal moral response profiles; such databases would be very useful for discovering how different abnormalities in development (due to injury, etc.) come together to cause severe moral pathology.

31. The angelic dilemmas that de Sousa mentions are ones where purely rational agents like the angels are faced with two equally compelling options. Whereas irrational creatures like Buridan's ass can just choose randomly or allow nonrational considerations to determine their choice, angels seem "stuck," forced to take no action by the demands of reason.

32. Lorenz (1996) discusses imprinting and also has much to say of general philosophical interest. Lorenz's vitriolic reaction to non-empirically informed philosophy is interesting: " . . . if Darwin discovers the fact that human beings owe their existence not to a unique act of creation but to an extremely drawn-out process of evolution, this fact has important consequences for our contemplation of '*a priori*' forms of thought and intuition. Yet in the humanities epistemological theory responds to these inevitable consequences in the most indolent manner possible: it simply ignores them!" Later, when discussing Max Planck's statistics-driven (and prescient) modification to Kant's categories, Lorenz says: "One might expect—indeed any reasonable person would expect—that in their thoughts and words the practitioners of epistemology on a Kantian basis would be vigorously exploiting this powerful new development of *their own school*. But what happens in reality? Living Kantians *ignore* Planck because he offends against the absolute mental necessity and truth of *a priori* schemata, because he has dared to *extend* and therefore *change* the theories of the master, which have now become a matter of faith. There is nothing that can be done with this kind of philosophical school. . . . In fact, however, Planck's results are in themselves already the *fruit* of a genuine synthesis between the natural sciences and the humanities, between highly specialized individual research and extremely general epistemology. As such, they bear witness to the fact that such a synthesis is really *possible*." (ibid., pp. 72–73) Fortunately, at least with regard to the possibility of fruitful interactions between the humanities and the sciences, things have changed somewhat since Lorenz's time (the late 1940s).

33. For a review of the experimental work surrounding children's abilities to detect lies, deceive others, and otherwise make inferences and engage in actions that require "full-on" theory of mind, see Astington 1996. I have such full-blown theory of mind capabilities "in mind" here; the precursors of theory of mind are present much earlier. Baron-Cohen (1995, p. 60) summarizes: "By the end of the first year of life, normal infants . . . can tell that they and someone else are attending to the same thing, and can read people's actions as directed at goals and as driven by desires. As toddlers, they can pretend and understand pretense. And by the time they begin school, around age 4, they can work out what people might know, think and believe."

34. This flexibility can often lead to confusion. Consider that Paul Churchland lays claim to theory-theory for connectionist reasons, but his theory-theory is not anything like (for example) Alison Gopnik's theory-theory, as Churchland has a very different spin on what it means to possess a theory and what a theory consists in than does Gopnik.

35. For a historical survey of theory-theory and simulation theory, see the introductory essay in Carruthers and Smith 1996.

36. Recall the discussion of concept formation earlier in this chapter and in chapter 3. Here is a quick recap from Paul Churchland (1989, p. 177): "An individual's overall theory-of-the-world, we might venture, is not a large collection or a long list of stored symbolic items. Rather, it is a specific point in that individual's synaptic weight space. It is a configuration of connection weights, a configuration that partitions the system's activation-vector space(s) into useful divisions and subdivisions relative to the inputs typically fed the system."

37. The circuit formed by the last two structures may mediate direction-of-gaze detection, all three locations probably are involved in mediating shared attention, and the specially coordinated action of all three regions might thus subserve theory of mind processing. See Baron-Cohen 1995.

38. For a brief review of this literature, see Brothers 1995. For a well-developed model of theory of mind with neurobiological plausibility, see Baron-Cohen 1995.

39. Consider the successes of conventional symbol systems such as Anderson's ACT and Newell's SOAR (Smith and Osherson 1995, pp. 267–296).

40. See Fodor and Pylyshyn 1988, particularly pp. 64–66.

41. See e.g. Clark 1989, Smolensky's rejoinder (1988), or volume 2 of the journal *Philosophy and Psychology* (1995). See also chapter 8 of Flanagan 1996a.

42. See p. 43 of chapter 14 of McClelland et al. 1986. Also see the last half of Gardenfors 2000, particularly the summary chapter "In Chase of Space."

Chapter 6

1. For concise statements of both these views, see Honderich 1995.

2. One example: the concept of agency. (See Rottschaefer 1998.) For the practical legal upshot of modifying our legal concepts on the basis of neuroscientific findings, see Reider 1998.

3. See chapters 3–6 of Johnson 1993. "Cognitive science" here is construed narrowly to mean "metaphor theory," so Johnson never explicitly discusses many other results in cognitive science research that bear directly on ethics.

4. For works in this area, see, in addition to those cited in the preceding chapter, Forbus and Gentner 1989 and the first issue of *Cognitive Linguistics* (1990).

5. See P. S. Churchland 1996. See also Damasio 1994.

6. See pp. 150–175 of Bechtel and Abrahamsen 1991.

7. The *Groundwork* is confusing on this point. For a comprehensive discussion, see pp. 126–144 of O'Neill 1989.

8. Churchland cites de Sousa as calling such a person (or, in the original context, an angel) a "Kantian monster."

9. More generally, there are at least six aspects of moral cognition that our moral theories and their corresponding psychologies must be able to accommodate. Acts of moral cognition are hot (they involve affective, conative and emotional subsystems), social (they arise in an other-oriented context), distributed (multiple modalities are needed to effectively engage our moral cognitive capacity), organic (they are exquisitely context sensitive), genuine (they are about action in the world and are a response to bona fide "felt" problems in an agent), and directed (they are about the interface between the agent and the world, so, to use Kantian language, moral realism is a transcendental precondition of moral judgment). For more detail, see Casebeer and Churchland 2003.

10. The "frame problem" in artificial intelligence deals with just how difficult it is to get a computer to pick out the relevant items about which it must reason in order to accomplish a goal. Dan Dennett's amusing article on the frame problem is reprinted in Boden 1990.

11. See e.g. Herman 1993.

12. For more on an "ethic of care," see Gilligan 1982, 1987. Also, there is much excellent work detailing Kant's position in his *Anthropology* that has all too often been ignored by Kant scholars. Some of it saves Kant from charges of insensitivity to the "facts on the ground" about the moral life. See e.g. Munzel 1999. There may be enough ammunition here to begin a rebuttal of some of the charges I have made, but the mainstream "received version" of Kant is still, I believe, liable to them.

13. Two judgments that Kant mentions in his work are (1) that we should not violate the moral law "though the heavens may fall" and (2) that even if we were the last two people on earth, if I were with someone who was convicted by a just court of a capital crime, it would be my obligation to carry out sentence on her even though it would leave me the last surviving member of the human race. I have always found these conclusions to be, morally speaking, simply incredible. I think we would understandably all be quite morally indignant with someone who refused to lie even though it led to the destruction of the universe. Kant has the resources to handle some of the more down-to-earth objections, though. One famous example: the Nazi knocks on your door, asking you where the Jews are hidden. Can you lie to him? Kant has wiggle room here: the "perfect duties" generated by the categorical imperative are *prohibitions*. Thus, Kant would not require that you act positively to tell him the truth. You could remain silent, talk about the weather, or even hit the Nazi over the head with a stovepipe. And there are additional complications regarding how we can treat those who are themselves treating others as mere means. There is some non-trivial sense in which they are asking (e.g., consenting) to be treated as mere means also. See Rachels 1993 for an introduction to these issues; see Christine Korsgaard's essay "The Right to Lie: Kant on Dealing with Evil" (in her 1996 collection) for a detailed and provocative discussion.

14. For examples, see chapter 4 of MacIntyre 1999.

15. For more on this trematode, see pp. 146–148 of Buss 1987.

16. For an extended riff on this theme, see Misak 2000.

17. For more reasoning along these lines, see Dennett's "Moral First Aid Manual" in McMurrin 1988.

18. See Williams 1985, especially chapter 6.

19. See also Tooby and Cosmides 1996.

20. For other informative discussions from a perfectionist perspective that nonetheless would also be quite fruitful from the modern-history standpoint, see chapters 6, 7, and 10 of Hurka 1993. For example, Hurka advises: Be well rounded. You'll be more likely to satisfy your complex of proper functions in that case. (Of course, Hurka doesn't use my particular style of explanatory language.)

21. From "The First Rule of Logic," as published in Peirce 1877.

22. Although Juarrero doesn't cite Elman's findings, she has something similar in mind when she writes (1999, pp. 254–255): " . . . it is not an exclusive disjunction—nature *versus* nurture—it is both, and fortunately, if dynamical systems are an appropriate metaphor, nature appears to be very generous in the flexibility that it confers on its initial endowment. But that malleability narrows quickly as interactions lead to self-organized structures that lock in, and the dependencies children establish early on become increasingly . . . resistant to future modification. The social and educational implications of this discovery are truly sobering."

23. "What Is Morality?" is an illuminating essay by two Continental philosophers friendly to my conclusions in chapter 4 regarding the essential nature of moral judgment.

Chapter 7

1. See pp. 71–76 of Kitcher 1999.

2. For example: If I were asthmatic, I might decide to enter an oxygen bubble so as to restore proper functioning to my lungs even though doing so might cause short-term harm to the proper exfoliatory functioning of my skin, but the reason that I decide to enter the bubble is still nonetheless a functional one. Note how closely this argument resembles that of the misguided critic who says that the naturalist about norms can't thereby critique anything natural.

3. Kitcher argues we can sidestep the whole "reductivist challenge," explanatory awkwardness and all, by adopting a coherentist epistemology. But to do so, he argues, is just to open a whole epistemological can of worms that we had hoped to avoid by being foundationalists to begin with (1999, pp. 82–83). I think that we successfully put the worst worms back in the can simply by being Quinean fallibilists—we get the advantages of coherentism along with the strengths of having admittedly provisional foundations. This is a subject for another paper in moral epistemology, however.

4. For a discussion of Neurath's boat, see Zolo 1990.

5. I do not mean to allege that only or mostly apodictic moral systems are used to indoctrinate rather than educate. I merely mean to point out that both instructors and students of moral education can often understandably misinterpret moral systems of this character in epistemically unhealthy ways.

6. See Plato's *Republic,* 412c–417b. Robin Waterfield's translation (Oxford University Press, 1998) is especially good.

7. Lieberman (1998) makes several interesting arguments, including a transcendental one that a very condition of the existence of commitment is that we think of those things we are committed to as objectively valuable (ibid., pp. 132–133). Lieberman also acknowledges, but does not discuss in any depth, that developments in the cognitive sciences support his thesis. I quote from pp. 197–198: "The view that psychological plausibility does in fact serve as a constraint on theory-building is becoming more widely accepted with the increasing influence of cognitive science, especially in the field of ethics. As we learn more about how the mind forms and applies concepts, about the processes involved in identity constitution, and the ways in which the self is formed and influenced, we are in a better position to assess various theories on the basis of the kind of psychological assumptions implicit in their system. It seems only natural that if a theory is in fact not possible for beings like us—not that it is hard, or difficult, or demanding, but runs contrary to what we understand to be the requirements of stable identity, for example, or effective agency—then that theory is just wrong . . . our best knowledge of human psychology and of how the mind works will act as minimally necessary conditions that any theory regarding possible human conduct must meet. And since metaethical theories concern our normative practices—what it is we are doing when we say 'stealing is bad,' or when we make conversational demands on others, or are involved in expanding the scope of the term 'we liberals'—they too must pass the test of psychological plausibility. Contrary to what many antirealists in ethics say, logical possibility is not the only condition a theory must meet. Practice does in fact constrain theory."

8. See, e.g., Begley 2001, which is about the new field of "neurotheology." Contrast this with Begley 2000, which is about morality and moral development but which makes only passing reference to the cognitive sciences.

9. I have in mind Bryan Skyrms's work on the evolution of the social contract (1996, 2001). For a more technical version of the same points, see Skyrms and Pemantle 2000. See also Alexander 2000.

10. I say "more basic" because social structures act in service of the individuals who flourish (or fail to flourish) within them.

References

Ackrill, J. L., ed. 1987. *A New Aristotle Reader.* Princeton University Press.

Adolphs, R., D. Tranel, A. Bechara, H. Damasio, and A. Damasio. 1996. Neuropsychological Approaches to Reasoning and Decision Making. In *The Neurobiology of Decision-Making,* ed. A. Damasio et al. Springer-Verlag.

Ahlstron, Dick. 2001. Scientist on Trail of the Killer Instinct. *Irish Times,* March 16.

Akins, Kathleen. 1996a. *Perception.* Oxford University Press.

Akins, Kathleen. 1996b. On Sensory Systems and the "Aboutness" of Mental States. *Journal of Philosophy* 93, no. 7: 337–372.

Alexander, Jason. 2000. Volutionary Explanations of Distributive Justice. *Philosophy of Science* 67, no. 3: 490–516.

Alexander, Richard D. 1987. *The Biology of Moral Systems.* Aldine de Gruyter.

Alexander, Thomas M. 1993. John Dewey and the Moral Imagination: Beyond Putnam and Rorty toward a Postmodern Ethics. *Transactions of the Charles S. Peirce Society* 29, no. 3: 369–400.

Alldredge, Stacey, W. Pitt Derryberry, Michael Crowson, and Asghar Iran-Nejad. 2000. Rethinking the Origin of Morality and Moral Development. *Journal of Mind and Behavior* 20, no. 1–2: 105–128.

Allen, Colin, Mark Bekoff, and George Lauder, eds. 1998. *Nature's Purposes: Analyses of Function and Design in Biology.* MIT Press.

Amari, Shun-Ichi, and Nikola Kasabov, eds. 1998. *Brain-Like Computing and Intelligent Information Systems.* Springer-Verlag.

Anagnostopoulos, Georgios. 1994. *Aristotle on the Goals and Exactness of Ethics.* University of California Press.

Anagnostopoulos, Georgios. 1996. Aristotle on Canonical Science and Ethics. *Philosophical Inquiry* 18, no. 1–2: 61–76.

Anagnostopoulos, Georgios. 1998. Ethics and the Indispensability of Theory. *Topoi* 17: 149–166.

Appleman, Philip, ed. 2001. *Darwin. Texts, Commentary,* third edition. Norton.

Arbib, Michael A., ed. 1995. *The Handbook of Brain Theory and Neural Networks*. MIT Press.

Arbib, Michael A., and Peter Erdi. 2000. Précis of *Neural Organization: Structure, Function and Dynamics*. *Behavioral and Brain Sciences* 23: 513–571.

Aristotle. 1985. *Nicomachean Ethics*. Hackett.

Arkes, Hal, and Kenneth Hammond, eds. 1986. *Judgment and Decision Making: An Interdisciplinary Reader*. Cambridge University Press.

Arnhart, Larry. 1998. *Darwinian Natural Right: The Biological Ethics of Human Nature*. State University of New York Press.

Arrington, Robert L. 1989. *Rationalism, Realism, and Relativism: Perspectives in Contemporary Moral Epistemology*. Cornell University Press.

Astington, Janet. 1996. What Is Theoretical about the Child's Theory of Mind? In *Theories of Theories of Mind*, ed. P. Carruthers and K. Smith. Cambridge University Press.

Audi, Robert, ed. 1995. *The Cambridge Dictionary of Philosophy*. Cambridge University Press.

Bakhurst, David. 1998. Pragmatism and Moral Knowledge. *Canadian Journal of Philosophy* 24, supplement: 227–252.

Ball, Stephen W. 1991. Linguistic Intuitions and Varieties of Ethical Naturalism. *Philosophy and Phenomenological Research* 51, no. 1: 1–38.

Ballard, Dana H. 1997. *An Introduction to Natural Computation*. MIT Press.

Barash, David P. 2000. Evolutionary Existentialism, Sociobiology, and the Meaning of Life. *BioScience* 50, no. 11: 1012–1017.

Barlow, Connie, ed. 1994. *Evolution Extended: Biological Debates on the Meaning of Life*. MIT Press.

Barnes, Jonathan, ed. 1995. *The Cambridge Companion to Aristotle*. Cambridge University Press.

Baron-Cohen, Simon. 1995. *Mindblindness: An Essay on Autism and Theory of Mind*. MIT Press.

Barsalou, Lawrence W. 1999. Perceptual Symbol Systems. *Behavioral and Brain Sciences* 22: 577–660.

Barto, Andrew. 1995. Learning as Hill-Climbing in Weight Space. In *The Handbook of Brain Theory and Neural Networks*, ed. M. Arbib. MIT Press.

Batali, John, and William Noble Grundy. 1996. Modeling the Evolution of Motivation. *Evolutionary Computation* 4, no. 3: 235–270.

Bateson, P. P. G., and R. A. Hinde, eds. 1976. *Growing Points in Ethology*. Cambridge University Press.

Bechtel, William, and Adele Abrahamsen. 1991. *Connectionism and the Mind: An Introduction to Parallel Processing in Networks*. Blackwell.

Bechtel, William, and Jennifer Mundale. 1999. Multiple Realizability Revisited: Linking Cognitive and Neural States. *Philosophy of Science* 66, no. 2: 175–207.

Begley, Sharon. 2001. Religion and the Brain. *Newsweek,* May 7: 19.

Begley, Sharon, and Claudia Kalb. 2000. Learning Right from Wrong. *Newsweek,* March 13: 30–33.

Bekoff, Marc. 2001. Social Play Behavior: Cooperation, Fairness, Trust and the Evolution of Morality. *Journal of Consciousness Studies* 8, no. 2: 81–90.

Bickle, John. 1995. Psychoneural Reduction of the Genuinely Cognitive: Some Accomplished Facts. *Philosophical Psychology* 8, no. 3: 265–285.

Bickle, John. 1998. *Psychoneural Reduction: The New Wave.* MIT Press.

Blackburn, Simon. 1998. *Ruling Passions: A Theory of Practical Reasoning.* Clarendon.

Blum, Lawrence. 1994. *Moral Perception and Particularity.* Cambridge University Press.

Boden, Margaret, ed. 1990. *The Philosophy of Artificial Intelligence.* Oxford University Press.

Bogdon, Radu J. 2000. *Minding Minds: Evolving a Reflexive Mind by Interpreting Others.* MIT Press.

Boghossian, Paul. 1996. Analyticity Reconsidered. *Nous* 30: 360–391.

Boghossian, Paul, and Christopher Peacocke, eds. 2000. *New Essays on the A Priori.* Clarendon.

Boisvert, Raymond. 1988. *Dewey's Metaphysics.* Fordham University Press.

Botterill, George, and Peter Carruthers. 1999. *The Philosophy of Psychology.* Cambridge University Press.

Bower, Bruce. 2000. Culture of the Sea: Whales and Dolphins Strut Their Social Stuff for Scientists. *Science News* 158: 284–286.

Boyd, Richard. 1988. How to Be a Moral Realist. In *Moral Discourse and Practice,* ed. S. Darwall et al. Oxford University Press, 1997.

Braddon-Mitchell, David, and Frank Jackson. 1996. *Philosophy of Mind and Cognition.* Blackwell.

Braitenberg, Valentino. 1984. *Vehicles: Experiments in Synthetic Psychology.* MIT Press.

Brandon, Robert N. 1990. *Adaptation and Environment.* Princeton University Press.

Brandon, Robert N. 1996. *Concepts and Methods in Evolutionary Biology.* Cambridge University Press.

Bransford, John D., Ann L. Brown, and Rodney R. Cocking, eds. 1999. *How People Learn: Brain, Mind, Experience, and School.* National Academy Press.

Brewer, Paul R. 2001. Value Words and Lizard Brains: Do Citizens Deliberate about Appeals to Their Core Values? *Political Psychology* 22, no. 1: 45–64.

Brink, David O. 1989. *Moral Realism and the Foundations of Ethics.* Cambridge University Press.

Broadie, Sarah. 1991. *Ethics with Aristotle.* Oxford University Press.

Brommer, Jon E. 2000. The Evolution of Fitness in Life-History Theory. *Biological Review* 75: 377–404.

Brothers, Leslie. 1995. Neurophysiology of the Perception of Intentions by Primates. In *The Cognitive Neurosciences,* ed. M. Gazzaniga. MIT Press.

Brower, Bruce W. 1993. Dispositional Ethical Realism. *Ethics* 103, no. 2: 221–249.

Brown, Richard G., and Graham Pluck. 2000. Negative Symptoms: The "Pathology" of Motivation and Goal-Directed Behavior. *Trends in Neurosciences* 23, no. 9: 412–417.

Burke, Tom. 1991. Ecological Psychology and Dewey's Theory of Perception. Report CSLI-91-151, Center for the Study of Language and Information, Stanford University.

Burnham, Terry, and Jay Phelan. 2000. *Mean Genes: From Sex to Money to Food.* Perseus.

Buss, David M. 2000. The Evolution of Happiness. *American Psychologist* 55, no. 1: 15–23.

Buss, Leo W. 1987. *The Evolution of Individuality.* Princeton University Press.

Campbell, James. 1995. *Understanding John Dewey.* Open Court.

Campbell, Richmond, and Bruce Hunter, eds. 2000. *Moral Epistemology Naturalized. Canadian Journal of Philosophy,* supplementary volume 26: 1–317.

Capaldi, Nicholas. 1966. Hume's Rejection of 'Ought' as a Moral Category. *Journal of Philosophy* 63, no. 5: 126–137.

Caplan, Arthur L, ed. 1978. *The Sociobiology Debate: Readings on Ethical and Scientific Issues.* Harper & Row.

Carpenter, Gail A. 2001. Neural-Network Models of Learning and Memory: Leading Questions and an Emerging Framework. *Trends in Cognitive Science* 5, no. 3: 114–118.

Carruthers, Peter. 1996. *Language Thought and Consciousness: An Essay in Philosophical Psychology.* Cambridge University Press.

Carruthers, Peter, and Andrew Chamberlain, eds. 2000. *Evolution and the Human Mind: Modularity, Language and Meta-Cognition.* Cambridge University Press.

Carruthers, Peter, and K. Peter Smith, eds. 1996. *Theories of Theories of Mind.* Cambridge University Press.

Cartwright, John. 2000. *Evolution and Human Behavior.* MIT Press.

Casebeer, William. 2000. Bridging the Sensory-Motor and Ontological Gaps: On Relations and State Spaces. Unpublished.

Casebeer, William, and Patricia Churchland. 2003. The Neural Correlates of Moral Cognition: A Multiple-Aspect Theory of Moral Judgment and Decision-Making. *Biology and Philosophy* 18, no. 1.

Caspary, William. 2000. *Dewey on Democracy.* Cornell University Press.

Caygill, Howard. 1995. *A Kant Dictionary.* Blackwell.

Changeux, Jean-Pierre, and Stanislas Dehaene. 1993. Neuronal Models of Cognitive Function. In *Brain Development and Cognition,* ed. M. Johnson. Blackwell.

Charles, David. 1995. Aristotle. In *The Oxford Companion to Philosophy,* ed. T. Honderich. Oxford University Press.

Chisholm, James S. 1999. *Death, Hope and Sex: Steps to an Evolutionary Ecology of Mind and Morality.* Cambridge University Press.

Churchland, Patricia Smith. 1986. *Neurophilosophy: Toward a Unified Science of the Mind.* MIT Press.

Churchland, Patricia Smith. 1996. Feeling Reasons. In *Neurobiology of Decision-Making,* ed. A. Damasio et al. Springer-Verlag.

Churchland, Patricia Smith. 2002. *Brain-Wise: Studies in Neurophilosophy.* MIT Press.

Churchland, Patricia Smith, and Terrence Sejnowski. 1992. *The Computational Brain.* MIT Press.

Churchland, Paul M. 1989. *A Neurocomputational Perspective: The Nature of Mind and the Structure of Science.* MIT Press.

Churchland, Paul M. 1995. *The Engine of Reason, the Seat of the Soul.* MIT Press.

Churchland, Paul M. 1996a. Neural Representation of the Social World. In *Mind and Morals,* ed. L. May et al. MIT Press.

Churchland, Paul M. 1996b. Learning and Conceptual Change: The View from the Neurons. In *Connectionism, Concepts, and Folk Psychology,* volume 2, ed. A. Clark et al. Clarendon.

Churchland, Paul M. 1998a. Toward a Cognitive Neurobiology of the Moral Virtues. *Topoi* 17: 83–96.

Churchland, Paul M. 1998b. Conceptual Similarity across Sensory and Structural Diversity: The Lepore/Fodor Challenge Answered. *Journal of Philosophy* 95, no. 1: 5–32.

Churchland, Paul M. 2000. Rules, Know-How, and the Future of Moral Cognition. *Canadian Journal of Philosophy,* supplementary volume 26: 291–306.

Churchland, Paul M., and Patricia S. Churchland. 1998. *On the Contrary: Critical Essays, 1987–1997.* MIT Press.

Clark, Andy. 1989. *Microcognition: Philosophy, Cognitive Science, and Parallel Distributed Processing.* MIT Press.

Clark, Andy. 1993. *Associative Engines: Connectionism, Concepts, and Representational Change.* MIT Press.

Clark, Andy. 1995. Moving Minds: Situating Content in the Service of Real-Time Success. In *AI, Connectionism, and Philosophical Psychology* (Philosophical Perspectives, volume 9). Blackwell.

Clark, Andy. 2000a. Word and Action: Reconciling Rules and Know-How in Moral Cognition. *Canadian Journal of Philosophy,* supplementary volume 26: 267–289.

Clark, Andy. 2000b. Cognitive Incrementalism: The Big Issue. *Behavioral and Brain Sciences* 23, no. 4: 536–537.

Clark, Andy, and Chris Thornton. 1997. Trading Spaces: Computation, Representation, and the Limits of Uninformed Learning. *Behavioral and Brain Sciences* 20: 57–90.

Cohen, L. J. 1981. Can Human Irrationality Be Experimentally Demonstrated? *Behavioral and Brain Sciences* 4: 317–370.

Collier, John, and Michael Stingl. 1995. Evolutionary Naturalism and the Objectivity of Morality. In *Issues in Evolutionary Ethics,* ed. P. Thompson. State University of New York Press.

Connolly, Terry. 1999. Action as a Fast and Frugal Heuristic. *Minds and Machines* 9: 479–496.

Cook, John W. 1999. *Morality and Cultural Differences.* Oxford University Press.

Cooper, David E. 1990. *Existentialism: A Reconstruction.* Blackwell.

Cooper, John M. 1999. *Reason and Emotion: Essays on Ancient Moral Psychology and Ethical Reason.* Princeton University Press.

Corballis, Michael C., and Stephen E. G. Lea, eds. 1999. *The Descent of Mind: Psychological Perspectives on Hominid Evolution.* Oxford University Press.

Crespi, Bernard, J. 2001. The Evolution of Social Behavior in Microorganisms. *Trends in Ecology and Evolution* 16, no. 4: 178–183.

Crisp, Roger, and Michael Slote, eds. 1997. *Virtue Ethics.* Oxford University Press.

Cronin, Helena. 1991. *The Ant and the Peacock: Altruism and Sexual Selection from Darwin to Today.* Cambridge University Press.

Cullity, Garrett and Gaut, Berys. eds. 1997. *Ethics and Practical Reason.* Clarendon.

Cummins, Robert. 1995. Connectionism and the Rationale Constraint on Cognitive Explanation. In *AI, Connectionism, and Philosophical Psychology* (Philosophical Perspectives, volume 9). Blackwell.

Damasio, Antonio R. 1994. *Descartes' Error: Emotion, Reason, and the Human Brain.* Putnam.

Damasio, Antonio R., D. Tranel, and H. Damasio. 1991. Somatic Markers and the Guidance of Behavior. In *Frontal Lobe Function and Dysfunction,* ed. H. Levin et al. Oxford University Press.

Dancy, Jonathan. 2000. *Practical Reality.* Oxford University Press.

Danielson, Peter A, ed. 1998. *Modeling Rationality, Morality and Evolution.* Oxford University Press.

Davies, Paul Sheldon. 2000. Malfunctions. *Biology and Philosophy* 15: 19–38.

Dawkins, Richard. 1986. *The Blind Watchmaker.* Oxford University Press.

Deacon, Terrence W. 1997. *The Symbolic Species: The Co-Evolution of Language and the Brain.* Norton.

Dennett, Daniel. 1987. *The Intentional Stance.* MIT Press.

Dennett, Daniel. 1995. *Darwin's Dangerous Idea: Evolution and the Meanings of Life.* Simon and Schuster.

DePaul, Michael R., and William Ramsey, eds. 1998. *Rethinking Intuition: The Psychology of Intuition and Its Role in Philosophical Inquiry.* Rowman and Littlefield.

Depew, David J., and Bruce H. Weber, eds. 1985. *Evolution at a Crossroads: The New Biology and the New Philosophy of Science.* MIT Press.

Depew, David J., and Bruce H. Weber. 1997. *Darwinism Evolving: Systems Dynamics and the Genealogy of Natural Selection.* MIT Press.

DesAutel, Peggy. 1996. Gestalt Shifts in Moral Perception. In *Mind and Morals,* ed. L. May et al. MIT Press.

De Sousa, Ronald. 1997. *The Rationality of Emotion.* MIT Press.

de Waal, Frans. 1996. *Good Natured: The Origins of Right and Wrong in Humans and Other Animals.* Harvard University Press.

de Waal, Frans, and Filippo Aureli. 2000. Shared Principles and Unanswered Question. In *Natural Conflict Resolution,* ed. F. Aurreli et al. University of California Press.

Dewey, John. 1909. The Influence of Darwin on Philosophy and Other Essays in Contemporary Thought. In *Collected Works: The Middle Works,* volume 4. Southern Illinois University Press, 1988.

Dewey, John. 1922. Human Nature and Conduct. In *Collected Works: The Middle Works,* volume 14. Southern Illinois University Press, 1988.

Dewey, John. 1925. *Experience and Nature.* In *Collected Works: The Later Works,* volume 1. Southern Illinois University Press, 1988.

Dewey, John. 1929. The Quest for Certainty. In *Collected Works: The Later Works,* volume 4. Southern Illinois University Press, 1988.

Dewey, John. 1932. Ethics. In *Collected Works: The Later Works,* volume 7. Southern Illinois University Press, 1989.

Dewey, John. 1933–34. *Essays, Reviews, Miscellany and A Common Faith.* In *Collected Works: The Later Works,* volume 9. Southern Illinois University Press, 1989.

Dewey, John. 1938. Logic: The Theory of Inquiry. In *Collected Works: The Later Works,* volume 12. Southern Illinois University Press, 1991.

Dewey, John. 1942–1948. Essays, Reviews, and Miscellany. In *Collected Works: The Later Works,* volume 15. Southern Illinois University Press, 1991.

Dewey, John. 1949–1952. Essays, Typescripts, and Knowing and the Known. In *Collected Works: The Later Works,* volume 16. Southern Illinois University Press, 1991.

Dickstein, Morris, ed. 1998. *The Revival of Pragmatism: New Essays on Social Thought, Law, and Culture.* Duke University Press.

Diener, Ed, and Eunkook M. Suh, eds. 2000. *Culture and Subjective Well-Being.* MIT Press.

Dienes, Zoltan, and Josef Perner. 1999. A Theory of Implicit and Explicit Knowledge. *Behavioral and Brain Sciences* 22: 735–808.

Doris, John M. 1998. Persons, Situations, and Virtue Ethics. *Nous* 32, no. 4: 504–530.

Dreyfus, Herbert, with Stuart Dreyfus. 1990. What Is Morality? A Phenomenological Account of the Development of Ethical Expertise. In *Universalism vs. Communitarianism,* ed. D. Rasmussen. MIT Press.

Dreyfus, Hubert L. 1992. *What Computers Still Can't Do: A Critique of Artificial Reason.* MIT Press.

Duch, Wlodzislaw. 1998. Platonic Model of Mind as an Approximation to Neurodynamics. In *Brain-Like Computing and Intelligent Information Systems,* ed. S. Amari and N. Kasabov. Springer-Verlag.

Dukas, Reuven, ed. 1998. *Cognitive Ecology: The Evolutionary Ecology of Information Processing and Decision Making.* University of Chicago Press.

Dupre, John, ed. 1987. *The Latest on the Best: Essays on Evolution and Optimality.* MIT Press.

Dupre, John. 1993. *The Disorder of Things: Metaphysical Foundations of the Disunity of Science.* Harvard University Press.

Eakin, Emily. 2000. Looking for That Brain Wave Called Love. *New York Times,* October 28.

Eames, S. Morris. 1977. *Pragmatic Naturalism: An Introduction.* Southern Illinois University Press.

Edidin, Aron. 1985. Philosophy: Just Like Science Only Different. *Philosophy and Phenomenological Research* 45, no. 4: 537–552.

Edwards, Donald H. 1991. Mutual Inhibition among Neural Command systems as a Possible Mechanism for Behavioral Choice in Crayfish. *Journal of Neuroscience* 11, no. 5: 1210–1223.

Elman, Jeffrey. 1990. Finding structure in time. *Cognitive Science* 14: 179–212.

Elman, Jeffrey. 1992. Learning and Development in Neural Networks: The Importance of Starting Small. In Cognitive Science 201F Course Reader, University of California, San Diego.

Elman, Jeffrey L., et al. 1996. *Rethinking Innateness: A Connectionist Perspective on Development.* MIT Press.

Elster, Jon. 1999a. *Alchemies of the Mind: Rationality and the Emotions.* Cambridge University Press.

Elster, Jon. 1999b. *Strong Feelings: Emotion, Addiction, and Human Behavior.* MIT Press.

Empiricus, Sextus. 1994. *Sextus Empiricus—Outlines of Skepticism.* Cambridge University Press.

Fabian, A. C., ed. 1998. *Evolution: Society, Science and the Universe.* Cambridge University Press.

Fackelmann, Kathleen. 2001. A Different Take on Anger Abnormalities in Brain Region May Help Explain Some Violent or Other Troubling Behavior. *USA Today,* March 15.

Falkenhainer, B., K. Forbus, and D. Gentner. 1989. The Structure Mapping Engine: Algorithm and Examples. *Artificial Intelligence* 41: 1–63.

Farah, Martha J. 1999. *Visual Agnosia: Disorders of Object Recognition and What They Tell Us about Normal Vision.* MIT Press.

Farber, Ilya. 2000. Domain Integration in Life and Mind. Doctoral dissertation, University of California, San Diego.

Farber, Paul Lawrence. 1994. *The Temptations of Evolutionary Ethics.* University of California Press.

Faver, Till, Jasdan Joerges, and Randolf Menzel. 1999. Associative Learning Modifies Neural Representation of Odors in the Insect Brain. *Nature Neuroscience* 2, no. 1: 74–78.

Fesmire, Steven A. 1995. Dramatic Rehearsal and the Moral Artist: A Deweyan Theory of Moral Understanding. *Transactions of the Charles S. Peirce Society* 31, no. 3: 568–597.

Fesmire, Steven A. 1999. The Art of Moral Imagination. In *Dewey Reconfigured,* ed. C. Haskins and D. Seiple. State University of New York Press.

Finlay, B. L., R. B. Darlington, and N. Nicastro. 2001. Developmental Structure in Brain Evolution. *Behavioral and Brain Sciences* 24, no. 2: 263–308.

Flanagan, Owen. 1982. Quinean Ethics. *Ethics* 93: 56–74.

Flanagan, Owen. 1988. Pragmatism, Ethics, and Correspondence Truth: Response to Gibson and Quine. *Ethics* 98: 541–549.

Flanagan, Owen. 1991a. *Varieties of Moral Personality: Ethics and Psychological Realism,* Harvard University Press.

Flanagan, Owen. 1991b. *The Science of the Mind,* second edition. MIT Press.

Flanagan, Owen. 1996a. *Self Expressions: Mind, Morals, and the Meaning of Life.* Oxford University Press.

Flanagan, Owen. 1996b. Ethics Naturalized: Ethics as Human Ecology. In *Mind and Morals,* ed. L. May et al. MIT Press.

Flanagan, Owen. 1999. Science and the Human Image. Paper presented at Romanell Phi Beta Kappa Lectures, Duke University.

Flanagan, Owen. 2000. *Dreaming Souls: Sleep, Dreams, and the Evolution of the Conscious Mind.* Oxford University Press.

Flanagan, Owen, and Kathryn Jackson. 1990. Justice, Care, and Gender. In *Feminism and Political Theory,* ed. C. Sunstein. University of Chicago Press.

Flanagan, Owen, and Amelie Oksenberg Rorty, eds. 1990. *Identity, Character, and Morality: Essays in Moral Psychology.* MIT Press.

Floridi, Luciano. 1999. *Philosophy and Computing: An Introduction.* Routledge.

Fodor, J. A., and E. Lepore. 1992. *Holism: A Shopper's Guide.* Blackwell.

Fodor, J. A., and Z. W. Pylyshyn. 1988. Connectionism and Cognitive Architecture: A Critical Analysis. *Cognition* 28: 3–71.

Forbus, Kenneth D. 2001. Exploring Analogy in the Large. In *The Analogical Mind,* ed. D. Gentner et al. MIT Press.

Forbus, Kenneth D., and Dedre Gentner. 1989. Structural Evaluation of Analogies: What Counts? In *Proceedings of the Sixteenth Annual Conference of the Cognitive Science Society.* Erlbaum.

Forbus, Kenneth, D. Gentner, and K. Law. 1995. MAC/FAC: A Model of Similarity-Based Retrieval. *Cognitive Science* 19, no. 2: 141–205.

French, M. J. 1988. *Invention and Evolution: Design in Nature and Engineering.* Cambridge University Press.

French, Peter A., Theodore E. Uehling Jr., and Howard K. Wettstein, eds. 1990. *The Philosophy of the Human Sciences.* University of Notre Dame Press.

Fuster, Joaquin, Mark Bodner, and James K. Kroger. 2000. Cross-Modal and Cross-Temporal Associations in Neurons of Frontal Cortex. *Nature* 405, 18 May: 347–351.

Gardenfors, Peter. 2000. *Conceptual Spaces: The Geometry of Thought.* MIT Press.

Garfield, Jay L. 2000. The Meanings of Meaning: Dimensions of the Sciences of Mind. *Philosophical Psychology* 13, no. 4: 421–440.

Gazzaniga, Michael S., ed. 1995. *The Cognitive Neurosciences.* MIT Press.

Gentner, Dedre, Keith J. Holyoak, and Boicho N. Kokinov, eds. 2001. *The Analogic Mind: Perspectives from Cognitive Science.* MIT Press.

Gibbard, Allan. 1990. *Wise Choices, Apt Feelings: A Theory of Normative Judgment.* Harvard University Press.

Gibson, Roger F. 1988. Flanagan on Quinean Ethics. *Ethics* 98: 534–540.

Giere, Ronald. 1999. *Science without Laws.* University of Chicago Press.

Gigerenzer, Gerd. 2000. *Adaptive Thinking.* Oxford University Press.

Gilligan, Carol. 1982. *In a Different Voice: Psychological Theory and Women's Development.* Harvard University Press.

Gilligan, Carol. 1987. Moral Orientation and Moral Development. In *Women and Moral Theory,* ed. D. Meyers et al. Rowman and Littlefield.

Gilligan, Carol, et al. 1988. *Mapping the Moral Domain.* Harvard University Press.

Gintis, Herbert. 2000. *Game Theory Evolving: A Problem-Centered Introduction to Modeling Strategic Behavior.* Princeton University Press.

Glover, Jonathan. 1999. *Humanity: A Moral History of the Twentieth Century.* Yale University Press.

Glurfa, Martin, and Elizabeth A. Capaldi. 1999. Vectors, Routes and Maps: New Discoveries about Navigation in Insects. *Trends in Neurosciences* 22, no. 6: 237–242.

Godfrey-Smith, Peter. 1991. Signal, Decision, Action. *Journal of Philosophy* 88, no. 12: 709–722.

Godfrey-Smith, Peter. 1996. *Complexity and the Function of Mind in Nature.* Cambridge University Press.

Godfrey-Smith, Peter. 1997. Replies to Sober, Sterelny and Neander. *Biology and Philosophy* 12: 581–590.

Goldman, Alvin. 1993. *Philosophical applications of Cognitive Science.* Westview.

Goldsmith, Timothy H., and William F. Zimmerman. 2001. *Biology, Evolution, and Human Nature.* Wiley.

Goodman, Nelson. 1979. *Fact, Fiction and Forecast,* third edition. Harvard University Press.

Gouinlock, James. 1972. *John Dewey's Philosophy of Value.* Humanities Press.

Gouinlock, James. 1978. Dewey's Theory of Moral Deliberation. *Ethics* 88, no. 3: 218–228.

Gouinlock, James, ed. 1994. *The Moral Writings of John Dewey,* revised edition. Prometheus Books.

Gould, Stephen J. 1977. *Ontogeny and Phylogeny.* Belknap.

Grayling, A. C. 1995. Psychologism. In *The Oxford Companion to Philosophy,* ed. T. Honderich. Oxford University Press.

Grice, H. Paul. 1989. *Studies in the Way of Words.* Harvard University Press.

Griffin, James. 1996. *Value Judgment: Improving Our Ethical Beliefs.* Clarendon.

Grusec, Joan E., and Leon Luczynski, eds. 1997. *Parenting and Children's Internalization of Values: A Handbook of Contemporary Theory.* Wiley.

Gutting, Gary. 1999. *Pragmatic Liberalism and the Critique of Modernity.* Cambridge University Press.

Haliday, T. R., and P. J. B. Slater, eds. 1983. *Genes, Development and Learning.* Freeman.

Hammond, K., G. McClelland, and J. Mumpower. 1980. *Human Judgment and Decision Making: Theories, Methods, and Procedures.* Praeger.

Hammer, M. 1993. An Identified Neuron Mediates the Unconditioned Stimulus in Associative Olfactory Learning in Honeybees. *Nature* 366: 59–63.

Handy, Rollo. 1956. The Naturalistic Reduction of Ethics to Science. *Journal of Philosophy* 53, no. 26: 829–835.

Hardcastle, Valerie Gray, ed. 1999. *Where Biology Meets Psychology: Philosophical Essays.* MIT Press.

Harman, Gilbert. 1999. *Reasoning, Meaning, and Mind.* Oxford University Press.

Harms, William F. 2000. Adaptation and Moral Realism. *Biology and Philosophy* 15: 699–712.

Haskins, Casey. 1999. *Dewey Reconfigured: Essays on Deweyan Pragmatism.* State University of New York Press.

Haugeland, John. 1985. *Artificial Intelligence: The Very Idea.* MIT Press.

Haugeland, John. 1998. *Having Thought: Essays in the Metaphysics of Mind.* Harvard University Press.

Heath, P. L. 1967. Boole, George. In *The Encyclopedia of Philosophy.* Macmillan.

Heidegger, Martin. 1975. *The Basic Problems of Phenomenology.* Indiana University Press.

Heidegger, Martin. 1978. *The Metaphysical Foundations of Logic.* Indiana University Press.

Heil, John. 1992. *The Nature of True Minds.* Cambridge University Press.

Heinaman, Robert, ed. 1995. *Aristotle and Moral Realism.* Westview.

Held, Virginia. 1996. Whose Agenda? Ethics versus Cognitive Science. In *Mind and Morals,* ed. L. May et al.. MIT Press.

Henle, M. 1978. Foreword to *Human Reasoning,* ed. R. Revlin and R. Mayer. Winston .

Hendriks-Jansen, Horst. 1996. *Catching Ourselves in the Act: Situated Activity, Interactive Emergence, Evolution and Human Thought.* MIT Press.

Herman, Barbara. 1993. *The Practice of Moral Judgment.* Harvard University Press.

Hertz, J., A. Krogh, and R. Palmer. 1991. *Introduction to the Theory of Neural Computation.* Addison-Wesley.

Heynen, Hilde. 1999. *Architecture and Modernity: A Critique.* MIT Press.

Hickman, Larry A., ed. 1998. *Reading Dewey: Interpretations for a Postmodern Generation.* Indiana University Press.

Hintikka, Jaakko. 1999. The Emperor's New Intuitions. *Journal of Philosophy* 96, no. 3: 127–147.

Hinton, Geoffrey, and Terrence Sejnowski, eds. 1999. *Unsupervised Learning: Foundations of Neural Computation.* MIT Press.

Hirschfeld, Lawrence A., and Susan A. Gelman. 1994. *Mapping the Mind: Domain Specificity in Cognition and Culture.* Cambridge University Press.

Hoffman, R. E. 1992. Attractor Neural Networks and Psychotic Disorders. *Psychiatric Annals* 22, no. 3: 119–124.

Hoffman, R. E., and T. McGlashan. 1993. Parallel Distributed Processing and the Emergence of Schizophrenic Systems. *Schizophrenia Bulletin* 19, no. 1: 119–240.

Holyoak, Keith. 1995. Problem Solving. In *An Invitation to Cognitive Science,* volume 3: *Thinking,* ed. E. Smith and D. Osherson, second edition. MIT Press.

Holyoak, Keith J., and Paul Thagard. 1996. *Mental Leaps: Analogy in Creative Thought.* MIT Press.

Holyoak, Keith J., and John E. Hummel. 2001. Toward an Understanding of Analogy within a Biological Symbol System. In *The Analogical Mind,* ed. D. Gentner et al. MIT Press.

Honderich, Ted, ed. 1995. *The Oxford Companion to Philosophy.* Oxford University Press.

Hook, Sidney, ed. 1950. *John Dewey: Philosopher of Science and Freedom.* Dial.

Hooker, C. A. 1995. *Reason, Regulation, and Realism: Toward a Regulatory Systems Theory of Reason and Evolutionary Epistemology.* State University of New York Press.

Hooker, Brad, and Margaret Olivia Little, eds. 2000. *Moral Particularism.* Clarendon.

Horgan, Terence, and John Tienson. 1996. *Connectionism and the Philosophy of Psychology.* MIT Press.

Hoy, Terry. 2000. *Toward a Naturalistic Political Theory: Aristotle, Hume, Dewey, Evolutionary Biology, and Deep Ecology.* Praeger.

Hubbard, Ed. 2000. Connectionism and Akins' Ontological Gap. Course paper for Cognitive Science 200, University of California, San Diego.

Hull, David L. 2001. *Science and Selection: Essays on Biological Evolution and the Philosophy of Science.* Cambridge University Press.

Hull, David L., and Michael Ruse, eds. 1998. *The Philosophy of Biology.* Oxford University Press.

Hume, David. 1739. *A Treatise of Human Nature.* Clarendon, 1985.

Hurd, James P., ed. 1996. *Investigating the Biological Foundations of Human Morality.* Edwin Mellen.

Hurka, Thomas. 1993. *Perfectionism.* Oxford University Press.

Husserl, Edmund. 1967. *The Encyclopedia of Philosophy,* volumes 3 and 4. Macmillan.

Husserl, Edmund. 1994. The Deductive Calculus and the Logic of Contents. In *Collected Works V: Early Writings in the Philosophy of Logic and Mathematics.* Kluwer.

Hutchinson, D. S. 1995. Ethics. In *The Cambridge Companion to Aristotle,* ed. J. Barnes. Cambridge University Press.

Hutchins, Edwin. 1995. *Cognition in the Wild.* MIT Press.

Jackson, Frank. 2000. *From Metaphysics to Ethics: A Defence of Conceptual Analysis.* Clarendon.

Jackson, Frank, and Philip Pettit. 1995. Moral Functionalism and Moral Motivation. *Philosophical Quarterly* 45, no. 178: 20–40.

Johnson, Mark. 1993. *Moral Imagination: Implications of Cognitive Science for Ethics.* University of Chicago Press.

Johnson, Mark H., ed. 1993. *Brain Development and Cognition: A Reader.* Blackwell.

Johnson-Laird, Philip N., and Ruth M. Byrne. 1998. The Cognitive Science of Deduction. In *Mind Readings,* ed. P. Thagard. MIT Press.

Jonsen, Albert R., and Stephen Toulmin. 1988. *The Abuse of Casuistry: A History of Moral Reasoning.* University of California Press.

Joyce, R. 2000. Darwinian Ethics and Error. *Biology and Philosophy* 15: 713–732.

Juarrero, Alicia. 1999. *Dynamics in Action: Intentional Behavior as a Complex System.* MIT Press.

Kahneman, Dan, Paul Slovic, and Amos Tversky, eds. 1982. *Judgment under Uncertainty: Heuristics and Biases.* Cambridge University Press.

Kahneman, Dan, and Amos Tversky, eds. 2000. *Choices, Values, and Frames.* Cambridge University Press.

Kandel, Eric R., James H. Schwartz, and Thomas M. Jessell, eds. 2000. *Principles of Neural Science,* fourth edition. McGraw-Hill.

Kant, Immanuel. 1786. *Groundwork of the Metaphysics of Morals.* Harper Torchbooks, 1964.

Kaplan, Jonathan Michael. 2001. Genes for Phenotypes: A Modern History View. *Biology and Philosophy* 16, no. 2: 189–213.

Katz, Leonard D., ed. 2000. *Evolutionary Origins of Morality: Cross-Disciplinary Perspectives.* Imprint Academic.

Keil, Frank C., and Robert A. Wilson, eds. 2000. *Explanation and Cognition.* MIT Press.

Keller, Laurent, ed. 1999. *Levels of Selection in Evolution.* Princeton University Press.

Kennedy, Gail. 1954. Science and the Transformation of Common Sense: The Basic Problem of Dewey's Philosophy. *Journal of Philosophy* 51, no. 11: 313–325.

Khalil, Elias L., and Kenneth E. Boulding, eds. 1996. *Evolution, Order and Complexity.* Routledge.

Killen, Melanie, and Daniel Hart, eds. 1995. *Morality in Everyday Life: Developmental Perspectives.* Cambridge University Press.

Kim, Jaegwon. 1998. *Mind in a Physical World. An Essay on the Mind-Body Problem and Mental Causation.* MIT Press.

Kitcher, Philip. 1985. *Vaulting Ambition: Sociobiology and the Quest for Human Nature.* MIT Press.

Kitcher, Philip. 1999. Essence and Perfection. *Ethics* 110: 59–83.

Klein, Gary. 1999. *Sources of Power: How People Make Decisions.* MIT Press.

Kohlberg, Lawrence. 1981. *Essays on Moral Development,* volume 1: *The Philosophy of Moral Development.* Harper and Row.

Kokinov, Boicho N., and Alexander A. Petrov. 2001. Integrating Memory and Reasoning in Analogy-Making: The AMBR Model. In *The Analogical Mind,* ed. D. Gentner et al. MIT Press.

Kornblith, Hilary. 1993. *Inductive Inference and Its Natural Ground: An Essay in Naturalistic Epistemology.* MIT Press.

Kornblith, Hilary. 1999. Knowledge in Humans and Other Animals. In *Epistemology* (Philosophical Perspectives, volume 13). Blackwell.

Korsgaard, Christine. 1996. *Creating the Kingdom of Ends.* Cambridge University Press.

Kraut, Robert. 1990. Varieties of Pragmatism. *Mind* 99: 157–183.

Kurtines, William M., and Jacob L. Gewirtz. 1984. *Morality, Moral Behavior and Moral Development.* Wiley.

Kusch, Martin. 1995. *Psychologism: A Case Study in the Sociology of Philosophical Knowledge.* Routledge.

Laakso, Aarre, and Garrison W. Cottrell. 2000. Content and Cluster Analysis: Assessing Representational Similarity in Neural Systems. *Philosophical Psychology* 13, no. 1: 47–76.

LaFollette, Hugh. ed. 2000. *The Blackwell Guide to Ethical Theory.* Blackwell.

Lampmann, Jane. 2000. The Fittest Conscience: New Take on Evolution. *Christian Science Monitor,* electronic edition, August 5.

Lawrence, Eleanor. 1989. *A Guide to Modern Biology: Genetics, Cells and Systems.* Longman Scientific and Technical.

Lazarus, Richard S. 1991. *Emotion and Adaptation.* Oxford University Press.

LeDoux, Joseph. 1995. In Search of an Emotional System in the Brain. In *The Cognitive Neurosciences,* ed. M. Gazzaniga. MIT Press.

LeDoux, Joseph. 1996. *The Emotional Brain.* Simon and Schuster.

Leigh, Egbert Giles, Jr. 1995. Review of *The Major Transitions of Evolution. Evolution* 49, no. 6: 1302–1306.

Leiter, Brian, ed. 2001. *Objectivity in Law and Morals.* Cambridge University Press.

Lemos, John. 2000. Darwinian Natural Right and the Naturalistic Fallacy. *Biology and Philosophy* 15: 119–132.

Lemos, Noah M. 1994. *Intrinsic Value: Concept and Warrant.* Cambridge University Press.

Levins, Richard, and Richard Lewontin. 1985. *The Dialectical Biologist.* Harvard University Press.

Lieberman, Marcel. 1998. *Commitment, Value, and Moral Realism.* Cambridge University Press.

Lieberthal, Ed. 1983. *The Complete Book of Fingermath.* McGraw-Hill.

Livingston, Kenneth R. 1996. The Neurocomputational Mind Meets Normative Epistemology. *Philosophical Psychology* 9, no. 1: 33–59.

Lloyd, Dan. 1989. *Simple Minds.* MIT Press.

London, Alex John. 2000. Amenable to Reason: Aristotle's Rhetoric and the Moral Psychology of Practical Ethics. *Kennedy Institute of Ethics Journal* 10, no. 4: 287–305.

Lorenz, Konrad. 1996. *The Natural Sciences of the Human Species: An Introduction to Comparative Behavioral Research.* MIT Press.

Louden, Robert B. 1992. *Morality and Moral Theory.* Oxford University Press.

Lupia, Arthur, Mathew D. McCubbins, and Samuel L. Popkin, eds. 2000. *Elements of Reason: Cognition, Choice, and the Bounds of Rationality.* Cambridge University Press.

Mackie, J. L. 1977. *Ethics: Inventing Right and Wrong.* Penguin.

MacIntyre, Alasdaire. 1990. *Three Rival Versions of Moral Enquiry: Encyclopedia, Genealogy and Tradition.* University of Notre Dame Press.

MacIntyre, Alasdaire. 1999. *Dependent Rational Animals: Why Human Beings Need the Virtues.* Open Court.

Maienschein, Jane, and Michael Ruse, eds. 1999. *Biology and the Foundation of Ethics.* Cambridge University Press.

Marcus, Gary F. 1998. Rethinking Eliminative Connectionism. *Cognitive Psychology* 37: 243–282.

Margolis, Eric, and Stephen Laurence, eds. 1999. *Concepts: Core Readings.* MIT Press.

Margolis, Joseph. 1996. *Life without Principles: Reconciling Theory and Practice.* Blackwell.

Marr, David. 1982. *Vision: A Computational Investigation into the Human Representation and Processing of Visual Information.* Freeman.

Maryanski, Alexandra, and Turner, Jonathan H. 1992. *The Social Cage: Human Nature and The Evolution of Society.* Stanford University Press.

Maslow, Abraham. 1998. *Towards a Psychology of Being,* third edition. Wiley.

Masters, Roger D. 1993. *Beyond Relativism: Science and Human Values.* University Press of New England.

May, Larry, Marilyn Friedman, and Andy Clark, eds. 1996. *Mind and Morals: Essays on Ethics and Cognitive Science.* MIT Press.

Maynard Smith, John, and Eors Szathmary. 1995. *The Major Transitions in Evolution.* Freeman.

Mayr, Ernst. 1976. *Evolution and the Diversity of Life: Selected Essays.* Belknap.

Mayr, Ernst. 1982. *The Growth of Biological Thought: Diversity, Evolution and Inheritance.* Belknap.

McCauley, Robert N., ed. 1996. *The Churchlands and Their Critics.* Blackwell.

McCauley, Robert N., and William Bechtel. 1999. Heuristic Identity Theory (or Back to the Future): The Mind-Body Problem against the Background of

Research Strategies in Cognitive Neuroscience. In *Proceedings of the 21st Annual Meeting of the Cognitive Science Society.* Erlbaum, 1999.

McClamrock, Ron. 1995. *Existential Cognition: Computational Minds in the World.* University of Chicago Press.

McClelland, James L., David E. Rumelhart, and the PDP Research Group. 1986. *Parallel Distributed Processing: Explorations in the Microstructure of Cognition,* volume 2: *Psychological and Biological Models.* MIT Press.

McClelland, J. L. 1998. Connectionist Models and Bayesian Inference. In *Rational Models of Cognition,* ed. M. Oaksford and N. Chater. Oxford University Press.

McCleod, Peter, Kim Plunkett, and Edmund T. Rolls. 1998. *Introduction to Connectionist Modeling of Cognitive Processes.* Oxford University Press.

McClintock, Jack. 2000. Baywatch. *Discovery,* March: 76–83.

McDowell, John. 1998. *Mind, Value and Reality.* Harvard University Press.

McKinnon, Christine. 1999. *Character, Virtue Theories, and the Vices.* Broadview.

McMurrin, Sterling M., ed. 1988. *The Tanner Lectures on Human Values,* volume 7. University of Utah Press.

McNaughton, David. 1988. *Moral Vision.* Blackwell.

Menzel, Randolf, and Martin Giurfa. 2001. Cognitive Architecture of a Mini-Brain: The Honeybee. *Trends in Cognitive Science* 5, no. 2: 62–71.

Metzinger, Thomas, ed. 2000. *Neural Correlates of Consciousness.* MIT Press.

Michod, Richard E. 1999. *Darwinian Dynamics: Evolutionary Transitions in Fitness and Individuality.* Princeton University Press.

Midgley, Mary. 1978. *Beast and Man: The Roots of Human Nature.* Cornell University Press.

Midgley, Mary. 1985. *Evolution as a Religion: Strange Hopes and Stranger Fears.* Methuen.

Miller, Richard W. 1985. Ways of Moral Learning. *Philosophical Review* 94, no. 4: 507–556.

Millikan, Ruth Garrett. 1984. *Language, Thought, and Other Biological Categories.* MIT Press.

Millikan, Ruth Garrett. 1989. Biosemantics. *Journal of Philosophy* 86, no. 6: 281–297.

Millikan, Ruth Garrett. 1993. *White Queen Psychology and Other Essays for Alice.* MIT Press.

Millikan, Ruth Garrett. 2000. *On Clear and Confused Ideas: Essays About Substance Concepts.* Cambridge University Press.

Misak, Cheryl. 2000. *Truth, Politics and Morality: Pragmatism and Deliberation.* Routledge.

Miscevic, Nenad. 2000. *Rationality and Cognition: Against Relativism-Pragmatism.* University of Toronto Press.

Monan, J. Donald. 1968. *Moral Knowledge and Its Methodology in Aristotle.* Clarendon.

Moore, G. E. 1902. *Principia Ethica.* Prometheus Books, 1988.

Moore, G. E. 1994. *Principia Ethica,* revised edition. Cambridge University Press.

Morgenbesser, Sydney, ed. 1977. *Dewey and His Critics: Essays from the Journal of Philosophy.* Journal of Philosophy.

Motluck, Alison. 2001. Read My Mind. *New Scientist,* January 27: 22–26.

Muller, Alexandra, E., and Urs Thalmann. 2000. Origin and Evolution of Primate Social Organization: A Reconstruction. *Biological Reviews of the Cambridge Philosophical Society* 75: 405–435.

Munzel, G. Felicitas. 1999. *Kant's Conception of Moral Character: The Critical Link of Morality, Anthropology, and Reflective Judgment.* University of Chicago Press.

Murphy, Michael P., and Luke A. J. O'Neill, eds. 1995. *What Is Life? The Next Fifty Years.* Cambridge University Press.

Narveson, Jan. 2000. Evolutionary Biology, Altruism, and Moral Theory. *Biology and Philosophy* 15, no. 2: 259–274.

Neander, Karen. 1997. The Function of Cognition: Godfrey-Smith's Environmental Complexity Thesis. *Biology and Philosophy* 12: 567–580.

Nicholson, Kelly. 1997. *Body and Soul: The Transcendence of Materialism.* Westview.

Nietzsche, Friedrich. 1888. *Ecce Homo.* Penguin, 1993.

Nitecki, Mathew H., and Doris V. Nitecki, eds. 1993. *Evolutionary Ethics.* State University of New York Press.

Noam, Gil G., and Thomas E. Wren, eds. 1993. *The Moral Self.* MIT Press.

Norton, David Fate, ed. 1993. *The Cambridge Companion to Hume.* Cambridge University Press.

Nussbaum, Martha C., and Amelie Oksenberg Rorty, eds. 1999. *Essays on Aristotle's De Anima.* Clarendon.

O'Hear, Anthony. 1997. *Beyond Evolution: Human Nature and the Limits of Evolutionary Explanation.* Clarendon.

O'Neill, Onora. 1989. *Construction of Reason: Explorations of Kant's Practical Philosophy.* Cambridge University Press.

O'Reilly, Randall, and Yuko Munakata. 2000. *Computational Explorations in Cognitive Neuroscience: Understanding the Mind by Simulating the Brain.* MIT Press.

Oyama, Susan. 1985. *The Ontogeny of Information: Developmental Systems and Evolution.* Cambridge University Press.

Oyama, Susan. 2000. *Evolution's Eye: A Systems View of the Biology-Culture Divide.* Duke University Press.

Palmer, Stephen E. 1999. *Vision Science: Photons to Phenomenology.* MIT Press.

Papaj, D., and A. Lewis, eds. 1993. *Insect Learning: Ecological and Evolutionary Perspectives.* Chapman & Hall.

Papineau, David. 1993. *Philosophical Naturalism.* Blackwell.

Pappas, Gregory F. 1998. Dewey's Ethics: Morality as Experience. In *Reading Dewey,* ed. L. Hickman. Indiana University Press.

Paul, Ellen Frankel, Fred D. Miller Jr., and Jeffrey Paul, eds. 1999. *Human Flourishing.* Cambridge University Press.

Peirce, Charles S. 1868. *The Essential Peirce: Selected Philosophical Writings, 1867–1893,* volume 1. Indiana University Press, 1992.

Peirce, Charles S. 1877. *The Essential Peirce: Selected Philosophical Writings, 1867–1893,* volume 1. Indiana University Press, 1992.

Peirce, Charles S. 1898. *The Essential Peirce: Selected Philosophical Writings. 1893–1913,* volume 2. Indiana University Press, 1998.

Peterson, Grethe B., ed. 1999. *The Tanner Lectures on Human Values,* volume 20. University of Utah Press.

Petrinovich, Lewis. 1995. *Human Evolution, Reproduction and Morality.* Plenum.

Pfeifer, Rolf, and Christian Scheier. 1999. *Understanding Intelligence.* MIT Press.

Pigden, Charles. 1993. Naturalism. In *A Companion to Ethics,* ed. P. Singer. Blackwell.

Pincoffs, Edmund L. 1986. *Quandaries and Virtues: Against Reductivism in Ethics.* University Press of Kansas.

Pinker, Steven, and Alan Prince. 1988. On Language and Connectionism: Analysis of a Parallel Distributed Processing Model of Language Acquisition. *Cognition* 28: 73–193.

Pizarro, David. 2000. Nothing More Than Feelings? The Role of Emotions in Moral Judgment. *Journal for the Theory of Social Behavior* 30, no. 4: 355–375.

Port, Robert F., and Timothy Van Gelder, eds. 1995. *Mind as Motion: Explorations in the Dynamics of Cognition.* MIT Press.

Punzo, Vincent A. 1996. After Kohlberg: Virtue Ethics and the Recovery of the Moral Self. *Philosophical Psychology* 9, no. 1: 7–23.

Putnam, Hilary. 1990. *Realism with a Human Face.* Harvard University Press.

Quine, Willard Van Orman. 1953. *From a Logical Point of View,* second edition, revised. Harvard University Press, 1980.

Quine, Willard Van Orman. 1979. On the Nature of Moral Values. *Critical Inquiry* 5: 471–480.

Quine, Willard Van Orman. 1981. *Theories and Things.* Harvard University Press.

Quinn, Warren. 1993. *Morality and Action.* Cambridge University Press.

Rachels, James. 1993. *The Elements of Moral Philosophy,* second edition. McGraw-Hill.

Radick, Gregory. 2000. Two Explanations of Evolutionary Progress. *Biology and Philosophy* 15: 475–491.

Rasmussen, David M. 1990. *Universalism vs. Communitarianism: An Introduction.* MIT Press.

Reader, John. 1990. *Man on Earth.* Harper and Row.

Reader, Soran. 2000. New Directions in Ethics: Naturalism, Reasons and Virtue. *Ethical Theory and Moral Practice* 3: 341–364.

Reider, Laura. 1998. Toward a New Test for the Insanity Defense: Incorporating the Discoveries of Neuroscience into Moral and Legal Theories. *UCLA Law Review* 46, no. 1: 289–342.

Rendell, Luke, and Hal Whitehead. 2001. Culture in Whales and Dolphins. *Behavioral and Brain Sciences* 24, no. 2: 309–382.

Rey, Georges. 1997. *Contemporary Philosophy of Mind.* Blackwell.

Ribes, Bruno. 1978. *Biology and Ethics.* United Nations Educational, Scientific and Cultural Organization.

Richards, Robert. 1986a. A Defense of Evolutionary Ethics. *Biology and Philosophy* 1: 265–293.

Richards, Robert. 1986b. Justification through Biological Faith: A Rejoinder. *Biology and Philosophy* 1: 337–354.

Richards, Robert. 1987. *Darwin and the Emergence of Evolutionary Theories of Mind and Behavior.* University of Chicago Press.

Richardson, Henry S. 1994. *Practical Reasoning about Final Ends.* Cambridge University Press.

Ridley, Mark, ed. 1997. *Evolution: A Reader.* Oxford University Press.

Rips, Lance. 1995. Deduction and Cognition. In *An Invitation to Cognitive Science,* volume 3: *Thinking,* ed. E. Smith and D. Osherson, second edition. MIT Press.

Ripstein, Arthur. 1993. Questionable Objectivity. *Nous* 27, no. 3: 355–372.

Robinson, Daniel N. 1982. *Toward a Science of Human Nature: Essays on the Psychologies of Mill, Hegel, Wundt, and James.* Columbia University Press.

Rockefeller, Steven C. 1991. *John Dewey: Religious Faith and Democratic Humanism.* Columbia University Press.

Rojas, R. 1996. *Neural Networks: A Systematic Introduction.* Springer-Verlag.

Rorty, Amelie Oksenberg, ed. 1980. *Essays on Aristotle's Ethics.* University of California Press.

Rorty, Richard. 1993. Putnam and the Relativist Menace. *Journal of Philosophy* 90, no. 9: 443–461.

Rosch, Eleanor. 2000. The Brain between Two Paradigms: Can Biofunctionalism Join Wisdom Intuitions to Analytic Science? *Journal of Mind and Behavior* 21, no. 1, 2: 189–204.

Rosenberg, Alexander. 2000. *Darwinism in Philosophy. Social Science and Public Policy.* Cambridge University Press.

Rosenthal, Sandra B., Carl R. Hausman, and Douglas R. Anderson, eds. 1999. *Classical American Pragmatism: Its Contemporary Vitality.* University of Chicago Press.

Ross, Don, Andrew Brook, and David Thompson, eds. 2000. *Dennett's Philosophy: A Comprehensive Assessment*. MIT Press.

Rottschaefer, William A. 1997. Evolutionary Ethics: An Irresistible Temptation. *Biology and Philosophy* 12: 369–384.

Rottschaefer, William A. 1998. *The Biology and Psychology of Moral Agency*. Cambridge University Press.

Rottschaefer, William A. 1999. Moral Learning and Moral Realism: How Empirical Psychology Illuminates Issues in Moral Ontology. *Behavior and Philosophy* 27: 19–49.

Roweis, Sam T., and Lawrence K. Saul., 2000. Nonlinear Dimensionality Reduction by Locally Linear Embedding. *Science* 290, 2323–2326.

Rowlands, Mark. 1999. *The Body in Mind: Understanding Cognitive Processes*. Cambridge University Press.

Rumelhart, David, James L. McClelland, and the PDP Research Group. 1986. *Parallel Distributed Processing: Explorations in the Microstructure of Cognition*, Volume 1: *Foundations*. MIT Press.

Ruse, Michael and Wilson, E. O. 1986. Moral Philosophy as Applied Science. *Philosophy* 61: 173–192.

Rutkowska, Julie C. 1993. *The Computational Infant: Looking for Developmental Cognitive Science*. Harvester Wheatsheaf.

Ryle, Gilbert. 1949. *The Concept of Mind*. Hutchinson's University Library.

Salthe, Stanley N. 1993. *Development and Evolution: Complexity and Change in Biology*. MIT Press.

Sayre-McCord, Geoffrey, ed. 1988.) *Essays on Moral Realism*. Cornell University Press.

Schall, Jeffrey D. 2001. Neural Basis of Deciding, Choosing and Acting. *Neuroscience* 2, no. 1: 33–42.

Scheffler, Samuel. 1992. *Human Morality*. Oxford University Press.

Schilpp, Paul Arthur, and Lewis Edwin Hawn, eds. 1989. *The Philosophy of John Dewey*. Open Court.

Schmajuk, Nestor A. 1997. *Animal Learning and Cognition: A Neural Network Approach*. Cambridge University Press.

Schulkin, Jay. 2000. *Roots of Social Sensibility and Neural Function*. MIT Press.

Schulteis, G., S. Ahmed, A. Morse, G. Koob, and B. Everitt. 2000. Conditioning and Opiate Withdrawal: The Amygdala Links Neutral Stimuli with the Agony of Overcoming Drug Addiction. *Nature* 405: 1013.

Searle, John. 1964/1970. How to Derive 'Ought' From 'Is.' In *Readings in Ethical Theory*, ed. W. Sellars and J. Hospes. Appleton-Century-Crofts.

Searle, John. 1992. *The Rediscovery of the Mind*. MIT Press.

Sejnowski, T., and C. Rosenberg. 1986. NETtalk: A Parallel Network That Learns to Read Aloud. Technical Report JHU/EECS-86/01, Electrical Engineering and Computer Science, Johns Hopkins University.

Serafini, Anthony. 1993. *The Epic History of Biology.* Plenum.

Shook, John R. 2000. *Dewey's Empirical Theory of Knowledge and Reality.* Vanderbilt University Press.

Sim, May, ed. 1995. *The Crossroads of Norm and Nature: Essays on Aristotle's Ethics and Metaphysics.* Rowman and Littlefield.

Simpson, Peter. 1987. *Goodness and Nature.* Martinus Nijhoff.

Singer, Peter, ed. 1993. *A Companion to Ethics.* Blackwell.

Singer, Peter. 1999. *A Darwinian Left: Politics, Evolution and Cooperation.* Yale University Press.

Sinnott-Armstrong, Walter, and Mark Timmons, eds. 1996. *Moral Knowledge? New Readings in Moral Epistemology.* Oxford University Press.

Skyrms, Brian. 1996. *Evolution of the Social Contract.* Cambridge University Press.

Skyrms, Brian. 2001. The Stag Hunt. Presidential address to Pacific Division of American Philosophical Association.

Skyrms, Brian, and Robin Pemantle. 2000. A Dynamic Model of Social Network Formation. *Proceedings of the National Academy of Sciences* 97: 9340–9346.

Slote, Michael. 1992. Ethics Naturalized. In *Ethics* (Philosophical Perspectives, volume 6). Blackwell.

Smith, Edward E., and Daniel N. Osherson, eds. 1995. *An Invitation to Cognitive Science,* volume 3: *Thinking.* MIT Press.

Smith, Eric A., Monique Borgerhoff Mulder, and Kim Hill. 2001. Controversies in the Evolutionary Social Sciences: A Guide for the Perplexed. *Trends in Ecology and Evolution* 16, no. 3: 128–135.

Smolensky, Paul. 1988. On the Proper Treatment of Connectionism. *Behavioral and Brain Sciences* 11: 1–74.

Snare, Francis. 1991. *Morals, Motivation and Convention: Hume's Influential Doctrines.* Cambridge University Press.

Snow, C. P. 1959. *The Two Cultures.* Cambridge University Press, 1993.

Sober, Elliott. 1984. *The Nature of Selection: Evolutionary Theory in Philosophical Focus.* MIT Press.

Sober, Elliott. 1993. *Philosophy of Biology.* Westview.

Sober, Elliott. 1994. *From a Biological Point of View: Essays on Evolutionary Philosophy.* Cambridge University Press.

Sober, Elliott, ed. 1997a. *Conceptual Issues in Evolutionary Biology,* second edition. MIT Press.

Sober, Elliot. 1997b. Is the Mind an Adaptation for Coping with Environmental Complexity? *Biology and Philosophy* 12: 539–550.

Solomon, Robert. 1995. Living Well: The Virtues and the Good Life. In *A Handbook for Ethics.* Harcourt Brace Jovanovich.

Sommers, Christina, and Fred Sommers. 1993. Vice and Virtue in Everyday Life: Introductory Readings in Ethics, third edition. Harcourt Brace College.

Sorell, Tom. 2000. *Moral Theory and Anomaly.* Blackwell.

Spencer, Herbert. 1873. *Study of Sociology.* University of Michigan Press, 1961.

Spitzer, Manfred. 1999. *The Mind within the Net: Models of Learning, Thinking and Action.* MIT Press.

Statman, Daniel. 1997. *Virtue Ethics: A Critical Reader.* Georgetown University Press.

Stein, Dan J., and Jacques Ludik, eds. 1998. *Neural Networks and Psychopathology: Connectionist Models in Practice and Research.* Cambridge University Press.

Stein, Edward. 1996. *Without Good Reason: The Rationality Debate in Philosophy and Cognitive Science.* Oxford University Press.

Steiner, Gerhard. 1999. *Learning: Nineteen Scenarios from Everyday Life.* Cambridge University Press.

Stent, Gunther S. 1980. *Morality as a Biological Phenomenon.* University of California Press.

Sterba, James P. 2001. *Three Challenges to Ethics: Environmentalism, Feminism and Multiculturalism.* Oxford University Press.

Sterenly, Kim. 2001. *The Evolution of Agency and Other Essays.* Cambridge University Press.

Sterelny, Kim. 1997. Where Does Thinking Come From?: A Commentary on Peter Godfrey-Smith's *Complexity and the Function of Mind in Nature. Biology and Philosophy* 12: 551–566.

Sterelny, Kim, and Paul E. Griffiths, eds. 1999. *Sex and Death: An Introduction to Philosophy of Biology.* University of Chicago Press.

Sternberg, Robert J, ed. 1994. *Thinking and Problem Solving.* Academic Press.

Sternberg, Robert J, ed. 1999. *The Nature of Cognition.* MIT Press.

Stevenson, Charles L. 1963. *Facts and Values: Studies in Ethical Analysis.* Yale University Press.

Stich, Stephen. 1983. *From Folk Psychology to Cognitive Science: The Case against Belief.* MIT Press.

Stone, M. W. F., and Jonathan Wolff, eds. 2000. *The Proper Ambition of Science.* Routledge.

Strauss, Valerie. 2001. Brain Research Oversold, Experts Say: Despite Educational Sales Pitches and Anticipation, Not Enough Is Known to Help Most Students Learn Better. *Washington Post,* March 13.

Sylvester, Robert Peter. 1990. *The Moral Philosophy of G. E. Moore.* Temple University Press.

Tenenbaum, Joshua B., Vin de Silva, and John C. Langford. 2000. A Global Geometric Framework for Nonlinear Dimensionality Reduction. *Science* 290: 2319–2323.

Tesauro, G., and T. J. Sejnowski. 1990. Neurogammon: A Neural-Network Backgammon Program. *IJCNN Proceedings* 3: 33–39.

Thagard, Paul. 1998a. Ethical Coherence. *Philosophical Psychology* 11, no. 4: 405–422.

Thagard, Paul, ed. 1998b. *Mind Readings: Introductory Selections on Cognitive Science.* MIT Press.

Thagard, Paul. 2000. *Coherence in Thought and Action.* MIT Press.

Thoma, Stephen J. 2000. Models of Moral Development. *Journal of Mind and Behavior* 20, no. 1–2: 129–136.

Thomas, Laurence. 1996. Virtue Ethics and the Arc of Universality: Reflections on Punzo's Reading of Kantian Virtue Ethics. *Philosophical Psychology* 9, no. 1: 25–32.

Thompson, Norma, ed. 2000. *Instilling Ethics.* Rowman and Littlefield.

Thompson, Paul, ed. 1987. *Issues in Evolutionary Ethics.* State University of New York Press.

Tiles, J. E. 1988. *Dewey.* London: Routledge.

Tiles, J. E., ed. 1992. *John Dewey: Critical Assessments,* volume 1. Routledge.

Tiles, J. E., ed. 1992. *John Dewey: Critical Assessments,* volume 4. Routledge.

Timmons, Mark. 1997. Will Cognitive Science Change Ethics? *Philosophical Psychology* 10, no. 4: 531–540.

Tinbergen, N. 1989. *The Study of Instinct.* Clarendon.

Tooby, John, and Leda Cosmides. 1996. Friendship and the Banker's Paradox: Other Pathways to the Evolution of Adaptations for Altruism. *Proceedings of the British Academy* 88: 119–143.

Turner, Jonathan H. 2000. *On the Origins of Human Emotion: A Sociological Inquiry into the Evolution of Human Affect.* Stanford University Press.

Ullmann-Margalit, Edna, ed. 2000. *Reasoning Practically.* Oxford University Press.

Van de Vijver, Gertrudis, Stanley N. Salthe, and Manuela Delpos, eds. 1998. *Evolutionary Systems: Biological and Epistemological Perspectives on Selection and Self-Organization.* Kluwer.

Vicedo, Margaret. The Laws of Inheritance and the Rules of Morality: Early Geneticists on Evolution and Ethics. In *Biology and the Foundations of Ethics,* ed. J. Maienschein and M. Ruse. Cambridge University Press.

Wagner, Gunter P., ed. 2000. *The Character Concept in Evolutionary Biology.* Academic Press.

Wallace, James. 1978. *Virtues and Vices.* Cornell University Press.

Wallace, James. 1996. *Ethical Norms, Particular Cases.* Cornell University Press.

Waller, Bruce. 1997. What Rationality Adds to Animal Morality. *Biology and Philosophy* 12: 341–356.

Warnock, G. J. 1967. *Contemporary Moral Philosophy.* Oxford University Press.

Weber, Thomas P. 2000. Biological Objects, Units of Selection and Character Decomposition. *Tree* 15, no. 8: 304–305.

Weibel, Ewald, R. 2000. *Symmorphosis: On Form and Function in Shaping Life*. Harvard University Press.

Weingart, Peter, Sandra D. Mitchell, Peter J. Richerson, and Sabine Maasen, eds. 1997. *Human by Nature: Between Biology and the Social Sciences*. Erlbaum.

Welchman, Jennifer. 1995. *Dewey's Ethical Thought*. Cornell University Press.

Welchman, Jennifer. 2001. Minor Virtues: A Deweyan Approach. http://www.american-philosophy.org.

Westbrook, Robert B. 1991. *John Dewey and American Democracy*. Cornell University Press.

Whitman, Walt. 1855. Leaves of Grass. In *Walt Whitman: Complete Poetry and Selected Prose*. Library Classics of the United States.

Wiener, Philip, P. 1972. *Evolution and the Founders of Pragmatism*. University of Philadelphia Press.

Williams, Bernard. 1985. *Ethics and the Limits of Philosophy*. Fontana.

Williams, Bernard. 1994. Nietzsche's Minimalist Moral Psychology. In *Nietzsche, Genealogy, Morality*, ed. R. Schacht. University of California Press.

Williams, Bernard. 1995. *Making Sense of Humanity and Other Philosophical Papers*. Cambridge University Press.

Wilson, Edward O. 1975. *Sociobiology: The New Synthesis*, 25th-anniversary edition. Belknap, 2000.

Wilson, Edward O. 1978. *On Human Nature*. Harvard University Press.

Wilson, Edward O. 1998. The Biological Basis of Morality. *Atlantic Monthly* 281, no. 4: 53–70.

Wilson, Robert A., ed. 1999. *Species: New Interdisciplinary Essays*. MIT Press.

Wilson, Robert, and Frank Keil, eds. 1999. *The MIT Encyclopedia of the Cognitive Sciences*. MIT Press.

Winkler, Earl R., and Jerrold R. Coombs, eds. 1993. *Applied Ethics: A Reader*. Blackwell.

Witkowski, Ken. 1975. The Is-Ought Gap: Deduction or Justification? *Philosophy and Phenomenological Research* 36, no. 2: 233–245.

Wollheim, Richard. 1999. *On the Emotions*. Yale University Press.

Wolters, Gereon, and James G. Lennox, eds. 1995. *Concepts, Theories, and Rationality in the Biological Sciences*. University of Pittsburgh Press.

Woolcock, Peter G. 2000. Objectivity and Illusion in Evolutionary Ethics: Comments on Waller. *Biology and Philosophy* 15, no. 1: 39–60.

Wright, Robert. 1994. *The Moral Animal: Why We Are the Way We Are*. Vintage Books.

Wren, Thomas E. 1991. *Caring about Morality*. MIT Press.

Zolo, Danilo. 1990. *Reflexive Epistemology: The Philosophical Legacy of Otto Neurath*. Kluwer.

Index